D1564046

The Reflective Journey toward Order

❧Eliot, "Tradition and the Individual Talent"

The difference between the present and the past is that the conscious present is an awareness of the past in a way and to an extent which the past's awareness of itself cannot show.

❧Paul Ricoeur, *The Symbolism of Evil*

By retroaction from the successive "nows," our past never stops changing its meaning; the present appropriation of the past modifies that which motivates us from the depths of the past.

The Reflective Journey toward Order

ESSAYS ON DANTE, WORDSWORTH, ELIOT,
AND OTHERS

Marion Montgomery

University of Georgia Press, Athens

Library of Congress Catalog Card Number: 78-190048
International Standard Book Number: 0-8203-0299-6

The University of Georgia Press, Athens 30601

Copyright © 1973
by the University of Georgia Press

Printed in the United States of America

For
Robert Hunter West

I have tried to find words for true things under the burden
of paradoxical multiplicity, the burden of existence. I have
tried not to contradict myself.

ERRATA SHEET
The Reflective Journey toward Order

page 2, line 2: read 1822 for 1882
139.30: read *Finnegans* for *Finnigans*
153.2: read *Finnegans* for *Finnigans*
219.5: read *Andrewes* for *Andrews*
219.15: read quondam for quandam
232.31: read colon for semicolon
247.7: read timeless for timelesss
247-263 (recto running head): read Keats's for Keat's
257.17: read diametrically for diometrically
266.9: read principal for prinicpal
270.11: read transferral for transferal
298:11: read grateful for greatful

Acknowledgments

Earlier versions of many passages in this book have had the advantage of publication before this revision of them, and I wish to express gratitude for these preliminary showings in cold print: to the *Arizona Quarterly, Discourse: A Review of the Liberal Arts, Florida Quarterly, Georgia Review, Laurel Review, Midwest Quarterly, South Atlantic Bulletin, Southern Humanities Review, Southern Review, Southwest Review.*

I should like to express particular indebtedness to a number of persons who have encouraged this work and responded to it with an interest bringing it to this issue: to Charles Beaumont, M. E. Bradford, Ernest Bufkin, James Colvert, George Core, William Free, Edward Krickel, Thomas Landess, Warren Leamon, Harold Grier McCurdy, Boyd McWhorter, Charles Patterson, Robert Hunter West.

Contents

III

IV

Preface

Experience, and the accumulated voices of experience, teach us that one who knows nothing of his origins knows little of his options. Even the romanticized foundling—whether urn or a novel's comic hero—fascinates us by that always serious, if not always reverent, question: whose bastard is this? And even where silence and slow time make no reply, or only faint reply, the question is worth the asking. Indeed, cause, contingency, chance—those specters of the future— are more haunting, because more fundamental, than "Love, Ambition, Poesy." They will not allow the question to go unasked for long, the question of being and consciousness. To pursue it discursively, and with the burden of the mind as ceaselessly changing as any young river, is to court despair. Yet Prufrock's "Oh do not ask" is prelude to an oblivion which mind itself rejects. We hold joyfully and desperately to words, words, words.

There is a commonplace which the writer must perpetually recall in his attempt to comprehend—to embrace in words—the life of the mind. Particularly so as he presumes to record not his own mind primarily but aspects of some other. It is that the tapestry of mind which he figures forth is, by his very act, a distortion. No matter how careful his reading of evidence, the unsaid cries out from the critic's simplifications. For a mystery of human life is, among its other aspects, that the given mind is like Heraclitus' river, never the same twice, while in some undeniable way it remains always the same. Within that paradox lies the temptation to words, for in words resides our confidence; the poets of our own century in particular have been pressed to say, in their several ways, that words are at least some temporary stay against confusion in the ebb and flow of awareness.

And the measurer, the prospector, the plumber of words—the critic—as he deals with words other than his own, adds to the complications by his own changing mind, compounding the difficulty. To that double presence of mind in the words—the double jeopardy he puts words to—is finally added the complication of his reader's mind as it enters also upon the flow which words inadequately stay. To consider the complication is *almost* to be forced to silence. But not quite. Pound's Kung may remember "A day when the historians left blanks in their writings / . . . for things they didn't know." The same cannot be said for poet or critic, and especially for the critic.

The poet may on occasion escape the burden of words on the plea of desertion by the muse, or he may occasionally exult in the mystery of a high plateau of silence where vision is beyond the weak reach of any words. But the critic, professing reason's power, may not publicly plead desertion of inspiration or an escape through vision. He feels therefore that he must justify the vanity of words—the poet's or his own. He notes the likeness between childhood and adult photographs of face or mind, playing order through his own metaphors or progressions; he notes the advances or contradictions between his subject's argument today and yesterday: he follows the imitative flow of early lines as they move toward distinctive accomplishment.

At the best the critic's figuring of his subject's mind represents tendencies—his own included. In the end he hopes to have made some resemblance of that unique force that curves through time bearing a name—Dante or Wordsworth or Eliot. But always under the burden of that separate force bearing a separate name in time, his own. He emphasizes the evidence of tendency out of his interest in, or obsession with, the precise charting of the force—the mind. This word marks a line moving between birth and death, between thought and expression, whether that birth and death of mind be contained in the sequence of verses of a particular poem, the inclusive body of all the poet's days, or whether he presume even upon epochs of minds. But a line is not the many-dimensioned wave that is any mind. And one is more often than not tempted to his line-drawing by the very aspect of magnitude in his subject. Hence the dilemma, upon reflection, between the enthusiasm of attempt and the foreknowledge of impending failure. But a valid justification for undertaking sure failure is that mind warrants treasuring, and minds of larger magnitude particularly so. And words, alas, are the best repositories vouchsafed us in time.

Words—frail conductors of the force of life. No wonder one of our dreams of perfection is to move beyond their limits, whether by transcendence into that angelic mode Milton argues or by subverting words through the mysticism of a Lawrence's blood knowledge. Everywhere and always words decay under the force of mind. If it were not so, we should have no need of an Ezra Pound to remind us to make it new. We should finally come to one poem in which mind would burn, a wordless prayer, pure life. But Eden is more believable behind us than before us, and so we must celebrate mind as best we may. What we treasure without ever possessing, surely, is the true marriage of mind with whatever "Other" confronts it, a wedding which the great poet always affirms as vision. The pursuit of a final rest in order or harmony of mind, the wise passiveness dreamed by Dante or Wordsworth or Eliot, is the high quest of art no less than of philosophy. The warrior on the bright plains of Elysium; the clear rest of the multifoliate rose in the presence of light; the living soul unbound upon the banks of the Wye; the bright terraces of Ecbatan; the bitter furies out of gong-tormented seas; girl- or heron-priested shores; the still point beyond the limits of images: each is a great reaching of the mind, a movement of mind through words toward a release from all necessity of words. Of the making of books, therefore, there will be no end. Indeed our curse is that we publish as we perish, whether we celebrate blue girls and their chattering beauty or affirm an old garden of truth to which most wanderers return. Were we beyond the burden of words, we too might sing in full-throated ease, or shine, brilliant in the regions of the sun, or enter an unchanging garden with unchanging minds—those conditions of complete simplicity. But meanwhile we are burdened, since

> any action
> Is a step to the block, to the fire, down the sea's throat
> Or to an illegible stone: and that is where we start.

That is, once more, we risk our labor as we may.

Foreword

THE REFLECTIVE JOURNEY

꙳Saint Augustine, *The City of God*

> Sometimes, after much debate, the very meaning of the author
> himself is at length discovered; at other times, this meaning
> remains obscure, but at least the discussion of a profound
> obscurity serves on occasion for declaring other things that
> are true.

The central concern of these essays is the poet's continuing
quest for certitude, for a point of rest which reflects an
order and harmony of mind. Our critical tendency is to
categorize, to divide English and American literature into
a multitude of "Ages," a tendency which distorts that continuity which is tradition. These essays consider modern
literature as an integral part of a continuum more extensive
than generally taken. They are composed within a broad
spectrum marked at a beginning by Dante's journey out
of his dark wood and at the end by Jack Kerouac's pathetic
wanderings on the road. The development of English and
American literature in particular (these essays suggest) may
be considered as one movement. Those disturbing problems
of separation and alienation which so concern us are an
expected consequence of the direction chosen by that spirit
emerging from the Middle Ages which we so proudly name
the Renaissance. Indeed, one might consider the twentieth
century as the lag-end of the Renaissance, whether the
breadth of such a view be governed by a system such as
Yeats propounds in his *Vision* or by the arguments of
McLuhan, who sees us in the death throes of the Age of

Gutenberg. Given a certain temperament and certain principles, one might go so far as to call the whole of this period, from Dante to the present and perhaps beyond, the romantic age.

However hazardous such a broad view may be, there are advantages to it as we consider the development of particular minds within it. Poets in particular react to history in sweeping ways, a cause of irritation to historian and philosopher alike. The significant poet, the poet to whom subsequent ages return again and again, seems always pressed to reconcile his own vision to the general course of mind of which he is a particular issue, to reconcile his individual talent to the tradition. He seems bent on finding some way to transform history into a myth which is believed because it is true absolutely and not simply metaphorically. So he sets a Plato's or Newton's teeth on edge. It is this quest toward certitude as reflected particularly by William Wordsworth that gives this book its focus. It was for some time fashionable to deprecate Wordsworth, yet it is Wordsworth in the nineteenth century who is most central in a tradition that brings forth Eliot, Pound, Stevens, Joyce, Lawrence, Hemingway. One particular reason for a neglect of Wordsworth as precursor to these figures has been that Eliot's early criticism so influenced critical sensibilities that not even his own subsequent modifications have restored a balance. Consequently, another of the themes of these essays is Eliot's evolving discovery of a "romanticism" in himself and of a "classicism" in Wordsworth, neither of which the early Eliot seems to notice. It is a theme developed here not only directly in exposition, but also through the choice of many epigraphs from Eliot for use as prefaces, a device which he himself was fond of employing.

I have attempted in some degree to imitate the action of the particular quest in Wordsworth and Eliot, through allusive reflections and by avoiding a strict dictation by chronology. It is a procedure of homage to them, recognizing an indebtedness for that journey of the mind each made, a journey which many of us have shared at a level more fundamental than that of art. Mine is an approach which is also meant to argue the suitability of an epic and narrative movement to literary criticism itself. Although an Alexandrian structuring and development of this book might in some ways have been more convenient, and certainly more usual, I have rather chosen what might in better hands be called a Homeric mode. I trust that the reader, however he may demur along the way, will discover a form which is deliberate with variation so that a particular idea may appear more fully through progressive enlargement or by an address of the same idea or the same material from a different quarter. Having borrowed such devices from literature itself, I have hoped to afford my reader some pleasure, along with whatever of critical value he may discover in these pages. Through an imitation of the reflective journey of particular minds as they seek certitude, it is even possible that we may return to the present, familiar garden of our literature and see it in important ways for the first time.

Introduction

Ezra Pound, "Notes on Elizabethan Classicists"

> Only the mediocrity of a given time can drive the more intelligent men of that time to "break with tradition." I take it that the phrase "break with tradition" is currently used to mean "desert the more obvious imbecilities of one's immediate elders." ... Only the careful and critical mind will seek to know how much tradition inhered in the immediate elders.

Eliot, "Wordsworth and Coleridge"

> Those who speak of Wordsworth as the original Lost Leader ... should make pause and consider that when a man takes politics and social affairs seriously the difference between revolution and reaction may be the breadth of a hair.

How continuously contemporary, Wordsworth's letter to Walter Savage Landor in April of 1882:

> It is reported here that Byron, Shelley, Moore, Leigh Hunt ... are to lay their heads together in some Town in Italy, for the purpose of conducting a Journal to be directed against everything in religion, in morals and probably in government and literature, which our Forefathers have been accustomed to reverence,—the notion seems very extravagant but perhaps the more likely to be realized on that account.

With a substitution of names and places the same words are spoken in the 1970s. But versions of these charges were spoken before 1822 and will be spoken after the 1970s, whether the revolutionary of the moment be Socrates, Euripides, Dante, Milton, Pound. Or T. S. Eliot or William Wordsworth himself. It would seem one of the abiding ironies of the mind's engagement with the world that its revolutionary reaction to the current establishment leads it to discover itself fundamentally reactionary. The literary or political radical, almost as a rule, discovers himself really to have been an ignorant traditionalist. That is, as his ignorance of antecedents and of the premises of his own position is removed, he discovers that his "root" position relates him to his fathers more firmly than he wanted to suppose. Meanwhile, of course, one's sons are themselves in passionate revolt, charging the old revolutionary who claims to be their father with having sold out to the establishment. It takes them too awhile to discover, as Twain comments somewhere, how much a father can learn between the son's fifteenth and twenty-first years.

Eliot, relatively early in his attempt to place his own work, to understand his own revolutionary mind, wrote: "the difference between the present and the past is that the conscious present is an awareness of the past in a way and to an extent which the past's awareness of itself cannot show." The statement out of context is tinged with arrogance. Given a little time, such words become the speaker's accusation of himself, hurled back at him by his sons across the temporally eternal generation gap. Given a detachment, and enough time for the mind to move about in, such words usually appear comic, as when we notice Dryden faulting Chaucer for ignorance of meter. Pound calls Dryden "by nature a lunk-head" who may nevertheless in the midst of his "outstanding aridity" have said "some quite sensible remark about Chaucer." Pound's excoriation of Dryden echoes Wordsworth's against Dryden, though less precise than Wordsworth's. Eliot proves himself very much aware of the problem of the present's relationship to the past: "Someone said: 'The dead writers are remote from us because we *know* so much more than they did.' Precisely, and they are that which we know." Who is that "someone" speaking so knowingly? One person most certainly is the Eliot of yesterday or the year before. And Pound can find Dryden historically justifiable in the continuing battle against mediocrity, the struggle to make poetry in a dead time. Eliot's two statements dramatize the revolutionary poet coming to accept his roots in the past. It is a movement of the mind reflecting less a change than an enlargement, especially when we remark it in minds of magnitude. Failing to make that distinction, we overemphasize the difference in the early and late Eliot or Wordsworth or Pound. In those minds of less magnitude we sometimes encounter a more spectacular or comic difference. Karl Shapiro writes a passionate *Defense of Ignorance* against Eliot and Pound in the 1950s; in the 1970s he passionately charges youth with ignorance: "We have the most inarticulate generation of college students in history. They don't want to learn; they want to 'feel.' They don't want to read; they want to 'experience.' They have become almost impossible to teach." One wishes, viewing the eternal struggle of youth and age (most fascinating when the struggle is within the one "conscious present" of one mind—Dante's or Eliot's or Shapiro's) for that healthy wisdom in the consciously aging Falstaff, who declares "We young must live." One wishes, that is, to see parts in that fullness dissolving into whole, to see development. To see finally an organic fullness of that mind.

And so it is one of my purposes to pay tribute to the mind of William Wordsworth as a more important antecedent of modern literature in English than it has been popular to acknowledge. As an influence on our letters, as a part of what we know, he has been largely relegated to a secondary position by our principal men of letters, while Coleridge is more generously acknowledged. The rise of new attitudes in criticism in this young and vigorous century, accompanying and proceeding from the new literature so prominently associated with the names of Pound and Eliot in poetry and Joyce and Hemingway in fiction, have allowed less conscious sympathy for Wordsworth than is justified by kinship. Pound, though he shares Wordsworth's disdain of Dryden, cannot speak of Wordsworth except disparagingly, as "ole shepe Wordsworth." Eliot, though he shares with Wordsworth an intense concern for the decay of sensibility in the seventeenth and eighteenth centuries, also attacks Wordsworth, without bringing himself to speak his principal adversary's name, in that famous essay on the uses of the past from which we have already quoted.

We should remember that it was Wordsworth who concerned himself so largely with the wasteland imminent— with the social, economic, and political disintegration upon England as it moved into the nineteenth century—warning repeatedly in his verse of decay in the moral fiber of his countrymen. If he was not so acidly effective as Ezra Pound's early slashing verses, for instance "Pax Saturni," he nevertheless registers a vigorous kindred opposition. Wordsworth lacks the quick wit and audacity of Pound, whose prophetic cry is that to misuse language is to "bear false witness." But Wordsworth's early attack upon false diction displays the same concern. Nor has one escaped false use by proscribing it, as Pound in later years has come more fully to realize.

In retrospect—in survey (as in survey courses)—we have tended to place Wordsworth in the tradition of English letters as a revolutionary, exaggerating his reaction to his

4

immediate elders and to his eighteenth-century predecessors. We have his word for it, in the famous prefaces and in his letters and in the poems themselves. But we have obscured to ourselves, as he in a measure obscured to himself, the traditionalist that Wordsworth was from the beginning. He called forth responses from his immediate successors—from Shelley, Byron, Browning—that argue a marked, even sudden, fundamental change in him, but it is a change more imagined than real. Wordsworth was never so eager to let old things pass, like Chaucer's monk, as the young perpetually expect their revolutionary leaders to be. The charge that he deserted "just for a handful of silver," like the charge against Eliot that with *The Waste Land* he betrayed the modern movement to the academy, underlines less a fundamental change in Wordsworth or Eliot than a growing awareness of complexity in Browning and William Carlos Williams.

It is predictable in the light of human nature that Wordsworth excoriate his eighteenth-century fathers and go behind them to invoke Milton in an indictment of the England bequeathed him, that "fen / Of stagnant waters." It is to one's grandfathers—natural or elected—that one looks when one's fathers seem to have failed, Dante's Cacciaguida, Eliot's Dante and Donne. But the struggle to disassociate oneself from the immediate past, to which struggle we give the term revolution, is never so fullhearted a desire nor so possible of success as innocent desire believes possible. Wordsworth's eighteenth-century decorum, the desire for worldly order, are deeply engrained. Surely Eliot is right that "much of the poetry of Wordsworth and Coleridge is just as turgid and artificial and elegant as any eighteenth century die-hard could wish." Nor is this criticism, in Wordsworth's case, applicable only to "Descriptive Sketches." And while Eliot may attack Milton and Wordsworth initially, he too grows closer to them finally. There is the famous second essay on Milton. If we have as his opinion that Wordsworth and Coleridge "were just as eighteenth century as anybody," we are increasingly inclined to see Eliot as far more nineteenth century than he suspected or wished to be. And we notice in examining Eliot that his poetry certifies Wordsworth's predictions of decay in images that one can scarcely read effectively without Wordsworth's images in mind. There are for instance the two famous evenings: Wordsworth addresses a holy time "quiet as a Nun / Breathless with adoration"; Eliot gives us the evening "spread out against the sky / Like a patient etherized upon a table." Wordsworth on the beach in what is to him the temple of the world gives way to Prufrock in the city, spiritually anesthetized, despairing of ever hearing mermaids call him to associated sensibilities. Eliot's debt to Wordsworth is implied and is a part of the effectiveness of his figure. The two evenings attempt to find in sufficient correlatives a distinction, the one of a sensibility still alive though threatened with extinction, the other of a sensibility very nearly dead. In reading Eliot closely, one becomes increasingly aware just how much Milton and Wordsworth are a part of what he knows. It is a knowledge one may measure in Wordsworth's and Eliot's common concern for endangered sensibility as seen in the more commensurate figure of the speaker of those "Lines Composed a Few Miles above Tintern Abbey" compared to Eliot's "Love Song of J. Alfred Prufrock." If we see Prufrock's sad desire to have been a pair of ragged claws scuttling floors of silent seas as an inevitable extension of Wordsworth's remembered state in nature when like the roe he ranged the countryside, we will nevertheless discover Eliot coming to think Wordsworth's romanticism less the creator of Prufrock's world than he at first supposed.

Wordsworth, long before Eliot, is concerned with a decay in English poetry, though it was Eliot who was to argue its principle source in Milton, a disease Eliot made famous under the term "dissociation of sensibility." Eliot sees that split in sensibility occurring between Dryden and Milton, with Milton's blindness "the most important fact about Milton" since because of it this poet's "sensuousness, such as it was, had been withered early by book-learning." The suggestion is that, had Milton somewhat quit his books before his blindness and engaged life more directly, he would have escaped perhaps the artificial, the "literary," though Eliot is not of course prepared to declare with Wordsworth that books are "a dull and endless strife." While Eliot declares that "at no period is the visual imagination conspicuous in Milton's poetry," it is some time after that he is to say "the mystery of iniquity is a pit too deep for mortal eyes to plumb," appreciating more fully Milton's burden assumed in that attempt to justify God's ways to man. Wordsworth finds Dryden the blind one of the pair. "The poetry of the period intervening between the publication of *Paradise Lost* and *The Seasons* does not contain a single new image of external nature; and scarcely presents a familiar one from which it can be inferred that the eye of the Poet had been steadily fixed upon his object." If Wordsworth is as severe in his judgment of Dryden as Eliot of Milton, the more important point is still that both Eliot and Wordsworth are exploring an approximate area in the English literary tradition with a common agreement that something went wrong in that period.

Wordsworth turns our attention then to the appropriateness of thought to feelings. He attempts a philosophical justification of our responses to those sensory experiences he believes involve true callings to the spirit through the medium of nature, a position Eliot comes to occupy in the *Four Quartets* more fully than Wordsworth was capable of doing. Those callings are not to Wordsworth the consciously fanciful mermaids that Prufrock toys with. Not that one doesn't find fear, and sometimes terror, attendant upon the questions Wordsworth tries. Earlier than the publication of *Lyrical Ballads,* he wonders whether he might not be deluded by fancy in a way fundamentally destructive of mind as well as of art.

As Wordsworth laments England's decline, and the decline of his own powers, he concerns himself with the possible causes of that disassociated sensibility in the eighteenth- and nineteenth-century Englishman which leaves one in a

7

self-willed enslavement to the man-made world, whose manifestation is Eliot's "timekept city," our own world's nightmare. Eliot wrote of that city, in the voice of the leveling wind: "Here were decent godless people: / Their only monument the asphalt road / And a thousand lost golf balls." A variety of sciences since Wordsworth's day have examined both the city's powers to destroy nature and man's capacity to respond to nature. Bertrand Russell can promise man a future (in 1961): "We are suffering from indigested science. But in a world of more adventurous education this indigested mass would be enlarged to embrace new worlds to be depicted in new epics." At the present, when the constrictions upon life in the city make human life, even animal life, doubtful, the epics are not forthcoming nor like to be. The moon landing stirs the poetic mind a moment, and fades toward insignificance as we find mercury in our rivers and complex death in the city air we breathe. We look back toward our grandfathers, puzzled and angry. "Poets like Baudelaire and painters like Monet," Charles Madge wrote in the *Times Literary Supplement* (25 October 1963), "were able to assimilate at least a part of the new urban-industrial world into their art. . . . But it now seems as though they were only able to achieve it so long as enough of the imagery of the pre-industrial world remained active. It was possible to be poetic about railroads so long as horses were a part of everyday life. . . . No one now seems capable of doing for our period what they did for theirs. For one thing, the turnover of technology is too rapid. The process of 'digestion' has not even time to begin." And C. P. Snow, long embattled in the war of the two cultures, can but underline the impossibility of the poet's going hand in hand with the man of science, as Wordsworth had dreamed possible. In "A Second Look at *The Two Cultures,*" he says, "One word about another passage where I showed bad judgment. . . . I have regretted that I used as my test question about scientific literacy: 'What do you know of the Second Law of Thermodynamics?' " What one might better know, he says, are the secrets of DNA. But that was so long ago, in 1963. Not only does the modern world at this moment seem to preclude a Homer, but a Lucretius as well. The death in life of our literature's Sweeneys and Prufrocks is a death Wordsworth both announced and attempted to prevent, though with a mind not deliberately committed to the technically philosophical or theological defenses one finds in Milton or Eliot. Particularly do we need reminding as we read Eliot's indictments of the "unreal City," the "timekept City" that Wordsworth too stood on London Bridge disturbed by those whom death in life has undone. Eliot asks:

> When the Stranger says: "What is the meaning of this city?
> Do you huddle close together because you love each other?"
> What will you answer? "We all dwell together
> To make money from each other"?

That was the answer Wordsworth heard over a hundred years before Eliot's words. But standing on Westminster Bridge in 1802 he, a stranger in the city, saw, as Eliot was to do, another possibility of the city caught by the mind for a moment in harmony with nature, suggesting a possibility of the mind's joyful engagement with the world, even including the city. After Wordsworth's morning vision of the city, before Eliot's version of it "Under the brown fog" of winter crowded with the walking dead, Wordsworth resolutely announced man's mind as a creator capable of self-rescue from that death in Eliot's *Waste Land*. Heffernan, in *Wordsworth's Theory of Poetry: The Transforming Imagination* (1969) has detailed Wordsworth's developing affirmation, the details of which show not only why Wordsworth came to a rest in the established church, as did Eliot, but show as well by implication affinities in their growth and development. A belief in the transforming powers of the mind, which is so central a concern in Wordsworth's argument for the poet, developed from that early assertion that mind half perceives and half creates. It leads Wordsworth to his attempt to build that "Gothic Church" to which his *Prelude* was to be "Ante-chapel." Eliot also

9

praises man's creative powers in choruses of "The Rock," and in terms which Wordsworth would have surely recognized. In justifying the building of the temple in the midst of continuing decay, Eliot has his Son of Man say:

> The soul of Man must quicken to creation.
> Out of the formless stone, when the artist united himself with stone,
> Spring always new forms of life, from the soul of man that is joined to the soul of stone;
> Out of the meaningless practical shapes of all that is living or lifeless
> Joined with the artist's eye, new life, new forms, new colour.
> Out of the sea of sound the life of music,
> Out of the slimy mud of words, out of the sleet and hail of verbal imprecisions,
> Approximate thoughts and feelings, words that have taken the place of thoughts and feelings.
> There spring the perfect order of speech, and the beauty of incantation.

Not, of course, that correspondences of concern in Eliot and Wordsworth are identical. The slimy mud of words with which the poet as an image of God makes his poem (Eliot's metaphor makes the poem an Adam) is inevitably flawed, as the numerous parodies of Wordsworth and Eliot make all too obvious. Nor is either poet free of "verbal imprecisions." What is of importance, once more, is a common concern for the poet's powers of relating thoughts and feelings so that there may spring forth an order of speech which bears the beauty of incantation. In the 1970s, when the city is so ominously present as antagonist upon which we center the anger of our disassociated sensibilities, when the spectacular violence of self-justification and self-pity are abroad, signs and wonders are once more evident: we invoke the global village. But it may be that the errors of desire, controlled by sloth or panic, will overwhelm us. Ignorant trust of a negative capability through electronics, fed by sentimentality and ennui, make us proclaim that the media never will betray the mind that surrenders to it in pureness of heart. The word within the Media may save us, we seem to feel, since we have lost the Word within the word. Among our young who revolt in such fever pitch we note the turning is toward the past, toward their grandfathers. It would seem that for the first time in history there is a general concert to "turn back the clock," that derisive phrase no longer serving the forces of Progress against its opposition as it has so often since Bacon. The blindness of our turning to the past—and we are an age which has lost its history—no doubt makes it appear more a rejection of the past than it is. There is a great deal of violent stumbling in the dark. But among the interesting signs, upon which we may build some expectation, are a new interest in Pound, in Eliot, in Wordsworth. A new interest in knowing "how much tradition inhered in the immediate elders," as Pound says, even as we strive to throw off "the more obvious imbecilities of ... immediate elders." In a world whose hunger for new form, new objects of devotion, is at a critical pitch, what emerges more and more is that the hunger is for a reasonable and emotionally assuring sense of continuity. Still, the multitudinous quest of the moment is for a tradition suited to the individual talent which, one is instructed from of old, it is death to hide.

Though the concern is a hopeful one, our quest for community in which the individual may find a place and a sense of continuity is not wisely pursued. That we are in some measure, and in my view to a considerable measure, blind is suggested by our increasingly general attempt to restore Dame Fortune to her ancient position. This, we declare, is the Age of Aquarius. We might profitably recall something of the history of Boethius' Lady of the Moon in the light of our new interest in triangulation of the individual by the stars. The concept of capricious fortune, our pagan inheritance, was undermined in the late Middle Ages by a growing faith that the created world was an orderly extension of omnipotence and omniscience. Willard Farnham says in *The Medieval Heritage of Elizabethan Tragedy* in dis-

11

cussing Dante's presentation of Dame Fortune and Boccaccio's and Petrarch's denial of her in their philosophical and theological debates: "She whom men had been taught to think of as proof against understanding was fated to be ultimately denied in a world of new scientific confidence, which defined chance as an order only temporarily hidden from man's intellectual grasp and capable of being exposed by some triumphant discoverer of its laws." Or, one might say, Fortune was at first baptized out of paganism into Christianity, rose slowly out of the dying ashes of the fascination with nature and astrology, was reborn yet again as Natural Law. That new faith in orderliness of the created world under the power of God was prelude to a separation of the orderly world from God, as from pagan belief in chance. That was the work of Hobbes and Newton and Locke. By the end of the nineteenth century, however, one comes upon a greater terror than the old one which saw Fortune as capricious. Even Dame Fortune is preferable to a Hardy; but he can see only that "Crass Casualty obstructs the sun and rain, / And dicing Time for gladness casts a moan. . . ." So too a desperateness in Crane, Twain, the Naturalists. Boethius' wheel in Fortune's hand is now a wheel in neither Fortune's nor God's hand. It is precise, ordered, unwavering, but most terrible of all, indifferent. The marvels of physics, the mystery of astronomy, culminate in $E = MC^2$.

But more significant of our civilization, if less spectacular than man walking on Dame Fortune's moon, is the rebirth of astrology in our day. The Age of Aquarius knows more of conjunctions than of curved space. Tarot cards are more commanding of the sophisticated modern than either transubstantiation or Einstein's triumphant discovery, for the laws of Christ or of physics enjoin the question of free will which our age wishes least to hear. If we find the grosser measure of our existence by deterministic physics and biochemistry to be spiritually or psychologically indigestible, we yet commit ourselves to that determinism out of our old heritage of dark despair. We romanticize it by

12

enlarging science's determinism and dressing it in poetic abstraction; we enjoy it under the pretense of fancy—that is, we pretend to pretend to believe the ordered system of astrology. Our sophisticated detachment assumes that its stance is not *deluded* commitment, for it is a deliberate and knowing pretense. In other words, we play at astrology, as did legions in the twilight of the classical world when it became no longer possible to believe man had any influence upon his own circumstances or destiny. Whistling in the dark, we enter upon a new Chaldean mysticism, a game to while away sober thought. And so we forget how often such games presage avid and dogmatic commitment beyond the press of reason, with large effect upon the generality. Even the current horrors of mass murders we take as local aberration and not symptoms of pervasive disorder. But ulcers are not supernatural; they tell us something about the body.

One of the justifications for my present concern for Eliot and Wordsworth then is that I may suggest how they too were interested in community, interested in a possible meaning in the city of man larger than its appearance as a place where one huddles with his fellows "To make money from each other," the city of getting and spending. Their concern was more generally intelligent than our own frenzied concern. For Eliot and Wordsworth too, among others of our fathers, were concerned with community of minds and bodies as healthfully founded under the banner of that four letter word which has become so notoriously distorted by us—love. To begin to perceive that point is to begin to realize that we must not only recognize that the "times, they are a changing," but that those who are given to changing the times are themselves changing. The transformation that Wordsworth saw as so vitally present in the making of a poem, in which the poet himself is changed as he springs forth new forms of life, is a rich principle to the larger concerns of youth. What one anticipates, always hopefully in any dark age, is an accompanying recognition: our recent devotion to the idol Progress is a warping of a good inclination, an inclination through which we come to realize that the end of life is not simply change worshipped as progress, a movement toward some vague Utopia. It is fulfillment of that potential which is a mysterious gift perpetually celebrated by poet and saint according to his light, whether the Giver be called Nature or the Word. And with the recognition that the more things change the more they are the same, that there is nothing new under the sun, one eventually moves beyond both the shock and the burden of the clichés turning awfully, painfully true.

I

Shadows in the New Cave
THE POET AND THE REDUCTION OF MYTH

Leo Strauss, *Natural Right and History*

> No universal principle will ever sanction the acceptance of every historical standard or of every victorious cause; to conform with tradition or to jump on "the wave of the future" is not obviously better, and it is certainly not always better than to burn what one has worshipped or to resist the "trend of history."

Eliot, *For Lancelot Andrewes*

> To put the sentiments in order is a later and an immensely difficult task: intellectual freedom is earlier and easier than complete spiritual freedom.

The decay toward Eliot's unreal city is sufficiently advanced in Wordsworth's view of his world to make an invocation of an English bard, Milton, seemingly more suitable than an invocation of the Holy Spirit or Calliope. Those presiding spirits of the old epic seemed more remote and lost even than the heroes Carlyle was presently to celebrate with burning passion. High drama proved elusive as well, as Wordsworth discovered in his tragedy *The Borderers*. In the press to answer the question "Who clipped the lions wings / And flea'd his rump and pared his claws?" Wordsworth named his own nebulous Lucifer: industrialism, a popular villain who has become more popular than ever in our own day. But industrialism was a villian at once so worldly and so nebulous as to allow the growth of no informing myth that could sustain the old high style necessary to the celebration of the heroic wealth of hall and bower that had been England.

Already history had become the river of continuous event, washing individuals along inexorably, a view which might exhilarate the emerging historicist whom Leo Strauss has analyzed in *Natural Right and History*. For historicism finally comes to consider itself "a particular form of positivism, that is, of the school which held that theology and metaphysics had been superseded once and for all by positive science or which identified genuine knowledge of reality with the knowledge supplied by the empirical sciences." So it is that Wordsworth, in *The Borderers,* is divided in his attempt by a confusion of tragedy and history. His play is largely a history but not like Shakespeare's in which the dramatist manipulates large spectacular events of common knowledge to pose metaphysical mysteries. Wordsworth attempts to give the history of one mind's decay from the good. He attempts to explain psychological steps in the degeneration of the hero he posits, first to explain it in the play itself, then in a very interesting introduction to that play which we shall have occasion to examine at some length.

Man as a flow in nature—history—has never proved adequate to the poet, tragic or epic. Neither the narrative nor drama yields satisfactory results as an instrument of empirical science, for mind is always larger than its measure, since it is the measurer. The ambiguity of fate and will remains unriddled in Greek tragedy, as it does in the struggles of the nineteenth- and twentieth-century poet under the growing shadow of determinism which led to the dead end of naturalism. Wordsworth almost instinctively realized the limitations of such an approach to the mystery of man. Whatever we may say of him as a poet of nature, we cannot make of him a naturalist. But in the absence of a metaphysical position that would make him initially comfortable in the presence of mystery, and in the absence of heroes to celebrate as changeless in the rapidly changing world of the mind, he sought solution by posing the natural world against the world made by man's mind. In an age increasingly devoted to the dream of progress, he puzzled the decline of a society through a span of centuries, the decline of the individual mind from wise innocence of youth to the enslavement of sequential life in nature. He, too, sought a still point, what he called "spots of time," in which there was a harmony of mind in nature allowing a transcendence of time and place.

But how are such moments to be dramatized? For the concern is more philosophical than poetic. It may be that such moments allow lyric intensity. Whether or not the concern allows an epic of the mind such as Wordsworth wished to compose is another question—one still heatedly debated with Wordsworth as principal. Wordsworth may seek

To apprehend all passions and all moods
Which time, and place, and season do impress
Upon the visible universe, and work
Like changes there by force of my own mind.

But in withdrawing, at Cambridge, from his fellows to voyage through strange seas of his own thought, he has

19

difficulty speaking in any "higher language" that conveys what he feels,

> What independent solaces . . .
> To mitigate the injurious sway of place
> Or circumstance.

Wordsworth can report the experience of a higher summons, so interestingly paralleled in Stephen Dedalus' callings in Joyce's *Portrait,* but he seldom dramatizes them. For what he has to present us, he says

> in the main
> . . . lies far hidden from the reach of words.
> Points have we all of us within our souls
> Where all stand single; this I feel, and make
> Breathings for incommunicable powers;
> But is not each a memory to himself?

Indeed so. And it is the artist's task to find those means through words, to find the necessary "objective correlative" within whose boundaries each may breathe feelings with some confidence of a community of mind.

The problems Wordsworth reflects upon here are the problems Joyce, Eliot, Pound offer solutions to. What one acknowledges in tribute to Wordsworth finally may be less his accomplishment as poet, except in isolated lyrical passages and brief poems that carry "Breathings for incommunicable powers," than his recognition of impending problems and his concern that they be solved, not only in the interest of the artist, but mankind's interest as well. A part of his attempted solution was to pose the country against the city, a moment of time in harmony with nature against the suffocating flux overwhelming man with the pressures of getting and spending. In that context he contended with the starvation of sensibilities. His world was already fast approaching that moment when, as Yeats put it, "the center cannot hold." That moment where Baudelaire was to announce to the discomfort of the poet no less than of the community—since from that moment life seemed given over to inexorable flow—"The Devil's deepest wile is to persuade us that he does not exist."

Let us then consider the effect of the death of Satan, which preceded by some years our own announcement of the death of God, upon the possibilities of a poetry larger than the lyric song or cry. When the world thoroughly accepts the proposition that the Devil does not exist, as ours has come to do since Wordsworth's day, it becomes more safely possible to use old myths in our art: safely, because their use implies no commitment to them beyond what we are pleased to call the aesthetic. It becomes no longer expected of the artist that he seek a viable myth, as Blake and Yeats and Lawrence did under the embarrassment of a current myth's failure, for indeed Christianity did seem to have fallen beneath even the level of myth under the new science's onslaught. But myth, given such intellectual freedom with it as our age enjoys, tends to become merely background whose presence we discover through the artist's skill at indirection, though he may often give us a hint in his title or in symbols. Eliot recognizes in *Ulysses* a partial solution to a technical problem in modern literature. Reviewing that novel for the *Dial,* he declares: "[Using myth] is simply a way of controlling, of ordering, of giving a shape and a significance to the immense panorama of futility and anarchy which is contemporary history. . . . It is a method for which the horoscope is auspicious. . . . Instead of the narrative method, we may now use the mythical method. It is, I seriously believe, a step toward making a modern world possible for art." Rather clearly, Eliot sees myth at this point as a device. It is a shell forming, but not informing. Since *Ulysses,* myth has become an aesthetic game the mind plays: the hidden term of a larger metaphor whose end is metaphor itself. Or, when most highly refined, the end is the indirection of the metaphor, an illusion of order in disparity. What is assumed in such an attitude toward myth, whether found in the poet or the critical explicator, is an ultimate irrelevance of myth to what we call "reality," that vaguest of all our terms of escape. Of course, one might pursue myth as a figuring of Freudian "realities"—as a source of data out of which the immediate source of the myth (the artist) may be characterized. Such was a popular critical sport between the two world wars, before the coming of the Age of Aquarius into the popular imagination. The Freudian myth in literature seems to have run its course in criticism no less than in literature itself. Conrad Aiken recalls realizing, as early as 1927, that Freud, Einstein, Darwin, and Nietzsche "had suddenly turned our neat little religious or philosophic systems into something that looked alarmingly like pure mathematics." Whither the poet? Eliot's answer was the Church of England and a life of the mind accepted as larger than mythical.

The enthusiasm of a Lawrence in the pursuit of dark forces of the blood, a very intense commitment to myth on Lawrence's part, has no arresting parallels in current creative literature. And perhaps we shall presently come to the conclusion that Freud was himself the great artist of Freudianism, the great mythic poet of the twilight of determinism. Perhaps when one comes to use the term Freudian in literary criticism, it will carry the implication of the derivative, as Miltonic or Joycean now do. It seems to me, at any rate, that Freud's relation to the poet or novelist is analogous to that of Homer to Joyce. But the principal point here is that myth, whether Freudian or Homeric, is largely a mechanism of our art, rather than a vision related to it as may be said of Freud's or Lawrence's or Yeats's. Myth has become abstracted and intellectualized in the interest of an imposed form or order with an accompanying hypertrophy of the abstract. Its relevance to any attempt upon a reality tangent to the work of art becomes a question not to be asked. Generally, myth is to narrative and drama as meter is to verse. To the extent that one may concern himself with its sources or ends, myth is taken to be the slough of history.

To see myth, in effect, as a vestige of primitive ritual

and ceremony—to see myth as the mind's vestigial appendix—is actually to see it only as a residue of bothersome history at last turned to some intellectually entertaining use. What I want to affirm is that myth alive is history numinous. The element of myth which permeates the *Oresteia* trilogy or *The Iliad* is not to be come at simply by an enumeration of details of legend or delineation of theme. Myth as I mean it is signified by awe and piety in the medium itself—the mind of the poet; that is, it is a quality seen in the world by the poet and signified by the voice of the poet. My distinction can be perceived if one compares what is ordinarily meant by myth as applied to Eliot's *Waste Land* (myth as controlled by "intellectual freedom") and what I here mean by myth as it causes a shining forth in the *Four Quartets*. There is a very distinct difference in Eliot's sense of myth in the *Quartets,* a distinction to which our prefatory epigraph relates. One is not so much required to accept the shining forth as being from a true vision as to acknowledge that it seems so to Eliot. There results an intensity in the *Quartets* which cannot be explained by exhaustive analysis of the poems' techniques independent of the sense of commitment carried by those techniques.

Myth conceived merely as vestigial history, used as material for modern poem or narrative or play, is deceptive. It suggests a magnitude to the thing signified in the foreground figure—usually a figure we have come to call the antihero—in excess of what the foreground figure in fact allows if examined carefully. Given such circumstances, we no longer have myth but its dead skin and bones, within which a modern (if not synthetic) flesh is forced as toothpaste into its decorated tube. For myth is dead when it is reduced to no more than fancy's paraphernalia—when it does not compel us to that substantial truth of which myth is the shining forth. (I use *fancy* as the term is distinguished from imagination by Coleridge; a point one might make about Prufrock is that he sometimes cannot, and generally will not, make the distinction.) The effect of the false is to corrupt both that mind which is myth's

23

medium (the poet) and the audience that otherwise would receive those live projections which good art is.

To make my argument clearer, let me introduce a quotation from Wordsworth's 1802 "Appendix" to *Lyrical Ballads*. Here I translate his argument from its relation to "false diction" to my own argument with false myth. There is, when myth is skeleton or paraphernalia or stage background, and not an essential element of the insight that is projected, an unsettling of "ordinary habits of thinking, . . . thus assisting the Reader to approach to the perturbed and dizzy state of mind in which if he does not find himself, he imagines that he is balked of a peculiar enjoyment which poetry can and ought to bestow." For the "ordinary habits of thinking" do not lead one to think that a Leopold Bloom requires our consent as an Odysseus does, or Stephen as does Daedalus or Prometheus. The anonymous member of the chorus is not elevated to the status of hero by casting him against an Agamemnon. It is rather the other way round. In the modern procedure, in which the rule is to use myth as metaphor, the metaphor's terms become inverted. The major term of a metaphor, the center of poetry's definition, includes an aspect of the minor term: one's love is like a rose in respect to the blossoming of her youth. But we are in a strange world indeed when the rose becomes the major term. In that larger, more inclusive metaphor of the human condition which drama (and narrative) constitute there is a relation of two similar terms. While an Agamemnon wavers in action (and in this respect is like the chorus), the chorus's habitual nature is inaction. Our epics and tragedies, on the other hand, become a pursuit of a place of green roses, a private refuge of the mind, with each psyche its only acceptable god.

If the reader catches on to what has happened in the reduction of myth and the perversion of its skin and bones—if he overcomes his "perturbed and dizzy state of mind"—he realizes that he has been "balked" into looking through what purports to be a scientific instrument upon the human estate, a magic lantern of Darwinian or Freudian or Marxian origins as usually advanced. Finding himself, he recollects the strange sensation: it is as if he has looked at the figure of man through the proverbial wrong end of a telescope. If he has really found himself, he may resist with some effectiveness the behavioral aesthetic dodge (inherited from the naturalists and refined through the arguments of psychology) which holds that the instrument of art is really an electronic microscope rather than telescope; he may conclude that the enlarged segment (the isolated individual) under view, while complete in the minutiae of detail, is after all a segment of a view and not an image of the whole creature.

Wordsworth felt that the poet was obliged to define the difference between himself and the "ordinary" man in order to establish a conception of the poet as the medium to project that whole creature. He refused the conception of the poet as a specialized, unique creature in an order of creation separate from mankind, arguing that the poet differs from the ordinary man, not essentially, but in respect to the intensity of his perception. He was not only attempting to define the nature of the artist, but was acknowledging and attempting to overcome as well the gap between the artist and his audience, a separation whose cause would seem to lie largely at the poet's door. Even so, the poet, increasingly since Wordsworth's time and not without much justification, has directed blame for his own loss of station against this century's middleman and patron of the arts, personified as Advertising. Still, if we are to look critically at industry's handmaiden, advertising, or examine the threat to the artist of Guggenheims, Ford Grants, or National Humanities Awards, we must look as well to that threat of the artist to his audience, for which Marianne Moore's contracting to name a new automobile may serve as parable, the text of which is the correspondence between Miss Moore and the Ford Motor Company's Marketing Research Division. When myth is to the poet and to his audience larger and livelier than metaphor, art itself has an immediate relevance to life, though a sudden and excessive blooming is

25

often a sign of its death—as in Elizabethan times, or in the first quarter of the nineteenth century, or in the twenty-five years following World War I, in which sequence each "showing forth" of myth became progressively weaker. In Eliot, personal spiritual unrest leads to an awareness of the relevance of art to life, and a concern for their separation in western culture becomes a part of the matter of his verse. One notices in particular the succeeding stages of failure presented in "Sweeney Erect"; Ariadne, Aspatia, Sweeney's mate decline the emotions from a bang to a whimper. And in that poem with the Wordsworthian title, "Whispers of Immortality," Eliot is very much about the problem of language. The poem is a wry, self-deprecating comment on the inability of the finest minds to unite the metaphysical and physical in words, a subject he returns to in a new mode and with enthusiasm at the end of *Little Gidding*. "Whispers of Immortality" implies a decay in Webster and Donne, out of the seeds of decay of thought planted by Origen, whom Eliot specifically calls "enervate" (as does Saint Augustine). The end of that decay is the wasteland of the post-World War I decade. Even Eliot's much admired metaphysicals, those self-conscious romantics whose camouflage is wit, fail to express the essential soul that whispers below the sound of words, only "circumambulating" Grishkin's worldliness. One can, with the sophistication of the metaphysicals, see the mortality in flesh and express it in terms of the fleshly Grishkin plus marmoset. But Eliot is still some time conjugating the jaguar beyond Death to Christ. At the moment (1917) Grishkin is "nice," an effective understatement on the failure of words to express the whisper suspected beneath the whisper of flesh. Pound's later comment in *The Pisan Cantos* that there is more to Grishkin than Eliot's portrait shows is to the point. But Eliot is aware that there is more, even if in his youth he takes refuge in the detachment of wit and Bradleyan phenomenology. The reality he is haunted by will bear no definition in the words of either poetry or philosophy at that point in his thinking, and he hangs back, fearful of risk, as John Crowe Ransom and Donald Davidson were quick to notice.

The same unresolved awareness is in "The Hippopotamus," which is taken too simply when it is taken to represent Eliot's ridicule and rejection of the Church. The irony of the True Church's being likened to the hippopotamus protects the poet from the scorn of such intellectuals of the 1920s as those one finds represented in Aldous Huxley's early novels. What one recalls, however, and what Eliot later affirms in his own person as he comes to abandon the safety which a mask affords the poet in a skeptical age, is that Christ did not come to bring Heaven to earth but to make the earthly eligible for Heaven. That the hippopotamus should sprout wings is miracle almost beyond belief. While the figure is comic in its terms, the implications of the terms are no more wondrous than that man, the lowly worm, should sprout wings, become that angelic butterfly on which Dante lectures us early in *The Purgatorio*. Eliot makes witty sermon of his figure of the Church as hippopotamus: "God works in a mysterious way— / The Church can sleep and feed at once." These lines, generally taken as sardonic, mark the end of the surface satire in the poem. The final three stanzas are in the tone of revelation, of a transport beyond that which the intellect can know into the region of that knowledge which passes understanding. It is as if the speaker of the lines, come to scoff, has remained at least to wonder. Man's soul, the angelic butterfly, which seems to the eyes of man more like a winged hippopotamus than the delicate creature of flowers Dante calls it, is released in spite of the obfuscation of the "True Church" in the "old miasmal mist" of this world. Eliot, who remarks that the present is an "awareness of the past . . . which the past's awareness of itself cannot show," adopts an ironic perspective upon the past. But irony is never simply historical. It necessarily involves a dissociation from personality at the present moment of its enactment, allowing a perspective upon the medium—ironic historian or poet—to a degree that the poet or historian is unaware

27

of. It is later that Eliot can describe the poet as "occupied with frontiers of consciousness beyond which words fail" and conclude that "ambiguities may be due to the fact that the poem means more, not less, than ordinary speech can communicate." That is, it is much later that Eliot is able to move beyond a dependence upon irony. But the reflective mind is never likely to move purely beyond the touch of irony, for the presentness of the past and the presentness of the present involve inevitable juxtaposition in the reflective poet. Yesterday's poem is never today's, though its words be irrevocably fixed.

Deliberate irony involves some mask that hides a pharisee, a point upon which it is not easy to meet a reader honestly and directly, as Gerontion acknowledges. That it is a concern increasingly disturbing to Eliot is reflected in his first two volumes of poems in which is revealed a poet very much at war with himself. He recognizes that the enemy within, his special burden, is the intellect, and he recognizes it long before William Carlos Williams or Karl Shapiro raises that alarm. The inevitable enemy—as Dante also becomes aware, regretfully releasing Virgil back to Limbo and turning to Beatrice—is the intellect. For the intellect has as its special charge that language which "Whispers of Immortality" finds inadequate, since intellect alone cannot go so far as to touch the essential Grishkin or say the true name of the jaguar, in which names reside the possible name of Beatrice or Christ. The final lines are again sardonic, directed at the intellectual poet:

> And even the Abstract Entities
> Circumambulate her charm;
> But our lot crawls between dry ribs
> To keep our metaphysics warm.

How myth's truth is destroyed by the intellect is the theme of "Mr. Eliot's Sunday Morning Service," in which poem we see those "Polyphiloprogenitive / ... sapient sutlers of the Lord" submitting myth to autopsy by intellect: "Superfetation of ["the One"] / Produced enervate Origen." The masters of the subtle schools are inevitably oblivious both to Sweeney in his bath and to those souls of the devout that "Burn invisible and dim," perhaps even in a Grishkin.

The decay of language concerned Wordsworth at the time of *Lyrical Ballads,* as it did Eliot at the time of his volume *Ara Vos Prec.* But the decay was associated in his mind not with the failures of certain scholastics or intellectual poets but with the general decay of society. Out of this concern he turned to an interest in the individual, and with the fervor of a Dante; but he is a Dante who is looking for and expecting (in his initial period) a temporal revolution and a general return to the old high ways. In this respect he is closer to Pound and to Pound's pursuit of the City of Dioce than to Eliot and a vision of the City of God. Wordsworth's poetry in this early stage is full of the spirit of reform, as even the most casual reader knows. For that old sense of hierarchal order and individual responsibility, whether of pagan or Christian origin, which had informed literature even into Wordsworth's day and which is of such interest to Shakespeare and Milton, had given way. By the beginning of the nineteenth century it was so far removed from the common mind that Wordsworth's first impulsive action was to commit himself to that attempt at a new order and unity in the world which we call the French Revolution. Of course, he reacts almost at once against that new thought. But it was a force not to be withstood by any common community of mind so that by the end of the century, the diversity of acceptable orders and responsibilities, of which the French Revolution was a part, had had its way. The diversity, our scientific heritage from Bacon through Darwin and our philosophical heritage from Origen through William James, was exemplified in the nationalistic spirit that exhibited itself in the realm of the state and that excessive protestantism that embraced a spectrum of belief from Catholic to atheist. The changed condition of the mind's world largely prevented our acceptance of a Hopkins in terms of his commitment.

His sense of hierarchy can be safely taken only as a gimmick for literary structure, as a mask assumed. The commitment explained away, the poetry presumably becomes more generally acceptable to an indefinite audience. But the consequence of explaining away the reality which myth plumbs has been not so much to make a Dante aesthetically acceptable to Protestant or atheist as to loose (in Yeats's words once more) "Mere anarchy . . . upon the world" in which flood all "ceremony of innocence is drowned."

The old system which placed man in a hierarchy and gave structure to the thought of Dante and Chaucer and Shakespeare ceases to be viable in the nineteenth century, particularly following the 1850s. A new and more terrifying allegory of the cave emerges, signaled pathetically in Arnold's dark view of the shadows in "Dover Beach." The old system which was still enough alive to give power to a drama of its violation in a *Macbeth* or *Lear* or *Paradise Lost* becomes a dead thing—sometimes used as wall props for an echo chamber into which new ideas are thrown. But in the new cave the shadows seen are taken to have no relation to a light that might be transcendentally true. Futile attempts to rescue the ceremonies of innocence are made by Emerson or Thoreau or Carlyle. But inevitably the dramatic possibilities of our literature lead to a Leopold Bloom to be played against Odysseus, a Sweeney to be played against Agamemnon, a Prufrock against Hamlet. The faint echo and exaggerated gesture result in queer shadows, themselves taken as the new reality, and the center of meaning and art. Pathos succeeds tragedy. Finally the existentialist nightmare seizes literature and life. The hero's grand act is to rise from his chair or, if a truly grand hero, to remain in his chair. And when we discover that an Eliot is serious about there being life and substance to the old myths, we feel betrayed, as William Carlos Williams avows his generation to have been by *The Waste Land*. For if the work of the new movement in our literature "staggered to a halt for a moment under the blast of Eliot's genius which gave the poem back to the academics," as Williams says, it was not so much that Eliot interfered with metrical freedoms and introduced anew the allusion which required explication, but that he cast a cold light on what was an attempt to deny three thousand years of history. "Critically," says Williams, "Eliot returned us to the classroom just at a moment when I felt that we were on the point of escape to matters much closer to the essence of a new art form itself—rooted in the locality which should give it fruit." But one wonders whether it was Eliot who "had turned his back on the possibility of reviving [Williams's] world," or Williams and Hemingway (whose reminiscences of Eliot in *A Moveable Feast* show his rancor). Such members of the Lost Generation were forced to admit or pretend not to notice that they were too knowledgeable to pose convincingly as Grandma Moses.

Though the term is not his, it was against Absurdity (as the term is generally applied to our theater) that Wordsworth protested, as have Eliot and Pound. "I'd rather be a pagan" could almost be the motto Pound set out to follow in rescuing the old and making it new. As prophet, and the agent—character—in his own poetry, Wordsworth predicted our Prufrocks and our Molloys and Estragons. There is to be understood of course a basic difference in the "protestantism" of Wordsworth as compared to Pound, as of Pound compared to Eliot. Wordsworth's great concern is, finally, like Eliot's, less a literary or political than a religious one; the old hierarchy that Milton believed in did not sustain Wordsworth in his early years so that he turned toward a salvation through the individual's relationship to whatever higher force he could perceive through emotional intuition. He seems to perceive in nature what Hopkins would hold to be a presence of the Holy Spirit. Pound is not religious in this sense. His concern is to deny any hierarchy of values in literature. There is that which is superlative, and there is the rest—to be cast into outer darkness. Pound's literary puritanism is really a new scholasticism in the arts. It leads him to editing the world, prescribing and translating the "Authorized Version," himself providing

31

a *Summa* for the true and lively word of the imagination. He is not so much opposed to Wordsworth's doctrine, actually, as to the weakness of Wordsworth's witness of that doctrine. Thus we may have him declare: "Wordsworth, emotion almost null, emotional element scarcely present and evaluation largely humbug." In the same passage he has just declared, "The poetic sense, almost the sole thing which one can postulate as underlying all great poetry and indispensable to it, is simply the sense of overwhelming emotional values." And for those "who must have definitions: Poetry is a verbal statement of emotional values. . . . Good art is expression of emotional values which do not give way to the intellect. Bad art is merely an assertion of emotion, which intellect, common-sense, knocks into a cocked hat." Wordsworth's famous prefaces are also a part of what Pound knows. It is then to Wordsworth at the halfway house of English letters, between Chaucer and Pound, Shakespeare and Eliot, that we now turn to consider in more detail both how traditional and how modern he is.

Innocence Abroad

諈Dylan Thomas, "Fern Hill"

> Time held me green and dying
> Though I sang in my chains like the sea.

諈Eliot, "A Dialogue on Dramatic Poetry"

> As for us, we know too much, and are convinced of too little.

諈Robert Herrick, "The Argument of His Book"

> I write of hell; I sing . . .
> Of heaven, and hope to have it after all.

Innocence is not necessarily a derogatory term, though it commonly carries that overtone in our age. For the concept of innocence has been terribly eroded through a superficial sophistication which confuses innocence with naiveté. We might well recall then what we know or have known traditionally about that concept. A high and serious concern for innocence is most conspicuously a theme in the literature we commonly agree upon as our landmarks. Given a loss of a high sense of innocence, we have since Wordsworth's interest in the child as blessed seer devoted a considerable talent upon the child. "Huck Finn as Hero" could almost be made an inclusive title for the study of our century's fiction and poetry, whose elegiac note laments the loss of naiveté rather than the loss of that innocence I shall presently define. From "Tintern Abbey" to "Sailing to Byzantium" to "Fern Hill"; from *Great Expectations* and *The American* to *Catcher in the Rye* and *Lord of the Flies*. And with attention to such a diversity of complex and simple figurings of Huck Finn as Housman's "lads," Conrad's Lord Jim, Joyce's Stephen Dedalus, Hemingway's Jake Barnes.

What is significant is the range and multitude of literature that may be included in such a consideration. But one aspect they have in common, with varying degrees of intensity: a suspicion that to know is to be robbed, to be reduced. Indeed, one of our most generally available aphorisms, one that comes easily to the lips of the unlettered and semiliterate, no less than to the semisophisticated, is characteristic of the distortion. It is difficult to convince these that the poet did not in fact say "ignorance is bliss." And if "a *little learning* is a dangerous thing" it follows as the night the day that deepest wisdom lies in total abstinence. So thoroughly are we given to a desire that ignorance be supreme that Huck Finn has in our day come into his own, being the principle authority consulted by the professionals on questions of educational content or foreign policy. But a reading of innocence as ignorance is quite separate from the innocence I wish to consider. The high innocence of my concern is one in which full knowledge is ultimately engaged toward its recovery, a recognition which Wordsworth had come to acknowledge in "Tintern Abbey" when he justifies "thought." The fall from innocence here is a fall into ignorance. One can make the distinction I intend by reference to Dante's *New Life,* in which work there is present both the transcendent mind of the poet (what we shall be calling with Eliot's term *the medium* of the poem) and an agent depicted under the name of Dante. The mind of the poet is one consciously intent upon the high innocence which is the theme of the *Divine Comedy,* that is, intent upon the restoration of the soul to its proper estate. On the other hand *The New Life* has in its foreground the figure of the naive lover pursuing the beloved, in a pursuit which in the course of the work undergoes a profound transformation. There is a distinct separation of the voice giving the account from the history of the agent of whom the work is an account. The history of the lover's metamorphosis to the higher love is indeed contained within the voice of the poet; it is this very relationship which makes possible the dramatic effectiveness of *The New Life.* For what Dante the poet does in the work is dramatize how Dante the man came to be a poet. In the progress of the work the character who is dramatized—love's pilgrim—rises out of his initial naiveté to meld finally with the inclusive medium of the poem, the poet's mind. In the work, Dante the poet is setting down that portion of his imaginative autobiography that is relevant to his estate as poet.

We have in *The New Life* an analogue to a vast body of literature since Dante's time, but in particular the literature of American Innocence. If Whitman's "Out of the Cradle Endlessly Rocking" or "Song of Myself" are not deliberate literary descendants of *The New Life,* they are significantly related to it. That is, Whitman's poems are consequences of that milieu which Dante, and later Wordsworth, saw condensing on the western horizon. There was a new world dawning in which naive innocence was to be sharply divorced from the high innocence that was Dante's concern in the *Divine Comedy*. We can see now that it was an inevitable separation, since the end, the final cause, which gave order to that archetypal wandering of innocence which is Dante's theme, was being separated from the wandering itself. Here one notices an unfortunate effect of the Renaissance upon literature, the marks of which are most conspicuous in our own day. For Dante wrote from a position transcending the wandering itself, with a sufficient understanding of and detachment from the pattern to enable him to give aesthetic form to that wandering. It is surely a primary part of his intention to argue for that elevated position in the face of the growing confusions in the Western mind as to man's proper end. The seeking by the individual of his proper end, represented in primitive and sophisticated art alike by the journey, is an aspect of life which is universally recognized. In Dante's day it was recognized almost universally in relation to a defined and accepted end to that seeking, rationalized by scholastic thought. This circumstance made possible to the poet a common ground with his audience. But by the time of Whitman the high innocence involved in the soul's proper relation to its source, through which it achieved its proper end, had been rejected. The center of innocence and the end of innocence was the self. The poet's position, relative to the theme of wandering innocence, was no longer that detached state of Dante the poet, toward which the wandering character Dante grew in the course of the work itself. It was rather a condition of the poet's mind deliberately changed back toward naive innocence. There was an almost insurmountable handicap attendant upon the new condition the poet found himself in, a handicap which technique has attempted to solve, as in the devices developed by James and Joyce in particular. The device of the related point of view, of ironic detachment, works marvelously well in the interest of art, but it lacks any assurance of commitment to the world, without which art does not finally satisfy the hungers it arouses. And in those poets who reflect a commitment, there is no assurance of a position from which to make that commitment, the self being finally so private, and, as Wordsworth said, "hidden from the reach of words." There is neverthe-less an uneasiness which does come through. We recover the past of the self, versions of recollections of early and later childhood. But in the re-creation, we become uneasily aware that the very moment of recovery is being lost, that the remembering self is itself already changing and slipping away. Further, as Paul Ricoeur says in *The Symbolism of Evil*, "by retroaction from the successive 'nows,' our past never stops changing its meaning; the present appropriation of the past modifies that which motivates us from the depths of the past."

The mark on our poetry of this submergence of awareness into time and place, the infinitely fleeting "now" which is comfortable only in the past tense, is a new kind of invoca-tion, unfamiliar to Homer, Virgil, Dante, Milton. Its techni-cal ritual is the incantation, self-hypnotism, a chanting toward enchantment. But the poet, revisiting the memory, does not record "the book of memory" from a station con-fidently superior to memory, such as Dante's in *The New Life*. He rather attempts to relive the naive innocence. We see such chanting in Whitman's first paragraph to "Out of the Cradle Endlessly Rocking," that early version of *A Portrait of the Artist as a Young Man*. The difficulty of the recovery is reflected by the length of the incantation, in which the rhetorical movement, the rhythms of memory, are of fundamental importance. One contrasts Whitman's remembering to that undeniably pedestrian recollection that prolongs *The Prelude*. The flatness in Wordsworth is out of his attempt to focus rational understanding upon experi-ence. For by the time Wordsworth writes *The Prelude*, thought is made a supreme value as a control of emotion. It is worth our recalling Whitman's initial paragraph for a subsequent point:

Out of the cradle endlessly rocking,
Out of the mocking-bird's throat, the musical shuttle,
Out of the Ninth-month midnight,

Over the sterile sands and the fields beyond, where the child
    leaving his bed wander'd alone, bareheaded, barefoot,
Down from the shower'd halo,
Up from the mystic play of shadows twining and twisting
    as if they were alive.
Out from the patches of briers and blackberries,
From the memories of the bird that chanted to me,
From your memories sad brother, from the fitful risings and
    fallings I heard,
From under the yellow half-moon late-risen and swollen as if
    with tears,
From those beginning notes of yearning and love there in the
    mist.
From the thousand responses of my heart never to cease,
From the myriad thence-arous'd words,
From the word stronger and more delicious than any,
From such as now they start the scene revisiting,
As a flock, twittering, rising, or overhead passing,
Borne hither, ere all eludes me, hurriedly,
A man, yet by these tears a little boy again,
Throwing myself on the sand, confronting the waves,
I, chanter of pains and joys, uniter of here and hereafter,
Taking all hints to use them, but swiftly leaping beyond them,
A reminiscence sing.

How far we have come from Dante needs only Dante's
first paragraph of *The New Life* to show: "Early on in
the book of my memory—almost before anything else can
be read there—is a rubric which says: 'The New Life begins.' Under this rubric I find written the words which I
intend to reassemble in this short book; or if not all of
them, at least their meaning." Whitman's materials are
recollected images colored by the recollection of that first
emotion. In other words, the attempt is primarily one aimed
at recovering that lost state of naive innocence, through
which the present moment is obliterated, rather than an
attempt to transcend that state to a knowledge of the causes
of that innocence which can include it. This aspect in our
literature in English since Wordsworth's day, and particularly in the American version of it, tempts one to suggest

it as the nineteenth and twentieth centuries' major contribution to Western literature; the figure of the adolescent arrested in his development abounds wherever one turns: Huckleberry Finn, Young Goodman Brown, Walt Whitman, Christopher Newman, J. Alfred Prufrock, Jake Barnes, Jack Burden, Bayard Sartoris, Holden Caulfield, Dean Moriarty.

These are characters out of a literature that is primarily lyric, whether one name a poem by Whitman or a novel or story by Hemingway. It is lyric in that the essential materials and the sensibility are derived primarily out of the temporal life of the poet. There is about that literature the uneasiness of the aimless quest. That much of it is forceful is beyond question; but it seems evident that its force is that of verisimilitude, a verisimilitude in which one feels the emotions of a quest which is finally unrelated to any ultimate end. Literature reaches a dead end in such writings as "Song of Myself" and *The Adventures of Huckleberry Finn,* after which there is a technical refinement of the retrogression of the mind implicit in those works, as in the fiction of Hemingway and Salinger, or a deliberate rejection of technical refinement, as in the fiction of Jack Kerouac or in the poetry of Allen Ginsberg.

Wordsworth reflects an awareness of this approaching dead end, brought about by the poet's changed relationship to his materials. The child as father of the man is an upsidedown relationship when compared to Dante's relation to the figure of himself in *The New Life.* That the relationship was less than suitable to Wordsworth's mind is reflected in many poems from the late 1790s on, but nowhere more revealingly reflected than in "Tintern Abbey," which poem puzzles the relation of the poet to himself as child and man. But the riddling is not completed there. It continues in *The Prelude.* It goes on and on in *The Excursion.*

Vaguely Realizing Westward

Wordsworth, *The Excursion*

> The tenour . . .
> Which my life holds. . . .
> Inverted trees, rocks, clouds, and azure sky
> . . . specks of foam, . . .
> And conglobated bubbles undissolved,
> Numerous as stars. . . .

Michael Polanyi, *The Tacit Dimension*

> Minds and problems possess a deeper reality than cobblestones.

In book 3 of *The Excursion,* Wordsworth has his Solitary relate his own history from an early enthusiasm engendered by the French Revolution, through a recovery after dejection, to his voyage to America in search of the noble savage. Finally the Solitary reflects, as Wordsworth puts it in the argument of the book, "His languor and depression of mind, from want of confidence in the virtue of Mankind." The history is Wordsworth's figuring of his own loss of innocent expectation, and the extended reflection of the Solitary upon a mountain brook in England is a reflection upon his own temptation to abandon exploration. The end of the Solitary's exploring is rather certainly not that he has arrived where he started in such a way as to see it for the first time. He hears a "softened roar, or murmur," but though the sound is soothing and though it is charged by nature with the "same pensive office" as when he first set forth upon his journeying, his only expectation now is that his "particular current soon will reach / The unfathomable gulf, where all is still!" The hopeful inland murmur on the banks of the Wye has led now to a state in which he looks languidly "Upon the visible fabric of the world."

What is of present interest to us out of this passage is the final disillusionment that led the Solitary to his retirement. His is a disillusionment such as Hawthorne was to deal with in his fiction, and Wordsworth's Solitary and Hawthorne's Young Goodman Brown end up in very similar spiritual states, both from an experience in the primeval forest. The Solitary, disappointed by the failures of the French Revolution, journeyed to America in quest of the noble savage, the natural man, more enthusiastically and with less misgiving than Young Goodman Brown undertook his journey. "There," says the Solitary, "Man abides, Primeval Nature's child." He anticipates the encounter:

> ... having gained the top
> Of some commanding eminence, which yet
> Intruder ne'er beheld, he thence surveys
> Regions of wood and wide savannah, vast

41

> Expanse of unappropriated earth,
> With mind that sheds a light on what he sees;
> Free as the sun, and lonely as the sun.

The expectation of the Solitary is that he may realize that ecstatic state of Keats's "stout Cortez," in discovering the red man in his natural habitat. But alas,

> That pure archetype of human greatness,
> I found him not. There, in his stead, appeared
> A creature, squalid, vengeful, and impure;
> Remorseless, and submissive to no law
> But superstitious fear, and abject sloth.

A dying spiritual state is the end to which the Solitary has come, though he cannot see the squalid creature he encountered as a figuring of himself. At a similar point in Goodman Brown's journeying, there is a recognition, the effect of which is to put him in that spiritual gloom from which he never recovers, leading his neighbors upon his death to carve "no hopeful verse upon his tombstone."

We may observe a parallel, with a significant difference, between Wordsworth's and Hawthorne's pilgrims on the one hand and Dante's on the other. Wordsworth's and Hawthorne's pilgrims have reached an end which is Dante's beginning: "Midway this life we're bound upon, / I woke to find myself in a dark wood." The parallel is obvious; the difference one with which we are so generally out of tune as perhaps to be hidden from us. For our interest in the innocence I have called naiveté inclines us to conclude life's richness ended as one reaches thirty; to Dante the richness has only become possible midway this life. (Pound, approaching that point remarked in 1913, "Most important poetry has been written by men over thirty.") Wordsworth stands at a midpoint between us and Dante, and consequently he writes a poetry complex in its relation to the question of innocence. The complexity is not of that formal kind involved in the allegorical dimensions Dante controlled and Hawthorne wished to command. It is rather a complexity out of a very real kinship with his Solitary. On the one hand, Wordsworth involves some degree of that high concern for innocence which is Dante's principle burden. But he also is, to a considerable degree, captive to that innocence which Hemingway's Jake Barnes characterizes as "arrested development." The loss of innocence and the heroic attempt at its recovery through the faculties of the mind—these are the burden of an order of literature which stretches from Aeschylus to Eliot, an order to which Wordsworth aspires. It is a literature of self-awareness, but not that self-awareness which is content with self-awareness as an end, as may be said of Huck Finn's sophisticated cousin Stephen Dedalus, and of that line of existential fiction descended from Huck and Stephen into the work of Samuel Beckett and to Holden Caulfield. That Wordsworth should use the "American Dream" as his Solitary's final disillusionment seems prophetic of the triumph of naiveté. The expense of that conception of lost innocence is something larger than cause for weeping.

I have suggested that the conspicuous mark of American literature is the tone of nostalgia; it is related to the central fact of our history: that we were granted what we believed a New Eden, during and after the early stages of which grant we became intoxicated by Eden as essentially worldly—that is Utopian. Seeking a worldly Eden, which became progressively more worldly, we moved westward. Ours was an intoxication which was initially a dream such as that which fascinated Coleridge and Wordsworth into considering emigration to America, or the dream which in our own day involved Aldous Huxley, D. H. Lawrence, and Bertrand Russell in similar wild surmises. But the actual accomplishment was other than Edenesque. Frost points to it in that poem celebrated for having become a part of a presidential inauguration. "The Gift Outright" is far less optimistic than generally taken to be in an easy reading of the poem, a reading Frost himself on occasion encouraged. For the manner in which we gave ourselves outright has, as we have come to see, made of our Eden the flat, if "profitable," land of despond. "The land was ours before we were the land's," and it was so through our "vaguely realizing westward, . . . still unstoried, artless, unenhanced." For we are a people for whom the realities of history are disproportionate to the innocent dream we professed. And so history became one thing for us and the dream another. The separation was one convenient to expediency, of course; for if one's concept of Eden is divorced from the land that lies immediately before him, he can dismiss from his mind the possible relation of the dream to that land. So Eden may be deforested and its streams polluted without one's having to face the issue of his own responsibility for desecration of the world's body. We evolved materialistic capitalism whose evolution can be remarked in the schizophrenic nature of our Horatio Algers on the one hand, whose final acts of conscience are the establishment of foundations for the arts, or on the other hand in the act of denial of an Ike McCaslin whose conscience leads him to a denial of all responsibility, in an attempt to emulate Christ while denying his own humanness.

The erosion of a common ground to the poet and his audience is evident much earlier, of course. Even Wyatt and Surrey see themselves in the roles of both Solomon and David, Surrey putting Ecclesiastes and the Psalms into verse, Wyatt the Psalms. The ambivalent role of the poet in society is present in them, as it is in Sidney, who must at once defend the poet against Plato while enjoying the playful extravagance of the sonnet. At the same time he is compelled to insist upon the poet's high calling. The divided view, which Wordsworth and Coleridge struggle to make viably whole, was transplanted to America, the Puritan version in the East to plague Hawthorne and James, the older Elizabethan version in the South where it somewhat comforted courtiers without courts at which to sing—poets like Timrod and Hayne. Hawthorne is acutely aware of the ambiguous position of the poet in that society so contradictorily given to building New Eden. (Eden must be a given, not a built.) James likewise wrestles with the problem of the relation of history to the dream, the made to the given, and decides that our history is not extensive enough or complex enough to provide in itself the necessary materials of art. His own accomplishment argues against his fear.

There is schizophrenia in James himself, evidenced by his concern over the separation of romance from realism, a question much troubling him. It is a separation which is inevitable, it seems to me, when the dream and the reality of the immediate world are rudely separated from each other. For the wholeness of vision that is necessary to the highest art requires a seeing through the realities of the world toward a reality which is not a dream. That is to say, art must have firm anchor first in the life of the artist and second in the life of his audience. I have pointed first to Eliot's America rather than to Wordsworth's England, since I wish particularly to relate Eliot to Wordsworth and since Eliot conspicuously inherits this very divorce which makes Hawthorne what we call a romantic and James a realist. We see how those two terms—romantic and realist—decay when we attempt to apply them to Chaucer or Dante. But we see how parallel the terms are in both American and English literature when we see their emerging conflict in Wordsworth, trace it through Keats's one theme—"Do I wake or dream"—through the rude awakening out of romance that is in Tennyson's *In Memoriam* and Arnold's "Dover Beach," to the realism of Conrad and Thomas Hardy. In American literature there is recently a significant move toward seeing a higher reality through the immediate materials of history, as in the work of William Faulkner, whose burden of history is a retribution for our "vaguely realizing westward." Faulkner is our Old Testament prophet. A writer who can be examined to show a return through Faulkner's beginnings toward the clearer examination of the dream by means of a Christian vision is Flannery O'Connor, whose fiction moves us to the threshold of Dante's *Purgatorio* and perhaps prepares us again for those larger visions within which high tragedy is possible as it has not been since Shakespeare. Both Faulkner, with his Old Testament voice of prophecy, and Flannery O'Connor, with her addition of the New Testament's vision, deal with the excesses of self, caused by the very awareness of self, and deal as well, though on different planes, with the expiation required for such excesses.

I can think of no more serviceable statement of the nature of this self-awareness and its relation to the dream—which in my own belief is not Keats's waking dream, but true vision—than that of C. S. Lewis, a hard-minded critic of dreams and visions and a man we might remember as holding Wordsworth in high esteem. In fact the reader might be interested, in the light of what I shall have to say in these next few pages, to recall that Lewis chooses as title to his autobiography a phrase from a Wordsworth poem which records an awakening from an innocent dream: *Surprised by Joy.* The title is appropriate in that Lewis's autobiography records a progress of his own awareness, which has repeated points of analogy to that of Wordsworth's—the child awed in nature, the young intellectual revolutionary, the older man pursuing orthodoxy. Let us recall as well how often this is the modern pattern, but more generally in the lives of the poets than in the life of a particular agent or mask of their art. The effect upon such a poet's work is usually that he turns from poetry to criticism—he becomes an essayist of the imagination whether his name be C. S. Lewis writing prose or Wallace Stevens writing poetry.

Lewis, in *The Problem of Pain,* considers as the remarkable point in the history of the race the emergence of self-awareness. "God caused to descend upon this organism [man] both on its psychology and physiology, a new kind of consciousness which could say 'I' and 'me,' which could look upon itself as an object, which knew God, which could make judgments of truth, beauty, and goodness, and which was so far above time that it could perceive time flowing past." The conditions were thereby propitious, Lewis argues, for the possibility of the loss of innocence. Men now self aware "wanted, as we say, 'to call their souls their own.' " He continues:

> But that means to live a lie, for our souls are not, in fact, our own. . . . We have no idea in what particular act, or series of acts, the self-contradictory, impossible wish found expression. For all I can see, it might have concerned the literal eating of a fruit, but the question is of no consequence. This act of self-will on the part of the creature, which constitutes an utter falseness to its true creaturely position, is the only sin that can be conceived as the Fall. For the difficulty about the first sin is that it must be very heinous, or its consequences would not be so terrible, and yet it must be something which a being free from the temptations of fallen man could conceivably have committed. The turning from God to self fulfills both conditions. It is a sin possible even to Paradisal man, because the mere existence of a self—the mere fact that we call it "me"—includes, from the first, the danger of self-idolatry.

In consequence of self-awareness "a new species . . . had sinned itself into existence." That is to say, the new man by definition was man fallen from high innocence.

Lewis's argument has an interesting parallel in Teilhard de Chardin's *Phenomenon of Man,* published later than *The Problem of Pain.* Teilhard is interested in a vision of order that would reconcile the truth of science and the truth of theology and philosophy. He singles out as a most significant step in the universe's movement toward its final realization the emergence of self-awareness. There is a fundamental difference in the views of the two men, however, indicated by Lewis's title. While Teilhard's word is concerned for a process of evolution which includes the spirit, his mode is that of joyful song. The problem of evil is not reconciled to the song. It is precisely this problem that Lewis aims directly toward. If I may put it so, Teilhard's is the music of a spirit that has overcome the world, a music whose analogue (as Prof. Thomas Stritch has said) is the voice

47

of Gerard Manley Hopkins; while Lewis's is the sound of a voice explaining how the world may be overcome, his vision and concerns and hence his music, being closer to Dante's than to Hopkins's.

Now the state of high innocence which man strives to recover, when that state of innocence is a concern of art, involves the artist in a magnitude of vision which is more or less adequate to the treatment of that theme, according to the extent of grace that allows his vision and talent. In some artists, and in some ages as well, there is a vision sufficiently large to behold the complete course that man's self-consciousness describes. Among the requirements essential for the vision to be operative in a poet's art is a mind which is far enough above time so that, as Lewis says, it can perceive time flowing past. The vision is not large enough, for instance, in a Keats or a Yeats. Keats's poetry is indeed his repeated attempt to rise above time, and we recall another nightingale toward the same end in the image of a form Yeats would assume in a new life:

> Once out of nature I shall never take
> My bodily form from any natural thing,
> But such a form as Grecian goldsmiths make
> Of hammered gold and gold enamelling
> To keep a drowsy emperor awake;
> Or set upon a golden bough to sing
> To lords and ladies of Byzantium
> Of what is past, or passing, or to come.

What I am describing, in contradistinction to Yeats, Keats, Whitman, Hemingway, Joyce, is a range of vision necessary to the conception of tragedy or the conception of lyric joy which is as sustained as that of Sophocles or of Gerard Manley Hopkins. It requires a mind which is aware of history and history's relation to myth in a manner far different from the relation of history to *dream,* as I have used that term in relation to American culture. To point more firmly to this distinction, let me once more remind the reader of Dante, and of the metamorphosis of dream to vision which

Dante dramatizes by relating section 23 of *The New Life* to the three dreams of *The Purgatorio* and to the full vision of *Il Paradiso*. Afterward, we shall consider the question of tragedy in relation to the high innocence pursued by most poets when they discover the dark woods beyond their thirtieth year.

Looking for Universal Things

🌼Wordsworth, *The Prelude*

I looked for universal things; perused
The common countenance of earth and sky:
Earth, nowhere unembellished by some trace
Of that first Paradise whence man was driven;
And sky, whose beauty and bounty are expressed
By the proud name she bears—the name of Heaven.

🌼Dylan Thomas, "The Force that through the Green Fuse"

And I am dumb to tell a weather's wind
How time has ticked a heaven round the stars.

🌼Theodore Roethke, "The Waking"

I wake to sleep, and take my waking slow
I feel my fate in what I cannot fear.
I learn by going where I have to go.

We observe that when myth is alive, when it is a vital aspect of society's mind, it binds an audience to the poet. Also that in such rare points in history, art itself carries little self-consciousness on the part of its medium, the poet. Such conditions are true of *The Iliad,* of *The Song of Roland.* When that medium becomes uneasily aware of myth, when the poet feels history loom between himself and myth as a glass through which he sees myth darkly, the conditions of tragedy are present. It is at the nadir of that movement that the condition most appropriate to the literary embodiment of tragedy occurs, that point in the thought of a community of minds described by Willard Farnham when the "worth and meaning of man's activity in this world" is most severely tried by art. "The pessimistic tragic poet reaches that limit when he represents life as never justifying hope, yet ironically producing the momentary will to live and some consequent struggle." That quality in tragedy is a real presence of the poet's mind in its disturbed state. However little one may know historically of the poet, one feels his disturbed presence in his art. I do not mean that one feels a "personality." It is beside the point whether we name that medium with specific details of biography. What one feels is something of a dark vision almost turning light through the force with which the poet's sight holds the world. A part, and an important part, of what we come to know through the tragic poem is the nature of that awareness we call the poet, and though his vision be shadowed, though tragedy be pessimistic almost to the point of despair, there is present always in some manner a "momentary will to live and some consequent struggle." It may be present in such unheroic directness as the chorus in Aeschylus which declares that in somewise, he who dies last dies best. It may be present in that more comic note to Faulkner's shadowed view when he expresses a confidence that at the last ding-dong of the history of the human race there will be two men somewhere about to set out into space, arguing with each other. What we reflect upon, after experiencing a particular work and when our disbelief is no longer in a state of suspension, is the validity of that self-awareness which a mind has projected for us. I believe the technical genre finally makes no great difference in our reflection, whether upon medieval narrative tragedy or Greek or Shakespearean tragedy, or lyric poetry since the sixteenth century. For in each there is that presence of mind busily working out its salvation in fear and trembling, usually with a fading exhilaration.

That is why, though Etienne Gilson's position on the nature of lyric poetry (in *Forms and Substances in the Arts*) is helpful, it does not finally say enough. For the aesthetic moment of art is only a part of the spiritual moment of life, in which art must find its ordinate place. "Lyric poetry," Gilson says, "contents itself with artful variations on the classic platitudes about life and death, heaven and earth, the mutability of seasons and of the human heart." Well enough. But what of the lyric poet, whose mind is the medium of that poetry and more pervasive of the poetry than a catalyst is allowed by definition to be? That is quite another matter. He is never fully content with art as variation of classical platitudes. If he is not the philosopher, he nevertheless pursues a kind of truth which variation is insufficient to justify. For he is continually perplexed—and so are we—by the hints of profundity in those classic platitudes. That is why it is not conclusive to say that in poetry the intelligence "is employed, literally, to charm," as Gilson does, unless we extend the implications of the charming beyond the aesthetic limits of beauty. Mallarmé is, after all, a rarity among poets, but even he attempts with a religious zeal to limit poetry's charming powers to the end of beauty alone. To pursue and to defend such an end so fervently is to argue that which needs no argument if the position be truly held. If eyes were made for seeing, does one need to argue that beauty is its own excuse for being? The conditional clause enlarges the question, willy-nilly, beyond the limits of the aesthetic, though the aesthetic is a legitimate limitation *for the moment necessary to train the eyes.*

The pleasure that the poet seeks and seeks to transmit (except when he is merely the poet poseur) is a fulfillment of being, his own. There hovers about that sometimes useful distinction between prose and poetry which sets truth as the province of prose, beauty of poetry, the shadow of Arnold's Hebraism-Hellenism separation, an implication of a worldly efficiency in prose as an instrument. The distinction in our attitudes is warranted on every hand, from the proofs and products of empiricism to the purity of symbolic logic. But the haunting question which neither prose nor poetry can possibly escape, the question which thrusts its head rudely into any attempt to ignore its persistent presence in language itself, is what is being? And that is the question with which the poet, the lyric poet no less than the epic or tragic poet, is always contending in one degree or another. It seems more satisfactory then, though it necessarily clouds the attempt to distinguish the uses of prose and poetry, to conclude that the separate pursuits of beauty and truth are analogous in that each is a pursuit by the mind of a fullness of being. The first and last cause of that pursuit, witnessed by the actions and attitudes of innumerable poets no less than by philosophers, is fulfillment. A coming to rest in completion, the arriving at some still point from which the disturbing qualities of those classical platitudes about life, death, heaven, earth, mutability of seasons and the human heart are transcended in a peace of mind beyond understanding—through prose or poetry.

Sometimes we observe the embodying mind of the poet, troubled with the abiding question, becoming more desperate as history (including the poet's own moment of time) obfuscates his vision. We remark it in that medium called Sophocles between *Oedipus the King* and *Philoctetes*. In Shakespeare between *Romeo and Juliet* and *The Tempest*. Even in Mark Twain between *The Adventures of Huckleberry Finn* and *The Man That Corrupted Hadleyburg*. Not that there is of necessity a consistent pattern toward increasing darkness, though there may be such a pattern. Eliot for instance reflects a pattern the reverse of Twain's. If

53

we look to that change in the quality of vision or in the direction of vision as reflected by the movement of an epoch (rather than of a single mind), we may sometimes discover a consistent pattern reflecting upon the course of civilization. To do so, or at least to make the attempt to do so, may be to see more clearly through our own dark glass of history. Such a pattern, for instance, seems present in the sequence of the *Agamemnon, Philoctetes,* and *The Bacchae.* Aeschylus, whether because of the age in which he lived or the grace of his gift (and I assume both) was close enough to the living myth to transform intermediary history with it. Whatever the immediate involvements of Periclean Athens in his trilogy, we cannot fail to see how closely the decline of Agamemnon relates to what C. S. Lewis describes as the course of man's fall from innocence. How admirable a reading of the progress of Agamemnon's spirit and vision from Argos to Aulis, to the plains of Troy, to the purple carpet at Mycenae—a progress dramatically reproduced in the long speech Aeschylus puts into Agamemnon's mouth upon his return. It is a projection of character whose surface is Agamemnon's innocent naiveté as he records his progress from his high role as instrument of the gods to the self-centered arrogance of the conqueror of Troy. He reenacts his whole history, in the presence of the smouldering Clytemnestra, sealing his doom. In the following passage from C. S. Lewis, one need only substitute *soldier, self-gratification* and *responsibility* for *lover, sexual pleasure* and *beloved.* (Or to follow Aristotle's conclusions about the requirements of tragedy, one may substitute any title of high office.)

> A lover, in obedience to a quite uncalculating impulse, which may be full of good will as well as of desire and need not be forgetful of God, embraces his beloved, and then, quite innocently, experiences a thrill of sexual pleasure; but the second embrace may have that pleasure in view, may be a means to an end, may be the first downward step towards the state of regarding a fellow creature as a thing, as a machine to be used for his pleasure. Thus the bloom of innocence,

the element of obedience and the readiness to take what comes is rubbed off every activity. Thoughts undertaken, for God's sake—like that on which we are engaged at the moment—are continued as if they were an end in themselves, and then as if our pleasure in thinking were the end, and finally as if our pride or celebrity were the end.

Clytemnestra, we notice, reads Agamemnon exactly in this light, and because she does, through her adopted mask of womanliness, leads him by argument onto the waiting carpet and to the bloody bath. (The pertinence of Lewis's figure of the lover in his description of the fall from high innocence will be apparent when we come presently to a discussion of Dante's Beatrice and Wordsworth's Nature.)

Or consider a more recent historical sequence of the poet's relation to myth than that sequence in the Greek tragedies: a movement from the absence of self-consciousness in *The Song of Roland,* to the uneasy self-awareness which Shakespeare controls toward effective drama, to what might be termed the deliberate self-willing of a life to myth in Milton. And doesn't one sense a kinship of that medium we call Milton and that we call Euripides? The progression indicated is toward a more intense self-awareness in the artist. With self-awareness at its strongest, the poet is no longer capable of a fullness of vision necessary to high comedy like Dante's or high tragedy like Sophocles' or high lyric joy like Hopkins's. Try how one may to collect and order his emotions, tranquility cannot be ordered for the sake of art alone. With self-awareness at flood, the poet cannot rise above time. And again in Milton—since he was so important to Wordsworth and to Eliot and must be considered later—isn't it true that we find evidence of much self-awareness in the conflict between his political and social commitments which, in spite of his determination upon piety, drag him into the miasmal mists of the world and set themselves in conflict with the mythical scaffolding he erects in *Paradise Lost?* And doesn't *Paradise Lost* attempt the matter of Aeschylus in the manner of Homer, in which mixture the poet does not maintain his proper distance,

Eliot's old complaint? It is not until much later that Milton writes from a position above time in a work that ends with all passion spent.

The poet then may find himself committed to the quest for a state of high innocence which he senses as lost to him. It is not an accident that such a poet tends to be a lyric poet, though he may be argument-maker or satirist as well. It has been suggested by my colleague Calvin Brown that the essential difference between the lyric poet and the satiric poet is that "the satirist speaks to all right-thinking men, whereas the lyric poet speaks to anyone or no one for the benefit of all sensitive and perceptive men." The lyric, Professor Brown adds, "arises from a dissatisfaction caused by the absence of some desirable thing, but the satire arises from dissatisfaction caused by the presence of some undesirable thing." Now the key word here insofar as my argument is concerned is not *absent* or *present* or *desirable* or *undesirable*, but *dissatisfaction*. What I would point to is that in the song of joy, which I hear as the principal music of *Roland* or in the lyric of Hopkins, there is no dissatisfaction. In the music of the tragic poet there is a dissatisfaction which results from a sight of the undesirable and some insight into the desirable. The result is a combination of dissatisfaction caused by the presence of the undesirable and the absence of the desirable, both of which meet in some manner in his chief agent. In other words, there is some degree of awareness of history's important relation to myth. The satiric artist depends upon an acquired formality of language and an intellectual perception of history. The lyric poet, on the other hand, enacts a pursuit of history with a language acquired by the pursuit itself.

The satirist is most often a versifier, not a lyric poet, and one may make a distinction in the context of our argument to the point. Verse exists in consequence of a presupposition of form as an absolute applied to words. Its principle is that of technique abstracted from preexisting poetry and imposed upon elected materials. Hence verse's tendency to decorate the denotative while insisting nevertheless upon the denotative lyric. Poetry, on the other hand, discovers its limits from inside words. In poetry, form is released from words as the sculptor releases the figure from stone. It is a discovery of possibility out of the poet's uneasiness, an uneasiness combining joyful or fearful expectation and fearful or joyful discovery. In two specimens having the appearance of poetry, as for instance an iambic pentameter measure in that passage of Wordsworth's *Prelude* celebrating the crossing of the Alps and Wordsworth's "The Emigrant Mother," one has little difficulty distinguishing which is poetry and which is verse. This is another way of saying of the lyric poet that he seeks vital myth. The lyric poet is the poet in pursuit of Melpomene or Calliope.

If we could know sufficiently well the history of the individual poet's mind, I think we should discover that all poets are initially lyric, for the lyric mode is the mode of discovery of self which precedes and is later included in the other literary modes. But there comes a stage in the growth of the poet in which he must accommodate himself to self-knowledge, a part of which accommodation is the recognition of the particular graces of his talent. Whereupon as a rule he either turns toward drama or the epic which require an imagination above time; or he turns to satire, which always is more heavily rooted in his immediate history; or he turns toward a prose disguise of that lyric quest, that is to the essay, most usually to literary criticism. As history darkens and increasingly impinges upon the literature of an age, one can see such developments in the literature of that age, as when the metaphysicals and Milton move literature from Shakespeare's vision toward a Swift and Pope. The cycle is from lyric through high drama to lyric. (In high drama I would include both epic and tragedy, and such modern combinations as Faulkner's *Absalom, Absalom!*) And its course may be occasionally remarked in individual writers as well, though seldom does the cycle come back to the lyric in the career of one man, as it does in Hardy, a poet whom our age has yet to assimilate. Still,

57

very often it comes back to the lyric in prose, as in the essays of Swift or Coleridge or Tate. Sometimes there is a rarity such as Wordsworth, the bulk of whose lyric work (and much of it worthier than it has been popular to admit) comes after the point at which he recognized himself as having been a lyricist too innocently self-aware.

This aspect of the innocent (naive) quest of high innocence seems to me the principal mark of the lyric poet. When that poet is of sufficient magnitude, he becomes a hero to us in a drama whose medium is our own mind. This is particularly true of Wordsworth as we relate his mind to his accomplishment. There is a continuing suggestion in him of a mind which is a stranger in a world he never made, encountering strangers generously but warily at crossroads on his route to some Thebes. The limits of his vision then provide a pleasure akin to that of a dramatic narrative or to that of tragedy itself. For the reader may see, in the work, the mind of the poet as protagonist in such a way as to raise his separate lyrics toward a unity governed by the reader's own mind as medium. In pursuit of this idea, let us turn to the question of the pursuit of being by the lyric poet which moves him beyond the lyric. It is an aside which is relevant to our assimilation of our fathers and grandfathers, all of whom when worthy of their own fathers attempted to move beyond the lyric anchor of the self. One finally comes to the pursuit of Calliope or Melpomene, whether he be Whitman, Hart Crane, Pound, Eliot, or Joyce, James, Faulkner, Hemingway.

In Pursuit of Melpomene

Eliot, *Little Gidding*

> Every poem is an epitaph. And any action
> Is a step to the block, to the fires, down the sea's throat
> Or to an illegible stone: and that is where we start.
> We die with the dying.

Eliot, "A Dialogue on Dramatic Poetry"

> The consummation of the drama, the perfect and ideal drama, is
> to be found in the ceremony of the Mass. . . . And the only
> dramatic satisfaction that I find now is in a High Mass well
> performed.

I recall my dissatisfaction on seeing Samuel Beckett's *Waiting for Godot* some fifteen years ago. Well performed, but the dissatisfaction has continued with me as the Theater of the Absurd has increasingly commanded our serious attention. It was a curious experience, for it seemed not only a failure as drama, but somehow a very familiar failure in spite of all the celebration of its novelty. Willard Farnham's discussion of the limitations of Stoicism upon Senecan tragedy (in *The Medieval Heritage of Elizabethan Tragedy*) at last suggested why: the Theater of the Absurd depends upon an inverted Stoicism. It is not tragicomedy; it is rather farce haunted by a dream of tragedy, as Seneca's is tragedy haunted by a dream of comedy in Dante's sense of *comedy*. Farnham remarks that "in tragedy the only struggle which a Stoic hero could consistently make would be the effort to know that evil did not exist, that he ought to remain calm because his misfortunes were in no sense true misfortunes—in short, that the tragedy in which he was participating was no tragedy at all." Conversely, the only struggle which the hero of the Absurd can consistently maintain is an effort to know that *good* or *order* does not exist, that he must continue agitated with no apparent justification for the agitation, and with the implication through the static, chaotic language of the play itself that such agitation is ultimately silly—that is, naive. One waits for the illusional Godot, but waits in the character of a Boeotian. The nothing-to-know Stoicism of the Absurd is, on the surface, comic. But beneath its surface it carries the same defeat which Farnham describes in Greek tragedy as it "dissolved into pantomime"; "by all the signs that remain to us Greek tragedy . . . finally came to an emotional and intellectual conclusion beyond which it could say nothing new—the conclusion that man is blown hither and thither in an evil world by the winds of chance which cannot be charted and that his choice contributes nothing significant to the outcome." In the interval of dissolution current to us, the Theater of the Absurd gives way not to pantomime but to what is not very far removed, the Happening. In the Happening

60

we see the fundamental "theology" of the Absurd emerging: it is Nihilism, which has used (largely) Sartrean existentialism for comic effect.

Where Seneca turns his tragedy toward the absurdities of spectacle on the stage, the Theater of the Absurd reduces stage spectacle to zero in the interest of language as spectacle, void of movement or signification, though carrying strange echoes of movement out of historical patterns of language. Seneca adapts Euripides' *Medea* and reduces Medea's piercing cruelty to Jason in refusing the rites of burial for his sons, having her hurl their bodies from the battlements to his feet. Beckett, in *Endgame,* reduces the movement of language, which ordinarily bears mind's action, to empty chatter. If the Stoic's fascination—his obsession—with evil led him to an intense struggle to deny its existence and assert consistent good in a perfectly ordered world, the Absurdist's obsession is with the threat of good or order, which he must continually deny by ridicule in order to maintain an uninterrupted assertion of an exploding meaninglessness. In Stoicism, suffering is the illusion of an inadequate mind; in Absurdism, it is the hilarious "unway" of the "unworld," the great joke of unreality beyond laughter. As the obverse of Stoicism, Absurdism too is paradoxical extremism. One may say of Stoicism in serious jest (to quote Farnham once more), "For the Stoic this is the best of all possible worlds, and everything in it is a necessary evil." One may say of Absurdism that it posits the worst of all impossible worlds, one beneath the dignity of the belly laugh. For each is an oversimplification, significantly attractive to the "sophisticated" audience (i.e., the mentally jaded) in periods of radical social, philosophical, and theological decay. The Stoic's orderly outer wheel of inexorably good fortune is balanced by the Absurdist's interior grenade of unreason exploding in that vacuum we describe as alienation. Since both good and evil exist, neither Stoicism nor Absurdism in their extremities is equal to the realities of the human condition to any degree sufficient for our transcending or reconciling ourselves to the paradox

61

of good and evil. That is, neither is a satisfactory imitation of life in the high modes of comedy or tragedy.

The possibility of literary tragedy, and a catharsis resulting from it, presupposes that the literary vehicle be dramatic, though the term *dramatic literature* neither implies nor requires tragedy. The term *dramatic literature* I use here to designate that literature which presents a specific likeness of human beings (actual persons or agents) in actions or meditations. The presentation of specific characters reveals their peculiar action which is essentially an action of the will when the character is confronted either by the world external to the character (which circumstance provides a more obvious action) or by a part of the character's internal nature (which circumstance provides for psychological action, as when Hamlet considers suicide). The character's will is revealed (1) through overt act, with the body as its instrument, as in the gestures by a character on stage; (2) through the contemplative action of the mind which may be revealed as in dialogue or soliloquy; or (3) through whatever devices of words, expository or metaphorical, the particular form allows the author. The fundamental medium is always words, and consequently there is always a voice or voices, which exist only where the speaker exists. (Gestures where no words are must have had their tone established already. Gestures on the stage are a part of the play's language, sometimes actually transcribed in texts as such.) Therefore all literary work is dramatic, whether a particular man speak for himself as author or create agents to speak for him. Dramatic literature then consists of the presence before an audience (whether an audience of one person or many) of a particular character (either the author himself or an agent of the author), in specific action (signified by words individually selected) in a created world (which comes into being through all the words used in the work).

The world of the particular work is *more* or *less* self-contained in the work. Dramatic literature allows an audience to identify a character and also relate that character to the particular literary world inhabited by that character.

Depending upon the sophistication of the author and of the audience, the character may also be related to the world inhabited by the audience, that is to the natural and psychological world in which the audience itself exists.

All literature then is dramatic, since the use of words reflects a response of a mind to the world it finds itself in. The evidence of the existence of a mind is its action, which a separate mind perceives through barriers. Those barriers are the variety of means we call communication—the eye, the tongue, the movements of head or hand. The barriers I call language. Language I take to be both a necessity and a preparation: a necessity, given the infringement upon mind of time and place; and preparation, given the potential completeness of mind to which we give the worldly name *silence,* as in Hamlet's "The rest is silence" or Aquinas' seceding from words. Language then is a kind of clothing of the mind (and the body is a part of that language) that both resists mind and protects it while mind realizes itself—that is, learns to love itself as Christ commands it. Put another way, language is the mind's fig leaf, necessary since the fall, through which it makes itself ordinately active and attractive: mind is to language as Herrick's Julia is to her dress. Language is not, as we sometimes have argued to us, a creature such as things of nature are creatures; that is, it hasn't an essence of life that makes it distinct from mind. In another figure, it is the word in which a particular of the Word may make its presence known. Tragedy, as I conceive it, is a representation of a particular (Oedipus, perhaps even Macbeth) coming to love itself in the grace of that light which is called the Word. By its very nature, response is action, whether that response be an essay on the nature of tragedy, a love sonnet, or a five-act play presenting a hero's defeat—which three forms progressively tend toward disassociation of the responding mind (the author's) from its vehicle (the essay, sonnet, or play). Again the question arises: since dramatic literature is prerequisite to tragedy as a genre, are all forms capable of creating tragic effect? Can a lyric poem be tragic?

First of all the possibility of a tragic effect depends upon magnitude and duration of the dramatic work. The course of action in Milton's sonnet on his blindness parallels the movement of *Oedipus the King* insofar as the poem's and the drama's action and reaction are concerned. There are in the sonnet both recognition and reversal. There is a voice which comes to an awareness of self-error, thus allowing a dramatic irony to exist within the sonnet. But Milton's sonnet does not allow a sufficient creation of a world and a sufficient projection of that world's character as does Sophocles' play or Milton's own *Samson Agonistes*. It should be considered, however, that often a particular lyric is enlarged toward the possibilities of tragic effect in the reader by whatever world lies tangent to the lyric, as for instance the particular biography of the poet. The possibilities of such become greater when the voice of the poem becomes specifically that of the poet. An example to this point is in Wordsworth's "Tintern Abbey," which as we read it carries an irony that is similar to the irony in Sophocles' play or in Milton's sonnet though different in one important respect. In the instance of Milton's sonnet, the illusion represented in the first seven and a half lines and the dissolving of the illusion in the remaining lines is contained within the poem itself; the action is complete, whereas in Wordsworth's "Tintern Abbey" the illusion is maintained throughout the poem. When Wordsworth says in the poem, as a promise to the person addressed by the poem that "nature never did betray the heart that loved her," the reader is aware of what is impending for Wordsworth: as popularly known, the shock of his brother's death at sea and a subsequent modification in his feeling toward nature. Nevertheless in varying degrees the poem involves (though it does not contain) the parts of tragedy said necessary by Aristotle: plot, character, diction, thought, spectacle, the making of melody. Obviously these elements are considerably modified from what they are in relation to Sophocles' *Oedipus*. For instance, as indicated, a part of the plot is brought to a reading of the poem by the reader, since he recalls those lines from Wordsworth's "Elegiac Stanzas":

Farewell, farewell the heart that lives alone,
Housed in a dream, at distance from the Kind!
Such happiness, wherever it be known
Is to be pitied; for 'tis surely blind.

Not without hope we suffer and we mourn.

There is a significant circumstance affecting the presence of spectacle in a work which should also be mentioned. To Aristotle, the epic is a narrative recited by a man before an audience, while tragedy is a single point of narrative, an imitation of an action, enlarged before an audience by agents. Our experience tells us that a reader may respond to spectacle in epic or tragedy when there is no physical presence of bard or agents, literacy having introduced a concern not pressing Aristotle. Milton argues the point, in respect to drama, in his preface to *Samson Agonistes,* "Of That Sort of Dramatic Poem Which Is Called Tragedy." Very obviously, the circumstances differ when one reads a play and when one witnesses its presentation. But the emotional effect of the two differing participations by the same individual do not differ essentially. Indeed, it seems arguable that external spectacle, staging, is the most considerable hazard to the ordinate relationship of the six parts of tragedy.

Though there is a certain staging of "Tintern Abbey"— two characters in a given place indicating by the action of words part of the history of the characters—the completeness which Aristotle requires does not exist in the poem. The climax of Wordsworth's drama occurs somewhere between his incomplete awareness as he speaks and the reader's complete awareness as he listens. The action does not run its course within the dramatic vehicle in the manner required by Aristotle. But it does so through implication in the knowledgeable reader. Therefore there is a sense of completeness in that reader. Nevertheless, the possibility of tragic effect from this particular poem is limited; the world within which the poem's statement becomes ironic is not contained within the poem, for the dramatically relevant part of Wordsworth's life is not contained within it—as Oedipus' is in Sophocles' play. (Eliot's "Journey of the Magi" is ironic in a similar way, Eliot presenting an innocent voice speaking two thousand years ago and the reader hearing with the advantage of the intervening years. The effect in both Wordsworth's and Eliot's two poems is pathetic rather than tragic, and though this seems the effect Eliot consciously intends, Wordsworth intends neither.) The effect of Wordsworth's poem tends toward the tragic on that reader who is knowledgeable about the speaker of the poem, who is not a person but William Wordsworth commanding his faculties as well as he is able at the moment and intimately and personally engaged in the words of the poem. In the poem's favor also is the fact that, unlike Milton's sonnet, it has duration. One cannot experience Wordsworth's poem as quickly as Milton's sonnet.

A sufficient engagement of the reader or spectator in point of the literal time required to the experience of the work is necessary to the emotional conditioning out of which the tragic effect is produced in the reader or spectator. Yet Wordsworth's poem does not have the magnitude that Milton's poem has. Milton's sonnet cries out against God: Wordsworth's poem laments a lost state of innocence with a voice still largely innocent. A transgression larger than Wordsworth's is necessary to engage the reader in the possibility of the tragic effect. Magnitude, then, is determined not so much by the protagonist's station as king—as with Oedipus—but by the nature of his transgression as measured against the possibilities of transgression. Those possibilities are defined primarily, but not entirely, by the created world the character inhabits. It would seem then on first consideration that the "station" of a character is sufficiently high to allow tragic effect when the particular character transcends those among whom he appears, as Oedipus transcends in station Jocasta and Creon. In those dramatic works which depend upon enlargement of their world by reference external to the vehicle's world (as when the reader brings Wordsworth's subsequent life to a reading of "Tintern Abbey") the establishment of the world and the character's station in it becomes more complex. It is perhaps pertinent to Wordsworth's station, for instance, to consider Dorothy Wordsworth and Coleridge, while with Oedipus we consider Jocasta and Creon.

It would seem at this stage of my argument that, potentially, tragedy may arise out of the dramatic quality of lyric, since a lyric may serve as a center for the accumulation of a world that is dramatic, though a part of that world be external to the work itself. For as I shall presently consider, the tragic effect is properly measured in the spectator and not in the form of the work itself. All audiences bring knowledge more or less external to the play, and knowledge of Oedipus' history brought by the spectator is not radically different from the knowledge of Wordsworth's history which a reader brings to Wordsworth's poem.

At this point in our argument, Aristotle's comment on the relevance of historical or legendary characters to tragedy is interesting as a qualification of our preceding paragraph. Comedy, he says, employs random names. The writers of tragedy however "cling to the names of men who lived. The cause of this is that whatever is possible is persuasive. Therefore, while we do not as yet believe that those incidents are possible which have not come to be, it is apparent that incidents which have arisen are possible, for an incident does not arise if it is impossible." He adds that, though many tragedies use known characters, tragedies exist in which "both incidents and names are made up and it gives enjoyment nevertheless. Thus the poet must not seek to cling altogether to the traditional plots." The use of the known, then, is an economy to the playwright, whose requirements are such that he cannot create his character's world as leisurely as the epic poet or the novelist may. Even so, the advantage may be less than it seems. For as Aristotle says of the audiences he knew, "even the known plots are known only to a few and yet give enjoyment to all alike." The question now would seem to be whether the work is completely self-contained. One which is so contained obviously satisfies a larger audience than one which is not, for it is not dependent upon the necessity or advantage of prior knowledge. But nevertheless the concern for whether the effect of a particular work is tragic does not depend upon the numbers affected but upon whether a given person is affected. The minimum requirement for a fit audience is one.

In dramatic literature, whether sonnet or play, the particular work itself carries, and must carry, a measure of the character living in it. The work defines the world the character inhabits, and the first critical concern with the effectiveness of the work as drama is in terms of the character's action in and reaction to his world. Far more which is external to the world contained in Milton's sonnet must be brought to the sonnet by the reader than must be brought by the spectator to *Oedipus*. However, it should be stressed that what must be brought to the sonnet is less a knowledge of Milton's literal blindness, which is of sentimental relevance, than a knowledge of his world in which piety was requisite to order in individual and society. The critical explication of the lyric is part of the process of discovering its dramatic effectiveness. Explication brings close attention to the lyric's world through a concern for the implications of the poem's diction and its "making of melody." The uses of the *New English Dictionary* in hearing a poem by Donne or reference to the parable of the talents in reading Milton's sonnet on his blindness is an attempt to make available to the reader the world of the poem, which of course involves ultimately the world of John Donne or John Milton. The attempt is to establish the voice of the poem as that voice is defined by the world it speaks. The attempt, in other words, is to establish character and the character's world in the interest of dramatic tension. Whether one bring specific and personal events of the poet's life to the reading of the lyric, as with Wordsworth's "Tintern Abbey," or more general re-creations, as with Milton's sonnet, the history of the poet and of his particular world is inevitably implicated in the poem's drama. While one is justified in bringing whatever is suitable to the poem's effectiveness— whether the poet's biography or the currency of a word's meaning in his day related to that day's science and philosophy—the extent to which such a building up of the poem's world from the outside is necessary is an indication of the limitations of what I have called its duration and therefore a limitation of its dramatic immediacy. For ideally, though never in fact of accomplishment, a work is of its proper duration when it contains its character and the character's world within itself, each a complement to the other.

Concerning what is called magnitude: a work of dramatic literature presents characters whose actions may exist on a scale of relative significance to the actions of other characters in its world or in other literary worlds. Creon is a measure of Oedipus; Oedipus of Macbeth. But the character's actions are also relative to the literal actions of men in the natural world inhabited by the reader or spectator. The spectator, then, is conditioned by his knowledge and experience in such a way that the tragic effect of the particular work upon him is either magnified or modified by his own intellectual history. As it relates to the spectator's knowledge and experience, let us consider the state of the character's knowledge and experience relative to the world contained in the particular work. A character may dawn slowly to his world's "reality," as Oedipus does. Or the character may never realize the reality of the world his author has cast him in, a common presentation of character in much contemporary literature, particularly in short fiction. The difference is that in the one, the character's knowledge eventually coincides with the audience's, while in the other it never does. (There is the alternative possibility of the eventual dawning outside the literary work, as with Wordsworth's realization that nature is not as he supposed.) Now in addition to the necessities of duration and magnitude for a work to effect a catharsis (these necessities having to do with the vehicle that contains

69

the drama), a major consideration is the necessity of an eventual coincidence of knowledge of the audience and of the drama's character, whether he be Wordsworth or Oedipus. For the absence of a coincidence of knowledge prevents a purging of pity and fear, for reasons which I shall presently argue.

Since, once more, the cathartic effect is in the spectator, it must be urged that the particular work may effect a catharsis in a particular spectator in one confrontation and fail to affect the same spectator in another. One spectator at one instant may find the character's knowledge of his world coincident with his own, and at another find himself beyond the character's possibilities of knowledge. For while the coincidence of knowledge is a necessary one to catharsis, it does not necessarily lead to catharsis. As has already been stated, the conception of the world, and of the character that inhabits it, may be relatively insignificant, failing to be of a sufficiently high intellectual and moral magnitude. The spectator who has grown to the possibilities of an Oedipus finds it impossible to respond in the same manner to the intended tragedy of a weak agent whose act of transgression is to impulsively steal an item from a drugstore counter. We may note that the weak agent is not a modern invention, though he is prevalent in our literature since the intrusion of determinism a hundred years ago. He exists repeatedly in the person of the Greek Chorus, as in the *Agamemnon* or the *Medea*. The argument of the weak agent is basically that it is better to be an anonymous face in the crowd, neither rich nor poor, thereby escaping the wrath of man or the gods.

If tragedy's end is to give pleasure, as I believe it to be, if the spectator's response to tragedy is a pleasure, then it becomes imperative to know why it is a pleasure and to know the nature of the pleasure. Tragedy is a cause of pleasure but not the pleasure itself; the pleasure exists in the spectator. Consequently one must turn to the spectator to discover the nature of the pleasure which Aristotle has argued as a result of taking from the spectator the emotions of pity and fear. I am aware of the debate over the locus of catharsis in Aristotle's *Poetics,* whether in the play or in the audience or in both. My position is that it is immediately in the audience as it rightly sees the imitation—the play—which itself must be an imitation consistent with life. It is to this problem of the nature of tragedy's pleasure that we now turn.

While it is necessary to consider as separate, as Aristotle does, aesthetic theory and moral theory, as an act of the mind's understanding of its world, it is not necessary to conclude that a moral end is not fundamental to tragedy. For the effect of catharsis in tragedy as described by Aristotle, when effected in the spectator, is to restore him to moral health. The means to that end are of aesthetic concern. The artist as teacher of moral health and the philosopher as teacher of moral health are concerned with different routes to the cleansing and perfection of the soul by the will, and not with different ends. Their modes of persuading the intellect are different.

I accept it as true that some degree of willful moral failure of character in literature is necessary to that tragedy which is of sufficient magnitude to effect catharsis, as I have already indicated in the comments on the limitations of Wordsworth's "Tintern Abbey" as tragedy. To fail willfully and to fail knowingly we must remember are not identical. Concerning the restoration of the spectator's soul through tragedy, I begin with an exploration of Aristotle's statement that tragedy effects a proper catharsis by purging the emotions of fear and pity. The basic question toward which I tend is: What is the source of pity and fear in the spectator?

As every explicator knows, Aristotle's metaphor describing the effects of tragedy on the emotions is a medical one. Pity and fear in some manner are assumed to poison the soul's health. They are somehow either foreign wastes—like undigested food which the body has not passed—or improperly released juices of the soul—like acids of the stomach which have no food to work upon. The presence of pity and fear as elements in the soul is disturbing, preventing its health and order. Again we remember that we are talking now, not about the tragedy on the stage or the play's characters, but about the effect of tragedy upon the spectator. We are talking about the pity and fear "latent" in the spectator. (Butcher in his commentary says that tragedy "excites emotion . . . only to allay it. Pity and fear, artificially stirred, expel the latent pity and fear which we bring with us from real life. . . . In the pleasurable calm which follows when the passion is spent, an emotional cure has been wrought. . . . Pity and fear are purged of the impure element which clings to them in life." But I take it that pity and fear, following catharsis, do not remain in a cleansed state but that the emotions in general have pity and fear removed, as Aristotle says—though removed only temporarily.) What is necessary to our understanding of the medicine's effect—the play's effect—is the nature of and cause of the infection in the spectator. For pity and fear are somehow improperly isolated, suspended in more or less concentrated form, constituting a poison which if expelled or neutralized would leave the spectator's soul in a healthy state. If a satisfactory explanation of the presence of pity and fear in the spectator before the experience of the literary work can be found and if the state of the spectator's soul can be related to that of the tragedy's hero by analogy, perhaps an understanding of catharsis may result which is satisfying. We should then have a better understanding of the nature of and the coincidence of knowledge in the spectator and the drama's character.

Here we are concerned with the "good" spectator, as the tragedy is concerned with the "good" hero. Prerequisite to catharsis is a spectator inclined to moral righteousness. This is a concern far different from that for artistic rightness. The highest art achieves a moral end through consummate artistry. This is not to say that high art is didactic in the common sense of that word, but that it demonstrates rightness commensurate with and satisfactory to the formal powers of the intellect. There is required of tragedy's audience the piety in the presence of tragedy required of the suppliant in the Prayer of Invocation in the Communion Service. (Piety, we recall, is the persuasive spirit in Aeschylus and Sophocles.) Butcher remarks that tragedy, "according to the definition, acts on the feelings, not on the will." If so, this is not to say that the will is not involved in the ill health of the spectator's soul. It is only to say that the route of tragedy to the will is through the intellect influenced by the emotions. Again, the means and not the end constitute the difference. I hold that pity and fear, the poisons of the soul that waste the will from healthy action, accumulate in the soul as a consequence of inordinate desire. But the human desire which makes tragedy possible is not in itself in the wrong direction; it is wrong in its degree, just as the action of Oedipus is not in the wrong direction, but is rather excessive. It is so since absolute knowledge (which would make possible the absolute health of the soul) is impossible to the finite soul of the spectator, as it is to the tragic hero. Absolute knowledge makes possible the perfect reconciliation of mercy and justice, both concerns being uppermost always in moral problems, and being also always immediately considered in that dramatic tragedy which is of sufficient scope to command the spectator and effect a catharsis. But perfect reconciliation is available only to God, as Aeschylus argues in the *Agamemnon*.

Yet, man's movement is toward God: his inclination, when he is properly moved, is toward emulation. But the inclination toward emulation of the perfect Good is more difficult since the borders which are inevitably transgressed are so indefinite. One easily confuses, under the necessity of the act, the difference between being an instrument of the Good and being the Good. (Note Agamemnon's homecoming speech in Aeschylus, in which he moves from considering himself an instrument of the gods to considering himself as triumphant hero, thus preparing himself for destruction.) This is the most difficult of temptations to overcome since the limitations of self-perfection, the border toward which the good man sojourns, are not so obvious as those of self-destruction, the border crossed into knowingly willed damnation. For the good man, there is a point where transgression, or rather supragression, occurs without the man's knowledge of his excessive action. There are possible to man two extreme violations of his potential being, both of which are subject of dramatic literature, but only one of which is compatible to tragedy. The one involves a full knowledge of deliberated evil; the other a full knowledge of undeliberated evil. The one involves a character whose knowledge of evil action as evil is concurrent with the action; the other involves a character whose knowledge of the evil follows the evil action. To illustrate both borders of being that may be transgressed: Satan, in *Paradise Lost,* never supposes himself God, though his act is deliberate evil with full knowledge of the evil; on the other hand Oedipus unknowingly supposes himself a pure instrument of absolute justice and dawns slowly to his transgression.

It is to be understood, of course, that there are gradations between the two poles established here, gradations reflected in a variety of presentations of character. I state the two borders of the possible to indicate a necessary sequence of the character's *knowledge* of his evil will to the *existence* of the evil will, through which sequence tragedy is effected. This is a crucial distinction—between a person's or an agent's state of existence (which is the particular temporal achievement of his potential, the actual of his essence) and his awareness of his state of existence. Radical existentialism such as Sartre's confuses this issue by denying, as an act of its faith, both the separation of existence from awareness and the sequential relationship of the two as observed in the history of the race or the history of the individual. One observes that the infant is uncomfortable because it is hungry, and it is hungry because it is. It is not hungry because it is uncomfortable, the argument of the egocentric absolutist. Or to put the matter with materials compatible to the inclinations of radical existentialism: commonly the infant cries because its diaper is soiled; it does not soil its diaper because it cries. The pain to the existential ego is

74

both more reasonably and more sensibly *subsequent* than *prior*. Surely it is an arbitrary and perverted faith that contends *I am because I suffer,* rather than *I suffer because I am.*

Now any action of the will is potentially a violation, an infringement of God's prerogative. It may be a knowing infringement, as with Milton's Satan, or a blind infringement as with Oedipus, or there may be some varying combination—that is, action with varying degrees of knowledge of transgression. I distinguish between the evil action of a Macbeth and that of a Satan. Macbeth, though his thinking is confused, commits his terrible murder with a knowledge of its evilness but with the rationalization that the evil is committed for the sake of a higher good. The course of the play forces his reluctant acknowledgment that his transgression is monstrous and that his alternatives were not a lesser or a greater good as were Agamemnon's at Aulis. Only that kind of action ascribed to Oedipus can lead to tragedy. The career of the bad character such as Satan which follows his knowingly evil act leaves the spectator with the emotions of pity and fear. These emotions remain because the state of the spectator's soul has not been reconciled to the reality of the badness and the appropriateness of the bad end. The spectacle of a bad man's career is appropriate to comedy, and pity and fear are not so much purged by comedy as they are inappropriate to it, as Dante argues through the actions of his *Inferno.*

That any intended good action is potentially a violation accounts for our holding pride or hubris so deadly and omnipresent in the affairs of man. The central concern for hubris in Sophocles would also seem a clear indication of the moral foundation of that drama, in which the hero's health results from a correction of hubris. Now the attempt to escape violation is, in recent literature, through a character's avoiding all action, which while it makes dramatic literature, as in Conrad's *Lord Jim* and Eliot's "Love Song of J. Alfred Prufrock," leads not to peace and health of the soul, but to stagnation. There is no catharsis to follow the failures of Lord Jim or Prufrock, since their failure is a failure to act. The spectator's will either coincides with that of a Prufrock, dissolving to inaction, or it never becomes engaged at all, leaving the spectator in the state of mind of the Pharisee in Luke.

Action is therefore necessary to the state of man's soul, whether it be an ill or healthy state. High moral actions involve man in an infringement upon the absolute by acts of his finite mind. Tragedy is a consequence of such high actions. This is the frustrating idea at the heart of Aeschylus' *Agamemnon:* the necessity of imperfect action through which man's "awful wisdom" comes. The wisdom is the realization, not only of the necessity of action, but of the excess, or infringement through action. The eventual self-knowledge of Sophocles' Oedipus is more obvious than Agamemnon's in Aeschylus' play. Yet the knowledge is so often repeated by Aeschylus' chorus that it becomes a part of the air Agamemnon breathes on his return, and his awareness is manifest in the purple carpet scene. The focus of each play is different.

Now pity is a dangerous emotion to the health of the soul, as Dante indicates repeatedly in *The Inferno.* For pity exists in man as an effect of the incomplete action of mercy. Pity, then, is an emotional residue. The act of mercy in man's will must also be compatible to the act of justice. (These acts are movements of the will, or as Aristotle puts it in the *Ethics,* "Volition is the essence of action.") But since perfect compatibility is impossible in the finite soul, the "waste" from the imperfect act remains. Coordinately, neither is justice perfectly moved by that finite will which is haunted by the expectation of excessiveness attendant upon action; its residue is the poison of fear. Again, there is no "emotion" in God; there is no residue, no waste—which waste necessarily results from incomplete being and the imperfect acts of the incomplete being. Fear and pity, however, are not in their most fundamental presence in the spectator as merely a fear of self-damnation or desire for self-salvation. Or if they are, they exist in a spectator whose inclination is not toward the good, a failure of the spectator which results from his perversion of potential good. Properly, the emotions of fear and pity exist as an awareness of incompleteness, an awareness of a failure through desire. For fundamentally the desire of the soul inclined to the good is to please God through perfect being, not to rescue itself from self-entrapment. The distinction here is between piety and cowardice, and we might once more recall how important piety is to the tragedy of Aeschylus and Sophocles.

The human actions of judgment and mercy involve the violation of perfect judgment and perfect mercy. That is made dramatically apparent by such a work as *Oedipus*. Yet after violation, Oedipus cures himself with his agonizing cry. Thus the staged action reenacts the history of the spectator's soul in an enlargement of that history that draws the spectator into a state of selflessness, which state is the one most nearly perfect act. Instead of the fear that he might be like Oedipus in the essence of Oedipus' failure (which failure in its essence is peculiar to all men, whether of high or low degree and regardless of their existence in point of time—whether B.C. or A.D.), or instead of pity for Oedipus, which would be an effect of disassociation from Oedipus, the spectator (when catharsis results) participates in that agonizing cry. Rather than an *emotional reaction* that might be expressed in words of pity or fear as "There but for the grace of God go I" there is a *religious action* which might be expressed "There go I." The state of knowledge in spectator and in hero coincide in such a way as to make words both futile and useless. Absent are both tears and laughter; by analogy, the effect is Eucharistic. The ritual of drama is fundamentally religious, its formality a disciplining of the soul. It is not accidental that dramatic literature evolves toward formal enactment whether in that sweep from hymns to Dionysus to the plays of Sophocles or in the work of a single mind such as T. S. Eliot's.

To summarize, it is the effect of tragedy upon the spectator which sets tragedy off from the effects of other modes of dramatic literature such as the essay or comedy or farce. The aesthetic form is not basic to the effect, but rather the moral implications of the tragedy and the spiritual state of the spectator are basic to it. The dramatic form used by Aeschylus is only the most economic form of tragedy, given his time and place. The effect is the result of a spiritual harmony between the tragic character's knowledge and the spectator's. The coincidence of knowledge effects an exorcism of pity and fear, restoring the spectator's soul to a moment of calm health. The end which tragedy achieves is a moral one, though its means depend upon aesthetic concerns. The moral end allows one to say, with Eliot in "East Coker":

> The poetry does not matter.
> It was not (to start again) what one had expected.
> What matters finally is
> The fight to recover what has been lost
> And found and lost again and again: and now, under
> conditions
> That seem unpropitious.

That fight may provide its own grounds in seemingly unpoetic and unheroic conditions. The prosaic necessity of economic survival, for instance, is always at hand for the poet no less than for the generality. Homer builds into his song high praise of the poet as useful to civilization, no doubt wondering always in what city he must next beg bread. It is late in Shakespeare's pursuit of security that he can give up his second-best bed for a final and enduring best one. The private documents of Coleridge or Pound or Joyce are dull with Homer's old concern. So then, let us turn to Wordsworth's condition as would-be bard, to the complex influence of rudimentary survival upon the intellectual and spiritual struggle his poetry reflects.

II

A Cow and Two or Three Other Little Comforts

John Wordsworth to William, January 24, 1805

My Investment is well laid in & my voyage thought by most persons the first of the season and if we are so fortunate as to get safe and soon to Bengall . . . I have no doubt but that I shall make a very good voyage of it if not a *very great* one. . . . In the Lyrical Ballads my favorites are the Mad mother part of the Indian Woman and Joanna.

Wordsworth, "Essay, Supplementary to the Preface"

Every Author, as far as he is great and at the same time *original*, has had the task of creating the taste by which he is to be enjoyed.

Wordsworth's alienation from his immediate antecedent poets, his unhappiness with what seemed to him the sterile formality of the eighteenth century, is most often made to revolve around his conception of nature and the mind's uses of it. Certainly one may agree with Geoffrey Durrant's impressive analysis of "Three Years She Grew" (*William Wordsworth,* 1969) and his conclusion that the poem asserts "that value has nothing to do with public judgment. The individual mind may create its own value.... This poem is a firm assertion of the validity of subjective judgments of value." But such poems are a minor portion of Wordsworth's body of work, a part of a complex whole. We shall presently consider at some length Wordsworth's subjectivity and the question of just how strong and continuing a confidence he places in it. For the moment we may recall another aspect of Wordsworth's thinking, the desire in him to be a public poet. He wanted sometimes a large audience, sometimes a fit audience, depending in part upon the fluctuation of his confidence in the subjective powers of the mind. His letters at the time of *Lyrical Ballads* carry this concern, and his famous prefaces to those volumes are public notices of it. The whole problem of divided inclination is further complicated by the problem of his and Dorothy's economic survival, which made this castigator of the world of getting and spending somewhat uncomfortable. But added to that mundane problem was the eager sacrifice of John on William's behalf. John, whom Coleridge declared "a *silent* poet," shy, reserved in the presence of the world outside the family, nevertheless engaged that world ambitiously on William's and Dorothy's behalf. "I will work for you ... and you shall attempt to do something for the world," William recalls his saying. Again, "Could I but see you with a green field of your own and a Cow and two or three other little comforts I should be happy." Far removed from Grasmere, John expresses anger at the news of the destruction of a copse he remembers as particularly pleasing to the eye, and from the heart of the commercial world warns of its encroachment upon the spirit. Meanwhile he pursues success in that world, having speculated in Spanish dollars to be bartered in China. He also encourages William in the expectation of making money from *Lyrical Ballads,* money which he will in turn use in the private bartering allowed captains of the East India Company. His resolution to make William's and Dorothy's fortune is undiminished by William's marrying Mary Hutchinson, with whom John was evidently in love. So that John's death off Portsmouth, at a point when the family fortune seemed reasonably assured, bears upon William in ways heavier than simply a disillusionment with the indifference of Nature. His position as poet in a secular, commercial age was complicated by a secular and commercial concern in his own heart, which came to a focus with the death of that generous brother who so hopefully expected William to create "something for the world."

As for the fit audience William wooed, it was one trained in certain tastes gone wrong in William's view. John recognized the limited audience whom the poetry would please as being "people of sense." It was an audience in intellectual positions of power. But it was not simply a concern for the correction of taste that made William engage the public mind; he wanted as well a reformation in social, political, and religious England that would return it to a piety forfeited by altar, sword, and pen.

Wordsworth's concern as poet-citizen in a state whose heritage was in decay led him to a concern for the history of that state as he sought an honorable and effective relationship of bard to the state. If Virgil may be taken as one of Wordsworth's fathers no less than Dante's, as Wordsworth took him to be, we may make a distinction that bears upon Wordsworth's difficulty with history, both personal and national. Virgil assumed Rome's history and myth with the confidence inspired by the accidents of his appearance upon the scene, Rome being at its high moment. But England seemed to have reached its high moment in Tudor days. Unlike Virgil, Wordsworth found it necessary to recover history before he could turn it to his uses. That concern is peripherally engaged in *The Borderers;* it is often the center of concern in *The Excursion.* If I am right in my reading of his concern for history, it is a part of what he came to consider his personal failure, a failure to see reality in relation to his dream of that happy community in nature which should have made the sacrifice of John unnecessary to the survival of the poet. The question became for him the relation of history to the myth he pursued, a very modern question, and one intimately related to Wordsworth's problem of justifying the mind's subjectivity.

By the time "Tintern Abbey" was composed, Wordsworth was beginning to realize that the self-willed turning of the Englishman from nature to his own made world carried evidence also of his own turning from God to the things of God, a turning to those things embraced by the term *Nature.* John could write enthusiastically of his engagement in usury, "my investment to China will amount to about 10,000 & the longer the war last the better it will be for me—that's some comfort." He could write also, "I only hope & trust that in the North of England you will never have a set of men supported by visitors to the Lakes—they will be the very ruin and the hearts of ruin of the country." What William saw as idolatry in his fellow Englishmen, whose ritual was getting and spending, was explicitly reflected in the career of John, a career whose primary energy was to justify William's genius by buying him time. That complication of purity in motive and action was so close to home as to raise the question of whether he himself was exempt from idolatry. John, about to set off on a voyage of conquest, looks over the side of his ship and sees in the calm waters Grasmere and its environs where he has recently helped Wordsworth and Dorothy settle in. Wordsworth uses that experience John told him of in "The Brothers," a poem which begins with a protest against "These Tourists" whom John has warned of. Though it is a poor poem, it contains a kind of uneasiness of mind in Wordsworth concerning his and John's relationship which makes it of particular interest to us. The "Shepherd-lad" brother, having left his quiet English world for sea life, becomes bored with the quest for riches and adventure, and

> would often hang
> Over the vessel's side, and gaze and gaze. . . .
> He, thus by feverish passion overcome,
> Even with the organs of his bodily eye,
> Below him, in the bosom of the deep,
> Saw mountains; saw the forms of sheep that grazed
> On verdant hills—with dwellings among trees
> And shepherds clad in the same country grey
> Which he himself had worn.

Wordsworth, in a note to these lines, gives a literary source for this description of the effect of a mild tropical fever on his homesick shepherd. But John's letters home are often enough laced with recollections of the landscape about Grasmere, of experiences in the English countryside when he goes ashore, to make him a more immediate source of the lines than "Mr. Gilbert, author of the Hurricane." An even more telling indication of Wordsworth's uneasiness in the personal circumstances is his inversion of the brother's roles in his poem. His shepherd-sailor returns

> From perils manifold, with some small wealth
> Acquired by traffic 'mid the Indian Isles,
> To his paternal home.

There he expects to pick up the shepherd's life again, with his beloved brother. But there is "Strange alteration wrought on every side." Woods are felled that he remembers, and even the "everlasting hills themselves were changed," to the imagination, the "confused . . . memory" of this wanderer. In a long, dull conversation with the village priest, in which the attempt at dramatic suspense through our secretly knowing this stranger to be the prodigal brother returned (as the priest does not), we learn that the younger brother pined excessively for his brother at sea, until one day he fell from a precipice and was mangled. The returned

85

brother now becomes "The Stranger" in the poem, takes his leave of the priest, goes back to sea, "and is now / A seaman, a grey-headed Mariner." John, reading *Lyrical Ballads,* found it a more striking poem than "Michael," though "Michael" is "much better" and indeed soon becomes his "first and greatest favourite." One may reasonably suppose the inferior poem is the more striking to John not only because he meets in it personal experiences and reflections shared with William, but more particularly because of the burden of guilt which the poem places on the Stranger's shoulders as consequence of desertion of "the younger" brother upon the English heaths. There is almost a note of accusation in the poem, which would be more apparent to John in the texture of a poem so heavy with private experiences turned to public verse. Even the awkward insistence upon the seafarer's being older than the abandoned brother, "the elder by just eighteen months," but "two years taller," seems a calculated reversal of the literal relationship.

If the older brother upon his return finds himself a stranger in his own home country, the priest's prolonged recollections of the younger brother show the younger brother no less so. The family dead and he the sole survivor—having heard his brother "was in slavery among the Moors"—he becomes ward of the country folk, staying first with one and then with another, exiled in his local home. Though "not sickly," he is "delicate," seeming rather happy, though the priest suspects it an appearance of happiness only. He sleepwalks, and "sleeping . . . sought his brother." His death is out of a "disquietude and grief" that led him on a May morning to walk over the precipice in his sleep. His shepherd's staff, caught halfway down, moulders away in the interval of his brother's absence. Sad story indeed, for the shepherd who stayed home has fed no hungry sheep.

Wordsworth's growing awareness of the complex role of the poet in society did not lead him to a poetry so great in its concerns for reformation as Milton's. His elegy for lost brothers carries no stern implications of duty and responsibility. There is failure in the presence of a complex world, whose moral import will slowly emerge in Wordsworth's poetry to become an open call to shepherds in those sonnets two years in the future. There is nevertheless in such poems as "The Brothers" and "Michael" the beginning of an unquiet note about his personal situation which does not allow his state in nature to be one of perfect peace. The famous prefaces also, while they have much to do with poetry, become rather heavily concerned with poetry in society, with the poet's place among men like John. Wordsworth, by the time he wrote his first preface, had come to a deeper understanding of the nature of the English mind than he had had before; it was an insight into the separation of history from myth occasioned by the rise of empiricism, that enemy of the mind and of poetry which had triumphed in the eighteenth century in Wordsworth's view of the matter. Its immediate spawn was the commercial mind, whose confusion is exemplified in that "*quiet* poet" John Wordsworth, looking over the side of his ship and seeing in his mind's eye Grasmere. If I am my brother's enemy, may I not also be my own? What price must be paid for "a green field . . . and a Cow and two or three other little comforts?"

As Reves Turn Lords

WORDSWORTH AND THE TUDOR INFECTION

Lawrence Stone, *The Crisis of the Aristocracy*

It is ... between 1560 and 1640, and more precisely between 1580 and 1620, that the real watershed between medieval and modern England must be placed.

Wordsworth, "The World Is Too Much with Us"

late and soon,
Getting and spending, we lay waste our powers:
Little we see in Nature that is ours.

Eliot, "Chorus" from *The Rock*

When the Stranger says: "What is the meaning of this city?
Do you huddle close together because you love each other?"
What will you answer? "We dwell together
To make money from each other?" Or "This is a community?"

The evolution of empiricism toward materialism affects the development of English and American letters in very obvious ways, no less commanding or disturbing for their being obvious. That growth of materialism out of the empirical spirit of the Renaissance was well underway in Chaucer's day, with consequences of importance to the present study for two reasons. First, empiricism is directly related to the loss of audience which the poet has openly lamented with progressive alarm from Milton's defiant "fit audience though few" into our own day, a loss of acute concern to Wordsworth. Second, it needs to be pointed out that the rise of the empirical spirit is a conscious part of Wordsworth's awareness at a very early point in his career.

In the late "Preface" Wordsworth composed as an introduction to his attempt at tragedy, *The Borderers,* he analyzes the development of an inexplicably malevolent spirit remarkably like Iago. Wordsworth's protagonist has as chief source of power, as explained by Wordsworth, an empiricism completely divorced from any awareness of moral or spiritual concerns. Wordsworth explains: "Having indulged a habit, dangerous in a man who has fallen, of dallying with moral calculations, he becomes an empiric, and a daring and unfeeling empiric." What Wordsworth is arguing is the psychological process whereby a "fallen" man accomplished the dissociation of sensibility. The separation is one Wordsworth laments in his 1800 "Preface" to *Lyrical Ballads,* even as he expresses the belief that poetry, which is "the breath and finer spirit of all knowledge" and the "impassioned expression which is in the countenance of all Science," will once more assume its proper role in ordering the forms of knowledge. "The remotest discoveries of the Chemist, the Botanist, or Mineralogist, will be as proper objects of the Poet's art as any upon which it can be employed." It is as if Wordsworth were here pleading, while attacking the "false poets" who had separated poetry from poetry's true language, for a poetry not unlike that which one finds in Teilhard de Chardin's *Phenomenon of Man.*

The new empirical science, which we see adorned by art

in the work of Sir Francis Bacon, did not spring as full-blown theory before the fact, any more than it lacked immediate practical effects. The home freezer was a long way in the future of Bacon's experiments with refrigeration, but there was already all about him in the seventeenth century a general engagement of the worldly values of empiricism. The middle-class succession to power, the rise of the "gentry" which is a phenomenon much discussed among recent historians, was busily preparing the way for a theorist, and in a sense this aspect of English life was to Bacon's work what Sophocles' work was to Aristotle's *Poetics*, the phenomena out of which theory was abstracted. The rise of the gentry to power came about as a result of what would be called, in America, Yankee ingenuity, the quick skill of adapting empirical inclinations to land utilization, or to investments in the expanding empire, or to the development of the industrial factories that eventually proliferated on the English plains like Wordsworth's daffodils. In lamenting industry's desecration of nature, Wordsworth could still express thankfulness (in his essay on *The Excursion*) that the English streams had been spared when coal proved more suitable than water power. He had not to oppose private or state Tennessee Valley Authority, as some of his descendants in America were to do some hundred years later in their Agrarian arguments.

As the English rose to international power, the old power structure of the nobility decayed. The Church gave way under the ideological assault of militant Puritanism. The Crown gave way under that attack, with Milton writing an apology to the courts of Europe for the assault upon Charles I. But both Church and Crown had already been significantly invaded and weakened internally by the rise of new lords of the land and city, the nationalistic burghers. The nobility, whose role it had been to embody in its life an idealized accommodation of Church and State, and defend that ideal by force of arms, likewise gave way under the assault of the Puritans, but (again) not before its power had been already considerably reduced by the new burghers.

The nobility was reduced in part, of course, because of its private corruptions in a changing world, weaknesses which such minds as Milton's were quick to measure, the gap between professed responsibilities and the failure to exercise those responsibilities.

As much to the point on the political level of power, the nobility's position was destroyed by the new possibilities of brute power and the "technicians" such power called forth. Consider the category of the military. The old manifestation of power first displayed, if somewhat crudely, at Hastings in the weapons of the French adventurers were spear, sword, battle-ax, and, most important, the horse. After those two decisive flank attacks on Harold's too eager infantry axmen by mounted soldiers, the new system evolved smoothly. Behind the spear was the alignment of forces in a figurative lance, the lord at the point with his liegemen behind him, and behind the liegeman the echelons of his own retainers. Much later at Agincourt the longbow was as prophetic as William's horsemen in 1066; it spelled the end of such stirring presences as that of Henry v, the final subject, we notice, of Shakespeare's chronicles of English history. The longbow was followed by the cannon—and the structure of society which had empowered the nobility was at an end. The phalanx, not the wedge, became the image of the army, an image incorporating also the effective sea power of the English broadside. The professional soldier and sailor arose to replace the traditional lord as leader, military men whose primary commitment was increasingly to the state as represented in the King, but a King who less and less represented a conciliation of a universal Church and particular State, as the Tudors spectacularly demonstrated. The upshot is that Chaucer's Sailor and his Yeoman rise to become admiral and general, but they are no longer under as strong an influence by the Knight or the Parson. It is the Franklyn and the Merchant who assume the power or influence, whose retainers are the Reve and the Maunciple.

Wordsworth realized this shift of power, though he does

91

not notice the importance of the Tudor shift of power from Rome. In his "Preface" to *The Excursion,* one finds him expressing regret over the loss of spiritual and cultural influences upon the peasantry by the nobility.

> It has ever appeared to me highly favorable to the beneficial influence of the Church of England upon all gradations and classes of society, that the patronage of its benefices is in numerous instances attached to the estates of noble families of ancient gentry; and accordingly I am gratified by the opportunity afforded me in the "Excursion" to portray the character of a country clergyman of more than ordinary talents, born and bred in the upper ranks of society so as to partake of their refinements, and at the same time brought by his pastoral office and his love of rural life into intimate connection with the peasantry of his native district.

One remarks that though these are Wordsworth's words in old age they relate to a conception of character presented in *The Excursion* much earlier. And one notices as well that Wordsworth's conception of the good parson does not correspond exactly to Chaucer's, being the figure of a Knight in holy orders rather than Chaucer's Parson of homely origins. (Wordsworth was, we recall, reading Chaucer and translating him into verse soon after *Lyrical Ballads.*)

What is suggested by Wordsworth's use of the knight in holy orders, whose "intimate connection with the peasantry of his native district" is a consequence of his family heritage, is that Wordsworth was hopeful of a new alliance against the industrial modernism which the cities reeked of. One can see the point by contrasting the attitude of a young city poet much taken with recent sweeping social changes. John Keats, reflecting Leigh Hunt's politics, considered the shift of power accomplished in Tudor times with enthusiasm. He writes his brother George, in 1819, of being very happy that the nobility was reduced. That indeed was the first change for the better in the modern world, "the gradual annihilation of the tyranny of the nobles, when Kings found it in their interest to conciliate the common people, elevate them and be just to them. Just when baronial Power ceased and before standing armies were so dangerous, Taxes were few, Kings were lifted by people over the heads of their nobles, and those people held a rod over Kings." The next change, which Keats took to be peculiar to the continent, was not for the best he thought, though he hardly appreciates it as a possible consequence of the discomfiture of the nobility as did Wordsworth. It was the change to the "obligation of Kings to the Multitude" which led to what Keats seems to have taken as an accident of history, the abuses of power by the multitude in the rush of the French Revolution. Wordsworth's turning to *The Borderers,* in 1795, was the beginning of his pressing concern to understand his English origins, following more personal disappointments with the French Revolution than the detached ideological influences of Leigh Hunt upon Keats. Wordsworth was interested in a counter alliance as a possible steadying influence on England, the alliance of the remnants of the nobility and the peasantry, both of whom were closer by virtue of origins and circumstances to the "ancient English dower / Of inward happiness." It would be a few years (in 1802) before Wordsworth could be so explicit as to publicly condemn an age in which "the wealthiest man among us is the best" since "the homely beauty of the good old cause" is failed. As Lawrence Stone details it in *The Crisis of the Aristocracy* the courtier, particularly under James and Charles I, received control of the sale of titles almost as a modern entrepreneur receives concession rights at a stadium. The destructive effects upon the English peerage were increasingly apparent to Wordsworth in his perusal of history, though his emphasis upon those effects did not mean, as the young Browning or Shelley, and Keats on occasion, thought, that Wordsworth was committed to the "establishment" of his day.

The effects of those political and social revolutions in "our old home" (as Hawthorne termed England in his reflections upon his sojourn to England) were abiding in Western culture. Nor were they relevant simply to England as separate from the continent as Keats preferred to believe. Bloody destruction such as appalled Keats can only be taken as accidents of a happy progress if one increasingly loses the feeling of horror in spiritual destruction. If England escaped blood baths of a spectacular dimension and a ratified date, an appalling destruction nevertheless resulted, as Carlyle, Ruskin, Dickens, and others contemporary with and after Wordsworth began to declare angrily. Social and political evolution out of an empirically spawned laissez-faire economics was a law of the jungle increasingly oppressive to a spirit like Wordsworth's.

If we pursue the progress of empiricism westward to Hawthorne's new home, we may make observations suitable to American letters. From Agincourt to Appomattox is a long reach, but in a very real way the latter represents the last battle in the west of that "good old cause" Wordsworth lamented. That Hawthorne was aware of the complexity of this final battle, before the emergence of a victor, is reflected in his attack upon Northern ideology in the *Atlantic Monthly* (July 1862), an attack used as the starting point of George M. Fredrickson's richly helpful book *The Inner Civil War: Northern Intellectuals and the Crisis of the Union* (1965). Fredrickson's book, considered as complement to Stone's *Crisis of the Aristocracy*, helps show our American version of the Tudor triumph, the ascendancy between the 1850s and 1870s of an inimically materialistic nationalism.

From Appomattox we carry as part of our heritage remembrance of two men, Grant and Lee. But to understand what they may signify to the poet, to the Fugitives for instance and to a less explicit degree to Eliot, we must reflect upon the history of empiricism in America. Its most direct line of development on our shores, which touches directly upon the emergence of Grant and the industrial barons who succeed him, is the growth of pragmatism out of Puritanism. If we may pursue the matter in terms of our literature, rather than in terms of military or economic history (which would reflect much the same thing), we observe that here also the inevitable end upon which pragmatism settles with fascination is gross materialism. The threat to art of unassimilated cultural change which troubled Wordsworth is demonstrated in its American manifestation by Mark Twain's tramping through Europe in muddy shoes as well as in lesser writers' concern for the possibility of the best-seller. The general triumph of American pragmatism, surely the dominant religion to emerge out of the American experiment, owes a great deal to the ascendancy of the new gentry in England just before England's expansion on the American continent. The spiritual freedom, which we advertise as our cause of being, underwent a decided sea change toward economic license whose consequences are spectacularly upon us now in our ecological concerns.

A difference between Eliot's American and Wordsworth's English materialism which should be noted is this: the American materialist felt it necessary to celebrate his success in abusing the world's riches by importing culture over a relatively short period of time. For his advances through active empirical devotions were so sudden and large as to disallow cultural assimilation. From Kitty Hawk to Lindbergh to super transports, he moved through worlds incomprehensible so that men and actions and places and distances combine in quick mystery till now our Pilgrim Christian stands on the moon but with no including metaphysical understanding to suggest the implication of that marvelous event, at last very much disturbed by "future shock." Europe, as James pointed out in defense of America, was quick to enlarge our foolishness into caricature of the American, a portrait too loudly close to the truth to allow much attention to similar developments in Europe which were so intimately a part of the texture of *Madame Bovary*. The new English lord of wealth did not need to import a castle, as our nineteenth-century industrial barons were inclined to do. Nor did he have to run for election to the House of Lords. He had only to move into the castle at hand, and thereby inherit the office. In this process, the nobility was displaced by a new aristocracy who were "the best" in respect to worldly efficiency. They used the precedents of hierarchy in the interest of an orderly expansion of empire, appropriating at once whatever remained of the old sentiments. The decline of the English empire accelerates with the early nineteenth-century exploitation of empire under the assumed mask of paternal responsibilities, to which the history of the East India Company and its opium trade serve as paradigm.

America, through John Adams in particular, was the first colony to recognize this aspect of English power, with Edmund Burke, one of Wordsworth's heroes, defending America's position and distinguishing it from that of revolutionary France. Somewhat later Twain, aware of the duplicity in the European aristocracy, attacked it by exaggerating American vulgarity in order to shock English and European pretense of having refined sensibilities. While Hawthorne was more perceptively aware than Twain of the discrepancy in the new Englishman and new European, as his notebooks and essays reveal, it was Henry James who effectively brought the two together, highlighting the deficiencies of the new "nobility" emerging in America and the decayed European nobility whose origins lay largely in the sixteenth and early seventeenth centuries. To James, the failure of European culture is more shocking than the innocence of American character, since for James the American failure had at least the extenuating circumstance of our being a new country without ancient traditions.

Nor was this discrepancy between the pretended and the real in English culture lost on Pound or Eliot. Pound's *Mauberley* deals angrily with the matter. Eliot concerns himself with the Unreal City, that city which is to Augustine's City of God what Hawthorne's black mass (in "Young Goodman Brown") is to Sabbath Puritan service. He uses the twentieth-century London built on Chaucer's London. I shall return later to this subject as it relates to the development of Eliot's mind and poetry. But first I must return again to Wordsworth, Eliot's nineteenth-century counterpart in English letters, and to some aspects of his personal history as they relate to the rise of that materialism which so confounded his high concern. To do so, after this brief, ranging reflection upon the rise of empiricism, will help set Wordsworth more firmly in the tradition of contemporary letters.

96

In a Dark Wood

ⁱⁱDante, *Divine Comedy*

I woke to find myself in a dark wood,
Where the right road was wholly lost and gone.

ⁱⁱWordsworth, "How Sweet It Is"

How sweet it is, when mother Fancy rocks
The wayward brain, to saunter through a wood! . . .
Such place to me is sometimes like a dream
Or map of the whole world.
. . . at last in fear I shrink,
And leap at once from the delicious stream.

ⁱⁱEliot, *The Use of Poetry and the Use of Criticism*

The contemplation of the horrid or sordid or disgusting, by
an artist, is the necessary and negative aspect of the impulse
toward the pursuit of beauty. But not all succeed as did Dante
in expressing the complete scale from negative to positive.
The negative is the more importunate.

One wonders whether, when Wordsworth became concerned with the possibility of self-delusion, he may not have been shocked at the light his new awareness shed on that extraordinary preface he wrote to his play *The Borderers* (1795–1796). In the preface Wordsworth analyzes the stages whereby a particular individual degenerates toward the satanic. It is a remarkable analysis of such a character as one has in Shakespeare's Iago, Milton's Satan in *Paradise Regained,* Aldous Huxley's Coleman in *Antic Hay.* Wordsworth attempts to explain the psychology involved in a man who comes to that deliberately destructive malignancy which, since the Renaissance, has centered on Satan as a dramatic hero to replace Prometheus. Here is an important fragment from that preface:

> Being in the habit of considering the world as a body which is in some sort of war with him, he has a feeling borrowed from that habit which gives an additional zest to his own contempt of those whom he despises. Add to this, that a mind fond of nourishing sentiments of contempt will be prone to the admission of those feelings which are considered under any uncommon bond of relation (as must be the case with a man who has quarrelled with the world), and the feelings will mutually strengthen each other. In this morbid state of mind he cannot exist without occupation, he requires constant provocations, all his pleasures are prospective, he is perpetually invoking a phantom, he commits new crimes to drive away the memory of the past.... His appetite from being exhausted becomes unnatural. Accordingly he will struggle so to characterize and to exalt actions little in themselves by a forced greatness of manner, and will chequer and degrade enterprises great in their atrocity by grotesque littleness of manner and fantastic obliquities. He is like a worn out voluptuary—he finds his temptation in strangeness; he is unable to suppress a low hankering after the double entendre in vice; yet his thirst for the extraordinary buoys him up, and supported by the habit of constant reflexion he frequently breaks out into what has the appearance of greatness; and in sudden emergencies, when he is called upon by surprise and thrown out of the path of his regular habits, or when dormant associations

are awakened tracing the revolutions through which his character has passed, in painting his former self he really *is* great.

If this analysis does not fit all of the villains I named, it fits each in enough of its particulars to be arresting. But it fits much more. In the light of the final sentence here quoted, we see how such a malignant figure can indeed become great, and Wordsworth makes an attempt at presenting such a figure in the victim of *The Borderers*. Marmaduke is a character combining Hamlet's procrastination and Othello's innocence, though as a play Wordsworth's execution makes melodrama rather than tragedy of the possibilities. Nevertheless, Wordsworth carries us in the final sentence quoted above beyond Iago and into Macbeth and Othello, in whom "sudden emergencies" and "surprises" and "dormant associations" are instruments that break the character out of dominant habitual ways of looking at the world Shakespeare established in his plays. We move now beyond the hopelessly perverse, beyond Satan, for Wordsworth's argument holds the perverted love of an Iago capable of being shocked back into a right-mindedness. And surely we observe a depth greater than nihilistic despair in the final speeches of a Macbeth or Othello. What is far more interesting in Wordsworth's analysis than its application to such exaggerated figures of man as Iago, then, is its relation to the figure of man as hero. What Wordsworth has described is a course of action precisely paralleling that described by C. S. Lewis as the pattern of Original Sin, that turning toward the self, and the shocked return of the self to right-mindedness, which is the antithesis of self-mindedness.

We are safely comfortable when making such application of this pattern to the agent in a play, as Wordsworth does in his essay. But we should notice that while Wordsworth is attempting to explain how the particular villain of his drama came to be and to point to the first beginnings of such a decline in the hero of his play, he is doing so by trying to imagine the disintegration in the literal life of a man as that life relates to art. He is not simply justifying a literary character, but attempting to understand the workings of the human mind. What if one apply his argument not to Iago or Macbeth but to oneself?

When he came, in his extreme years, to publish *The Borderers* so as not to "impose upon my successors the task of deciding its fate," he nevertheless withheld that essay preface, which was not published until Professor Selincourt presented it in 1926. In a note composed for its first publication, Wordsworth points to the center of his interest in the play. "The study of human nature suggests this awful truth, that as in the trials to which life subjects us, sin and crime are apt to start from their very opposite qualities, so are there no limits to the hardening of the heart and the perversion of the understanding to which they may carry their slaves. During my long residence in France 1791–1792, while the Revolution was rapidly advancing to the extreme wickedness, I had frequent opportunities of being an eyewitness of this process, and it was while that knowledge was fresh upon my memory that the Tragedy of 'The Borderers' was composed."

The play is written then out of the shock of that "extreme wickedness" that had control of the revolution before Wordsworth's eyes, an "awful truth" indeed for one to contemplate who had his initial sympathy for the revolution out of a vague good will for the human race. His experiences forced him to look at individual men and try to account for sin and crime out of good intentions in the sinner. The next step, inevitably, given such a dedicated and committed man as Wordsworth, was to examine himself to see whether good deeds and virtuous intention possibly had in them the seed of error and sin. "Tintern Abbey" is precisely such an examination. It is a poem that is deeply concerned with conveying the shock of discovering that an unexamined, habitual way of looking at the world will no longer suffice. The poem attempts to discover in what manner the speaker has lost that "feeling of zest" which belonged to him earlier, the feeling he had tried to capture in *Descriptive Sketches* after his walking tour of the continent.

In "Tintern Abbey," Wordsworth stands, a new man, at a site ancient in memory and reflects upon that memory under the emotional strain of "many recognitions dim and faint" with "somewhat of a sad perplexity." The literal revisiting is a means to a revisiting of earlier emotional states. Looking at his young companion, he catches in her "wild" eyes "gleams / of past existence." That is, he sees that hers is the same emotional relation to nature that had once been his, for "past existence" here does not mean a Platonic existence prior to the earthly one. The poem attempts to juxtapose emotional states and examine them with a mind not seduced by the emotions, a mind which has come to acknowledge the necessity of thought. The poem begins with the eye turned outward: the details of imagery in the first twenty or so lines are the sharpest of the poem. But rapidly the seeming sharpness of detail begins to give way to vague adjectives before indefinite nouns.

The disparity between the literal environment in the vicinity of Tintern Abbey and Wordsworth's imagery in the poem is ironically remarkable. The river was heavy with commercial shipping as far inland as the Abbey. Gilpin's *Tour of the Wye,* a copy of which Wordsworth and Dorothy apparently had with them, points out that "many of the furnaces, on the banks of the river, consume charcoal, which is manufactured on the spot; and the smoke, which is frequently seen issuing from the sides of the hills; and spreading its thin veil over a part of them, beautifully breaks their lines, and unites them with the sky." Wordsworth's choice of *cliffs* over *smoke* as the agent binding earth to the sky echoes Gilpin but ignores those encroachments of industry upon the sylvan Wye of which he must have been aware. Nor does he suggest in the poem that the "wreaths of smoke / Sent up, in silence, from among the trees" have anything to do with charcoal furnaces. It has been suggested that the poem begins in the eighteenth-century landscape tradition. But Wordsworth is, as the poem soon reveals, presenting a landscape of the mind. Such a place as this above Tintern Abbey, he reflects in a sonnet some eight years later, "is sometime like a dream / Or map of the

whole world." In 1800 he says in a note to the poem that
"it was written with a hope that in the transitions, and
the impassioned music of versification, would be found the
principle requisites of [an ode.]" But the transitions and
the music alike seem rather the requisites of thought, of
the contemplation of a state of mind rather than an ode
to Psyche. The poem is not public as is an ode, nor are
its formalities those traditional to the ode. What happens
in the poem is that at once the mind turns in upon itself
as it attempts to measure the present sensations against those
of the past and thus justify a kind of thought beyond Wordsworth's beloved wise passiveness, since feeling alone no
longer suffices. To read the poem without remembering
Dorothy's presence is to be shocked by the turning outward
to address her late in the poem. It is a shock in the speaker
himself which leads him to "leap at once from the delicious
stream" in which "mother Fancy'" has rocked the "wayward
brain."

We may, at this point, shed some light on Wordsworth's
troubled poem by recalling a point from Eliot's 1936 essay
on Milton and a reflection from one of Wordsworth's "Miscellaneous Sonnets," used above as epigraph. In that sonnet
Wordsworth reflects upon the seduction of Fancy in nature,
in which "thoughts . . . Enter through ears and eyesight,
with such gleam / Of all things, that at last in fear I
shrink." Eliot, in his essay, argues that Milton's sensuousness
has been withered "by book-learning." He illustrates his argument in part by a citation from *L'Allegro:*

> . . . the plowman near at hand,
> Whistles o'er the furrowed land,
> And the milkmaid singeth blithe.

"It is not," Eliot says, "a particular ploughman, milkmaid,
and shepherd that Milton sees (as Wordsworth might see
them)." But Eliot is overrating Wordsworth's powers at
particularizing, just as he underestimates Milton's sensuousness in those twin experiments by Milton on the effect of

the heart's clouding the mind or the mind's clouding the heart—*L'Allegro* and *Il Penseroso*—poems in which the dissociation of sensibility is at deliberate issue. As soon as "Tintern Abbey" turns inward to the emotions, there begins to arise a strong current of what Eliot calls, when he finds it in Milton and Joyce, the "rhetorical style." Lamenting the loss of all those "aching joys" and "dizzy raptures," the poem rises toward an abstract thought which touches upon very general images of nature—"meadows" and "woods" and "mountains." It rises toward affirming the mind as "a mansion of all lovely forms" and the memory "a dwelling-place / For all sweet sounds and harmonies." What Wordsworth is doing is expressing with intensity what is more nearly a desire in him than a reality perceived: a desire that the mind have power to make for itself a pure estate like that which Dante's Pilgrim experienced after drinking Lethe and Eunoae. Now what is involved in Wordsworth's rhetoric is both an awareness of the past inadequacy of emotions alone, and, in spite of this larger awareness, a new seduction of the mind by the new emotion. It is the complicated experience in which present thought changes past experience, whereby past experience qualifies present thought as well. There is no still point possible, which means of course that confidence in the abiding qualities of the mind's experience, the reassurance of any dependability in the accuracy of memory, is fleeting. For, as Paul Ricoeur has said, "By retroaction from the successive 'nows,' our past never stops changing its meaning; the present appropriation of the past modifies that which motivates us from the depths of the past." It is at the crisis of this dilemma that the poem suddenly turns outward, to Dorothy, with a passionate assertion that the present moment does have abiding qualities, even as the speaker acknowledges that inevitably death will come and he no longer be where he can catch from Dorothy's eyes "these gleams / Of past experience." This desire for a steadiness in the flux of mind which troubles Wordsworth is not unique, but neither is it common: one finds it in sensitive, reflective minds, those minds troubled by the meaning of awareness. To dramatize the reflective struggle is a dominant theme of modern literature, and Wordsworth is our first major poet of that struggle. The assurance of the validity of experience to the awareness, with which "Tintern Abbey" concludes, is moving in large part because it protests too much. A less-troubled mind writes less impressive poetry, as Wordsworth may be said to do in that miniature summary of the "Tintern Abbey" experience, sonnet 2 of part 2 of his "Miscellaneous Sonnets." In that sonnet the poet maintains an ironic distance. The imagination, which he champions in impassioned moments, is here suspected of being in fact the machinations of "mother Fancy" who "rocks / The wayward brain." The kind of literary excessiveness with which Eliot charges Milton of being unaware in *L'Allegro* is parodied by Wordsworth here, in a mock epic simile describing a

> wild rose tip-toe upon hawthorne stocks,
> Like a bold Girl, who plays her agile pranks
> At Wakes and Fairs with wandering Mountebanks,—
> When she stands cresting the Clown's head, and mocks
> The crowd beneath her. Verily I think,
> Such place is sometimes like a dream
> Or map of the whole world.

Fear of delusion saves the poet: "I shrink, / And leap at once from the delicious stream." That delicious stream is not far removed from those soft inland murmurs heard along the Wye, murmurs inland of the mindscape. Nor is it far removed from the reflections of the Solitary in his depression of mind as he reflects upon the long history of his betrayal by the world of nature, no less than that by man. There in the presence of the memory of a stream's "softened roar, or murmur," a sound which "Though soothing," nevertheless is Nature's way of making known "perplexing labyrinths, abrupt Precipitations, and untoward straits," the Solitary turns with a hope that his "particular current" will soon reach "The unfathomable gulf, where all is still." Wordsworth is not always so despondent as he makes his Solitary out to be, but he is often so, and over the problem of whether the awareness itself distorts its experience in nature so that at "some still passage of the stream's course" it sees prophetic but unriddled: "Inverted trees, rocks, clouds, and azure sky."

I do not think that one has the same innocence in Milton's twin poems as in Wordsworth's "Tintern Abbey." Milton is more fully conscious of what he is doing than Wordsworth is capable of being or than Eliot gives Milton credit for being. Milton is performing as Eliot himself does in "Prufrock": he is dramatizing the emotional coloring of the world by an innocent consciousness, the poems' protagonists are clearly not John Milton. The plowman and milkmaid aren't particular. That is the point, as the voice of *Il Penseroso* emphasizes. For the voice which speaks in *L'Allegro* is one out of an "idle brain" intoxicated by "Deluding joys," even as the voice of *Il Penseroso* is one controlled by a "loathed Melancholy" that comes from too much bookishness. (Wordsworth's two poems "Expostulation and Reply" and "The Tables Turned" may be considered his version of Milton's experiment.) Milton too is concerned with the dissociation of sensibilities, and the rhetorical style of these poems is so much exaggerated that it calls attention to two ways of failing to maintain the necessary control by the mind: through an excess of emotions or by an absence of emotion. The poems show mood in command, emotion in control, and illustrate the artificiality which is the consequence. They reflect back upon the voice speaking, as Eliot's "Prufrock" reflects back upon its speaker. No doubt Eliot is right about the dangers of such a style as he described its application to such a work as *Paradise Lost* and *Finnegans Wake:* "A disadvantage of the rhetorical style appears to be, that a dislocation takes place, through the hypertrophy of the auditory imagination at the expense of the visual and tactile, so that the inner meaning is separated from the surface, and tends to become something occult, or at least without effect upon the reader until fully understood."

But it seems reasonably evident that Milton is deliberately dramatizing that disadvantage in *L'Allegro* and *Il Penseroso*, calling specific attention to it, however he may have failed to escape that danger in his more ambitious poetry. The poems with which one should compare Wordsworth's "Tintern Abbey" are not Milton's twin caricatures of mood, or Eliot's "Aunt Helen" or "Cousin Nancy" or "Mr. Apollinax." It is more ambitious poetry to which we must look: *Lycidas* and "The Love Song of J. Alfred Prufrock." For Wordsworth's is an attempt to comprehend that strain that is of a higher mood. He is attempting to present in perspective the stages of his changing awareness, not of nature itself, but of his own mind's change. It is an attempt to move from a reaction to nature to an action in nature. "Tintern Abbey," like *Lycidas* and "Prufrock," is introspective, but it is an introspection firmly pursued. Wordsworth too is called by mermaids; unlike Prufrock he takes the risk. Thus it is with "gleams of half-extinguished thought"—seen at the present moment of the poem in the eyes of his companion and recalled from the past by memory's eye—that he attempts to understand that early stage of his relationship to nature.

> ... when like a roe
> I bounded o'er the mountains, by the sides
> Of the deep rivers, and the lonely streams,
> Wherever nature led: more like a man
> Flying from something that he dreads than one
> Who sought the thing he loved.

That time being past, it becomes necessary to pursue the more remote charm with thought; which is to say, the necessity now is that one turn in the direction of first causes. The language of the lines which immediately follow suggest the pursuit as necessarily philosophically abstract. Indeed, the language of the memory in the passage quoted is itself far removed from imagery, even the adjectives being subjective, impressionistic: "*deep* rivers," "*lonely* streams," "*sounding* cataracts," "*tall* rock," "*deep* ... *gloomy* woods."

What is haunting at the present moment is an emotional residue in the memory, somehow suggesting profound implications of the mind's past experiences of the external world. But form is something more decisive in the existence of consciousness than is allowed when existence itself is suggested as accident, as when it is yoked with "colours" as an "appetite."

Wordsworth, turning toward the prime question *what is existence,* rests for the time being in affirming only the existence of some first cause, vaguely perceived now because he recognizes inadequacy in that early relationship to nature. He has learned to look on nature by 1798, "Not as in the hour / Of thoughtless youth"—a period surely including his involvement in the cause of the French Revolution—but hearing in nature now

> The still, sad music of humanity
> Nor harsh, nor grating, though of ample power
> To chasten and subdue.

And the new "feeling" he has, relative to nature, is toward something to which nature serves as a medium:

> I have felt
> A presence that disturbs me with the joy
> Of elevated thoughts; a sense sublime
> Of something far more deeply interfused,
> Whose dwelling is the light of setting suns,
> And the round ocean and the living air,
> And the blue sky, and in the mind of man;
> A motion and a spirit, that impels
> All thinking things, all objects of all thought,
> And rolls through all things.

This passage in particular is called upon to demonstrate the pagan element in Wordsworth, but it hardly requires that particular reading. It can surely be read as the first turning of the self from the self toward first cause and not an affirmation of spirit pervading matter. The poem, in fact, goes on to turn out of the self immediately to the companion, and the address on to the end of the poem is largely in her interest. One has not taken a giant step toward Christian orthodoxy perhaps, but the poem is considerably more of a stride in that direction than usually taken to be. For what Wordsworth is now seeing in the external world is precisely such a spirit as that which is described as "The Comforter," the "Life Giver," the very spirit which Milton invokes at the beginning of *Paradise Lost.*

Wordsworth argues, in his preface to *The Borderers,* the process whereby an individual develops out of initial failure, an initial "sin" as he says, into habitual malignancy. The individual's acute self-awareness leads to a shift away from whatever that "something" is (whose presence is signaled by the light of setting suns) to the self's state in nature where any thought separate from the joys of self are suspect. The concern is no longer for the end toward which one journeys but for the journey itself. The spiritually dangerous progression is from that interest in the journey as an end to that warm private glow of self within which the self warms, a rest from any journey at all. It is a pattern of intensifying egocentricity corresponding to that which C. S. Lewis presents as the pattern of the self ingrown which is called Original Sin. And this egocentricity is such that the particular mind is finally cut off from any world except that of its own making.

A more brilliant presentation of this process than Wordsworth can manage, let us recall, is Joyce's portrait of the romantic poet, *A Portrait of the Artist as a Young Man.* We notice in the account of Stephen Dedalus that by the end of the novel he too has moved toward coloring the world with his own eyes. He is capable of seeing green roses, as he has earlier been able only to desire such coloring, because he has discovered the process whereby roses of the world may be taken into the mind as a part of its private world. Stephen's too is the rhetorical process whereby the sensibilities are dissociated. His dislocation takes place "through the hypertrophy of the auditory imagination at the expense of the visual and tactile," but the cause is not primarily in the physical characteristics that he is imbued with—his weak eyes. The cause lies in the intensification of concern for the self, as Stephen affirms when he associates himself with Lucifer's *non serviam*. The novel's account of Stephen's development, given us in the limited third person, changes its point of view in the last few pages. There we have the actual voice of Stephen, addressing itself to his diary, so cryptic that a great deal of deciphering is necessary if the reader is to know what Stephen means. He does not mean to be heard by any save himself, for he has reached a point where not only is he incapable of communicating with anyone: he no longer wishes to.

The diary is a most suitable technical device for the ending of Joyce's particular fiction, but it is far more than a device. Nor are the many fictions since Joyce's *Portrait* that employ the interior monologue, often in the guise of a diary, merely copying Joyce. The monologue, which develops out of Browning and gets appropriated into fiction through James and Joyce, is a symptom of the extent to which the modern mind has turned in upon itself. We are dealing not simply with a literary convention as in that development of the epistolary novel. The diary, the voice speaking to one hearer or no hearer, is an extension both out of Milton's concern for fit audience though few and Lucifer's *non serviam*. It becomes so heavily a concern for the few that the poet such as Stephen is finally his own audience. One sees the process underway in *The Counterfeiters*, in *Point Counter Point*, more recently in *Molloy, Herzog, The Clown, The Tin Drum*, even in *Portnoy's Complaint*. One sees a form of it in Eliot's portrait of the artist as an old man, "Prufrock," and in those poems up to *Ash Wednesday*. There is a form of it displayed in *Hugh Selwyn Mauberley*, whose initials as someone has pointed out stand also for His Satanic Majesty.

But it is not, after all, an immediate modern device. Or rather, though it is modern, it is not twentieth century. The

109

first important period of this turning of the self to the self in English letters is the seventeenth century, particularly in John Milton, Wordsworth's spiritual patron.

Milton, some readers have suggested, was a victim of the Establishment. He seems to have felt himself so, and it brought him to a position of private concern analogous to that in which we find Stephen Dedalus at the end of the *Portrait.* In retreat at Horton, he devoted himself to history and to those monuments of the spirit's quest which Joyce and Eliot share a concern for—Aquinas and Augustine, for instance. At the same time Milton felt pressed by the immediate world of the Church Establishment as it had developed under the hand of Laud. At Horton he feels increasingly called upon to justify himself; he would publish, but is reluctant to do so. (We note by this that the "publish or perish" dilemma is not limited to the modern academy, our replacement of the Church as patron of the literary mind.) His sonnet which begins "How soon hath time the subtle thief of youth / Stolen on his wing my three and twentieth year" goes on to lament that his "late spring no bud or blossom showeth." It concludes with an emotionally flat assertion that the writer will try to ignore time and do what he can when he can, "however mean or high." As Milton later looks back on this period of his life, he chooses as the end of that part of it the death of his mother. What we choose to see as the end of his withdrawal from the world, of course, is *Lycidas;* that is the significant sign to us of Milton's breaking free of his "diary" stage. It contains in it an acknowledgment of his finally having been shocked out of his easy pattern by that calling of a higher strain beyond the praise a poet might desire. As Wordsworth is to lament later, there are those false poets who are poets only for the praise, and Eliot will shock us with his argument developed through his poetry and summarized in *Murder in the Cathedral* that the desire for praise is "the greatest treason," leading us "to do the right thing for the wrong reason." *Lycidas* is an action, not such as that in response to a Henry's saying

"Will no one rid me of this churlish priest," but an action in response to a sudden recognition of an almost fatal egocentricity in the poet. For the poet can analyze, weigh the Church and his own possible future, and be as indecisive withal as Hamlet or Prufrock. Horton is Milton's diary stage, in which we recall he spent some time corresponding with close private friends such as Charles Diodati, who may be called his Cranley.

Now in quoting from "Tintern Abbey" as I have done and going forward to similar states of mind in more recent writers, then going back to Milton, I am attempting to show an aspect of English poetry which reveals a pattern analogous to the one we have in both Lewis's account of man's first fall from grace and Wordsworth's account of a particular man's fall into evil where the self is its own and only guide. It is a significant pattern which we see developing. If we look closely at the body of poetry produced by some of the principal poets in this tradition, we see a struggle occurring at a key point in the career of each through which each attempts to break out of a mold of intellectual self-centeredness. Immediately following *Lycidas,* Milton visits the continent, returns to London, and (like Joyce) sets up as tutor (to a fit audience though few, we might note again). But Milton, unlike Joyce, immediately engages himself in the affairs of England, writing *Reason of Church Government.* Milton, after having retired to Horton, breaks out of the confusions of the self into larger attempts. Compare our own great city poet, Eliot, who goes through the same growing awareness, facing the complexities of self in that self-love song, "Prufrock." Eliot breaks out through history, the poems most relevant to the assault upon history being "Gerontion" and *The Waste Land,* his intellectual, spiritual versions of *Paradise Lost.* (These latter works follow Eliot's retirement to Margate and Switzerland at a time of spiritual crisis, which Pound mistakenly supposed to be as simple as "a nervous breakdown" brought on by Eliot's job as a clerk in a London bank.)

Wordsworth goes through a struggle essentially like that

111

of Milton and Eliot, and the evidence of his breaking out of habitual modes of thought is in part contained in "Tintern Abbey." As Milton moves on to *Paradise Lost* and Eliot on to *Four Quartets,* Wordsworth goes on to *The Prelude* and the dream of that larger poem for which it was to serve as prologue. What each has managed to do, to varying degrees of success in subsequent work—Milton's *Paradise Lost, Samson Agonistes,* Wordsworth's sonnets and some of the odes, Eliot's *Ash Wednesday* and *Four Quartets,* was to break out of the self and become engaged in the common motive of the "kind," as Wordsworth put it. In other words, each rejoined the human race in a way he could not before; each does so after a major spiritual crisis has occurred. Meanwhile, of course, there were writers who did not succeed in breaking away from the self, Joyce's own diary *Finnegans Wake* serving as an instance. (Joyce, by sheer force of will that often seems perverse, imposed a form on his uncertainties.) Wordsworth breaks away from self with no success corresponding to Milton's or Eliot's. Our next two essays are to concern themselves with the possible cause of Wordsworth's inability to emerge from his new awareness with sufficient powers to execute the large works he set for himself.

No Warre Woorse

WORDSWORTH ON THE BORDERS
OF ANTIROMANTICISM

Petrarch, *De Remediis Ultriusque Fortunae*

(translated by Thomas Twyne in 1579)

There is no warre woorse then this, no not civile warre: For
that is betweene factions of citizens in the streets of the cities,
but this is fought within the minde; between the parts of
the soule.

Eliot, *Burnt Norton*

Desire itself is a movement
Not in itself desirable.

There are two passages I wish to pose for consideration as we look further into the effect of that turning inward upon the self which is steadily accelerated in English letters from Tudor days to our own. The first is Eliot's distinction between the romantic and the classicist, to which distinction we shall return late in this chapter:

> The romantic is deficient or undeveloped in his ability to distinguish between fact and fancy, whereas the classicist, or adult mind, is thoroughly realist—without illusions, without daydreams, without hope, without bitterness, and with an abundance of resignation.

The second passage is Wordsworth's:

> It must be observed that to make the nonexistence of a common motive itself a motive to action [which is to say in our modern way of putting it: to make "alienation" a motive to action] is a practice which we are never so prone to attribute exclusively to madmen as when we forget ourselves [that is, when we forget that we are in this sense inclined to be madmen ourselves]. Our love of the marvelous is not confined to external things. There is no object on which it settles with more delight than on our own minds. This habit is in the very essence of the habit which we are delineating.

The human inclination to wrong-mindedness by Wordsworth's account (the passage is from the preface to *The Borderers*) involves two stages: first the defiant *non serviam* of Milton's Lucifer or Joyce's Stephen. Then the assertion that the mind is its own place, that state of mind in which, as C. S. Lewis says, we insist on calling our souls our own. Once the mind is so oriented, the orientation becomes the mind's habit. Reality is that which happens to lie in the color range the mind habitually sees: the rest is recolored to make a consistent, though false, whole. The mind "creates" its own world. Both truth and falsehood are, as Wordsworth says in his analysis, pressed into "the same service." The mind "looks at society through an optical glass of a peculiar tint: something of the forms of objects [it] takes from objects, but their colour is exclusively what [such a mind] gives them: it is one, and it is [the mind's] own. Having indulged a habit, dangerous in a man who has fallen, of dallying with moral calculations, he becomes an empiric, and a daring and unfeeling empiric."

Wordsworth, in these passages, is describing his conception of a deliberately malignant mind which nevertheless disguises from itself its own malignity "by assuming the character of a speculator in morals." But a startling fact about Wordsworth's portrait of his villain is that it implies a description of those aspects of the romantic temperament of which Eliot in particular was so sharply critical and against which Wordsworth himself reacted with progressive intensity. There is even the occurrence of particular words and phrases in Wordsworth's essay which one meets with in antiromantic criticism: *feeling* as opposed to *thought,* for instance; *a mind fond of nourishing sentiments; perpetually invoking a phantom; thirst for the extraordinary.* The reader may recall for himself the application of similar phrases—if indeed not identical phrases—to the poetry of Keats, Shelley, Wordsworth, Coleridge. To see how Eliot's criticism of the romantics has affinities to Wordsworth's own criticism, let us turn briefly to Eliot's description of the romantic mind, concerning ourselves with his attempt at dramatizing the romantic mind in his early poetry.

In such a poem as "Sweeney Erect," Eliot presents the history of the dissociation of sensibility, that decline of the classical intelligence toward romanticism. Assuming both the ballad form and the ballad maker's detachment, he records for us a decay of mind in a sweep of literary history. It is a descent of mind (1) from the mind's seeing its own workings in nature in a perspective that does not confuse mind with nature, (2) to the mind's coloring all nature with its private awareness of emotion, (3) to the final decay of both mind and emotion represented in the dead figure of Sweeney. For the final end of the unchecked turning inward upon the Self is to lose awareness of any possible Other. This is also finally to lose awareness of Self; it is the inevitable negation since there is no Other to make the Self a particular existence.

The epigraph of the poem is, as we have learned to expect in Eliot, a key. It is a speech from Beaumont and Fletcher's *The Maid's Tragedy,* the circumstances of which are important. Aspatia, deserted by her lover, looks on a tapestry depicting Ariadne lamenting the departure of Theseus and says:

> And the trees about me.
> Let them be dry and leafless; let the rocks
> Groan with continual surges; and behind us
> Make all a desolation. Look, look, wenches!

We recall that the tapestries out of the Middle Ages are in color but they are not, in Wordsworth's phrase, "one color." The medieval mind is one which looks more kindly upon pagan myth than our own age does pagan or Christian; that is, it sees a light in pagan myth which, though ultimately requiring the full light of Christ's descent into the world, was nevertheless commanding of respect. Dante, in *The Inferno,* makes this point through Virgil's apology for the souls in Limbo. So that a tapestry maker, the artist of the scholastics, could see the larger significance of Theseus' trials than one might imagine an Ariadne to see. Ariadne's emotional state does not lead the tapestry maker to color all her world black. Further, it is a virtue of the medieval mind that it is capable of seeing dimensions of reality that require an incorporation of time in timelessness, a consideration Eliot will argue in *Burnt Norton.* It can see Ariadne's immediate emotional state and see as well that the physical world is unaffected by it, though she herself might well see the world darkly. The tapestry maker can, with his perspective, give to his art those qualities of objectivity which Eliot is to discuss as having atrophied in literature. He has established, that is, the proper objective correlatives whereby the mind of the beholder may see a wholeness that involves the particular sorrows of Ariadne, the larger concerns of

116

Theseus, and both of these against a conception of a timelessness capable of containing them. It is precisely when the western mind begins to lose the tapestry maker's perspective that it begins to demand the "reality" of the three-dimensional art; there is a movement toward naturalism which one might chart from Chaucer's Miller with his wait to the elementary animalism of Theodore Dreiser's lobster and squid. What seems to us unsophisticated in the medieval mind—two-dimensional art such as that of the tapestry maker—was rather a seeing of the world of nature as related to the supernatural. Considering itself of and in two worlds simultaneously, the world of nature and the world of spirit, the medieval mind was intent upon a juxtaposition of those worlds in its art, with the result that the theory of art as a mirror of nature suffered in a higher cause. For it is foolishness, as we lately acknowledge, to imagine either that the medieval eye did not see three dimensions or that it was technically incapable of representing the three dimensional world of nature. If we are not aware of the nature of the medieval mind in respect to those two worlds which its imagination contained, we are hardly in a position to appreciate Eliot's poetry. Eliot is similarly concerned for that complexity of the rational mind caused by its existence in two worlds so radically different that the existences cannot even be spoken of as concurrent. His poetry is the attempt to shock the mind out of itself into the complexity of time and turn it to a new conception of self that embodies the timeless. That is what has happened when the mind finally arrives at the place "where we started" and knows the place "for the first time." But we are not yet ready for the timelessness of *Little Gidding*. For the present, the tapestry maker's world is of interest to us because it gives a clue to the technique of "Sweeney Erect." Eliot is juxtaposing Sweeney's world to that of Aspatia, and both to that world which the tapestry maker knows. He is calling our attention, in the epigraph, to the distinction between the actual rendering of the tapestry depicting Ariadne's sorrow and the coloring of that world

117

by Beaumont and Fletcher's bereaved maid. For the princess of myth has been reduced to a maid—Ariadne has become at this stage of seventeenth-century English letters Aspatia. And she requires dry and leafless trees, groaning rocks, a wild sea scene quite other in its coloring from that many-dimensioned scene of the mind in *Dry Salvages*. The voice of the poem, the medium through which these three worlds are brought into relationship in "Sweeney Erect," is a detached one. The first lines of Eliot's poem take up the romantic cry of Aspatia, and lest we be too susceptible to her emotions, recasts them in a language such as to force our seeing the diction as a sign of "dissociation of sensibility" in that voice.

> Paint me a cavernous waste shore
> Cast in the unstilled Cyclades,
> Paint me the bold anfractuous rocks
> Faced by the snarled and yelping seas.

But the voice of the poem is less coolly detached than it seems, though at first hearing it may seem detached if we compare it to the voice of *L'Allegro* and *Il Penseroso* or "The Eve of St. Agnes." We are given by that voice a means of measuring Aspatia's sorrowful cry which beseeches nature to bewail her. Aspatia's imperative mood is counteracted by the artist's imperative mood; the scene must balance one reality with another, without letting either deny the other's existence: Aspatia's groaning rocks are subdued to a proper relation to the whole by the poet's "anfractuous rocks."

We have already considered Milton's attempted perspective on emotional coloring in *L'Allegro* and *Il Penseroso*. Let us look for a moment at a much later romantic poem. In Keats's "Eve of St. Agnes" we might remark that there is not the same awareness of a necessity of perspective as in Milton. The poet's voice colors all, as the rose window bathes Madeline and all her room in the lover's eyes, and as Milton's melancholy Soul sees similar windows to different effect, where there are "Storied windows richly dight / Casting a dim religious light." The difference in Keats on the one hand and Milton or Eliot on the other is that Keats's whole poem is colored by a darkness deeper than the rose windows of Madeline's chamber. The sense of the action's being *now* isn't allowed to go with the reader, for the opening and closing stanzas are carefully used to set the whole irrevocably in the past: the lovers, like the beadsman and the old belledame, are dead long ago. The point is that Eliot, unlike Keats, attempts to establish a medium through which the poem can be seen "without illusions, without daydreams, without hope, without bitterness, and with an abundance of resignation." It is a point above time. The past tense of the poem does not signify a position of the medium (the voice through which the poem has its being) above time but one existing only at the latest moment from which there is a looking back. Keats as maker of poems cannot escape into that level of awareness Eliot means when he says in *Burnt Norton,* "To be conscious is not to be in time." Consequently, there is a feeling in Keats's poetry, even in "The Eve of St. Agnes," not of an abundance of resignation but of an abundance of despair. It is so since Keats has not, as that prose Keats—Ernest Hemingway— cannot, come to terms with history. The poet in such a position cannot distinguish between himself as the maker of the poem and the thing that the poem is, a most necessary distinction whenever the materials of the poem have their origin in the emotions of the poet himself. And the effect upon his poetry is that kind of malignancy which Eliot detected in romanticism and argued against: the coloring of the work by the poet's own emotions. That is, the tapestry is finally of one color, even if pastel. In the end the privacy of the poet's emotions destroys the perspective so that there is no trustworthy access to the poem by a mind other than the poet's. This is the argument that I take Eliot to have dramatized in his epigraph and the first two stanzas of "Sweeney Erect." The epigraph, followed by a carefully controlled tone in the opening lines of the poem proper, is a common device in the early Eliot, as when he plays Virgil to his reader in "Prufrock." It is a device developed as a reaction to that romantic involvement of the poem which prevents an aesthetic detachment. The coloring of poems by the optic glass of the romantic poet's emotions is (in the eyes of such a classicist as Eliot intends to be) an alarming tint in that it is a symptom of a malignancy in the self so far advanced that it is no longer capable of clear-sighted, conscious artistry. He indicates as an instance of that malignancy Emerson, a thinker disinclined to see that repulsive worldly reality in nature which cannot be denied:

> (The lengthened shadow of a man
> Is history, said Emerson
> Who had not seen the silhouette
> Of Sweeney straddled in the sun.)

For Emerson, as Randall Stewart has argued in *American Literature and Christian Doctrine,* would not see the Sweeney side of human existence, that "Gesture of orang-outang" that "Rises from the sheets in steam." The end of the dissociation of sensibility that we have come to, in Eliot's view, is the separation of Prufrock and Sweeney in the individual, as the final stanza of "Mr. Eliot's Sunday Morning" suggests: the cause of that separation in poetry is the decline of the classical mind into the romantic mind.

Both Wordsworth and Eliot, it would appear, are engaged upon an analysis of the romantic mind, though Eliot is more clearly aware of what he is about, having the advantage of an additional hundred years for hindsight. The striking thing about Wordsworth's analysis of his villain (whose final existence one might characterize as that of an intellectual Sweeney) is that it matches a concurrent development in his own mind, which he subsequently recognized and revolted against. A mind, while it may be in the habit of "coloring the world as a body which is in some sort of war with him," may make a parallel mistake and consider the world as a body at perfect peace with him. It is just this state of mind which we see Wordsworth recalling and rejecting in "Tintern Abbey." We should note that Wordsworth is aware of that earlier state (and it is a state developed beyond boyhood and its animal joys) as one in which he colored nature according to his established habit of mind. Now it is a habit which he rejects not only because he has grown beyond it but because, having grown beyond it, he sees it as false, despite the pleasures it had afforded him in that dreary existence in "the city of men." That old mode of existence required only the charm which the seeing eye gave to it, the happy pleasure of colors and forms. Though he does not reject nature as an object of poetry's address in "Tintern Abbey," he is beginning to seek a more faithful Beatrice in its stead. The mind must now deal more firmly with the world; Nature will be an anchor of his purest thought, but it is an anchor to prevent thought's being seduced by fancy. Nature never is again to Wordsworth the end that it had seemed to be.

What Wordsworth describes in "Tintern Abbey" as his earlier state is just such as we should have if Aspatia, happy in her lover and not deserted by him, should look upon the natural scene with Milton's "idle brain" and "deluding joys." As in the one instance all nature was colored by self-sorrow, now all nature would be colored by self-joy. Wordsworth has come back to that "still, sad music of humanity" which is not to his ears alone. That is, he has come back to the "common motive" that his figure of Iago in *The Borderers* had rejected, and in doing so he turns from nature to the "kind," which requires not a rejection of nature, but a firmer sight of man's relation to it. Incidentally, those who look with raised eyebrow at the relationship of Wordsworth and his sister, wondering, are misled by a coloring of their own "optic glass of peculiar tint" which has been prescribed for our age by our optometrist, Dr. Freud, and encouraged by the antics of Byron and, to a lesser degree, Shelley. A clearer reflection upon Wordsworth and Dorothy is to be found, I believe, in the fiction of James—in his repeated portrait of the innocent abroad, the young American girl who was his Beatrice. In James's discussion of the relation of realism and romance, we see a concern very like Wordsworth's in "Tintern Abbey." We remember that James insists that the artist's balloon of fiction, his imagination, needed a firm anchor in reality to prevent its escape into romance, into what Wordsworth would call fancy. Wordsworth, in making nature the "anchor of his purest thought," seems to me intent on the identical problem, and Dorothy almost becomes a sign for the embodiment of his concern. It is as if Dorothy's literal presence prevented his realization of this possibility, where Beatrice's absence brought the possibility sharply to Dante's attention.

Though the state of mind Wordsworth recalls in "Tintern Abbey" may not be deliberately malignant and is far from spectacular in the way that Iago's or Macbeth's is spectacular, still its necessities are precisely those of the deliberately malignant mind Wordsworth analyzed for us. For the mind "fond of nourishing sentiments" of innocent adulation (rather than "of contempt") will likewise be prone to the admission of those feelings which are considered under any common bond of relation (as opposed to "uncommon bond of relation"); and "the feelings will mutually strengthen each other." In other words, that mind which is, in Eliot's view of it, romantically inclined, while it may not through deliberate malignancy paint an evil world in which good is totally absent, is very likely through well-intentioned sentiments ("feelings") to paint a good world in which evil is colored good. But the peasant one takes to be a depressed angel may in fact be a rustic Sweeney. Neither can such a mind as this "exist without occupation"; for it too requires constant provocations, whose pleasures are "prospective," an element still present in "Tintern Abbey" as Wordsworth looks to future joys out of the present experience—future recollections of this present awareness. Such joys require the perpetual "invoking of a phantom," the phantom of past experience. (We note here a concern for history similar to that which we have already remarked in both Eliot and

Milton.) He, unlike the malignant romantic, invokes the phantom not to "drive away the memory of the past" but to recall the memory.

What I have been describing through this appropriation of Wordsworth's analysis of the malignant mind and Eliot's criticism of the romantic mind is that state of mind which one finds not only in the early Wordsworth, but subsequently in many writers who are unable to come to terms with history except through the process of divorcing the self from time and making self-history their concern. Such a mind is reflected in those works which attempt to arrest a moment of time and divorce it from time's flow without relating that moment to any dimension other than the temporal. Herein lies the cause of the development of a new style in fiction, beginning with James and Conrad (and Conrad predicts this new style in apology for what he considered his awkward uses of the old). Wordsworth's Iago "commits new crimes to drive away the memory of the past." Conrad's Lord Jim attempts to commit heroism to drive the memory of a failure away. Hemingway's heroes commit new acts to forget the fact that the last act was fleeting. Hemingway is himself "perpetually invoking a phantom," trying to recreate a moment that he would call "good," trying to recreate "the way it really was." In the matter of style, we see Conrad's convoluted indirection used to get at the moment that never was. Hemingway will "chequer and degrade enterprises" which, if not great in their "atrocity," are great in their engagement of courage "by grotesque littleness of manner and fantastic obliquities," of which the style of *The Sun Also Rises* and *A Moveable Feast* are sufficient examples. Wordsworth anticipates his own critics, including Coleridge, with his phrases "a forced greatness of manner" in the attempt "to exalt actions little in themselves," phrases one may apply with justness to "The Old Cumberland Beggar," "Goody Blake and Harry Gill," and even to such better poems as "Michael" and "The Leech-Gatherer."

If Wordsworth's malignant mind, his Iago, finally im-

presses one as being "like a worn out voluptuary" who finds
"temptation in strangeness" and is unable "to suppress a
low hankering after the double entendre in vice," so does
the innocent spirit of the early Wordsworth impress one
as being a "voluptuary" of the good, another way of describing sentimentality. The interest of the sentimentalist requires
a personification of strangeness through which one escapes
the necessity of giving the full attention of the mind to
the thing personified or to the motives and the feelings
that are involved in illusion. I am not being unduly harsh
to Wordsworth: I am only showing a course of his mind
which he rejected with very harsh criticism of himself. For
Wordsworth no less than Eliot became aware that a dissociation of sensibilities occurred in English letters between
Shakespeare's day and his own. His concern with that separation is on a level more radical than simply a concern for
poetics, and in this he is also close to Eliot. We recall how
severely he regrets that self-illusion which led him to be
"to myself a guide" in whom "Too blindly I have reposed
my trust." But that regret was well under way before the
death of his brother led him to "Elegiac Stanzas" or his
"Ode to Duty."

In *The Borderers* essay he has pointed to the failures
that result when one "disguises from himself his own malignity by assuming the character of a speculator in morals."
Malignancy causes a failure in the eye of the beholder as
Wordsworth argues in his essay, and certainly Wordsworth
considers his eyes affected. Certainly, too, he is "a speculator
in Morals," much of his argument having to do with the
moral value of that nature in which he early put his trust.
He castigates the Moralist in "A Poet's Epitaph" (1797)
in much the same way he rebukes himself later in "Ode
to Duty":

> Himself his world, and his own God
> One to whose smooth-rubbed soul can cling
> Nor form, nor feeling, great or small;
> A reasoning, self-sufficient thing,
> An intellectual All-in-all!

One notes a sting in such lines which Wordsworth is not so often thought of as carrying, and it is a sardonic sting. For the tone turns somewhat back upon the self; increasingly Wordsworth will be examining his own reaction to the world in a highly critical way, suspecting that his own joy or sadness colors nature. In 1803, looking back, he declares a "timely utterance" to have relieved the sadness with which he had come to receive nature; now he declares "No more shall grief of mine the season wrong." That "timely utterance" I do not take to be "My Heart Leaps Up," lines from which are given as prologue to the "Intimations Ode," for *timely* has as one of its meanings *early*. ("My Heart Leaps Up" does not precede the composition of the first four stanzas of the ode by much more than a year.) Besides which, the prayer, the desire, of the final lines do not sound convincing enough as the catharsis of that grief which the ode declares the utterance to have been.

> The child is father of the man;
> And I could wish my days to be
> Bound each to each by natural piety.

The ode, we notice, makes deliberate use of pastoral terms, especially in the first four stanzas, in a manner not unlike Milton's uses in *Lycidas:* the happy shepherd boy, tabors, trumpets. The address to the things of nature is with a deliberate enthusiasm. The poem is more consciously artificial by a considerable degree than is "Tintern Abbey." The thought which is the cause of the first four stanzas of the ode is of mortality. In a note to the "Intimations Ode" Wordsworth recalls that, as a child, he could not admit the "notion of death" into his thinking, feeling destined to ascend to heaven like Enoch and Elijah. "With a feeling congenial to this, I was often unable to think of external things as having external existence, and I communed with all that I saw as something not apart from, but inherent in, my own immaterial nature." The opposite tendency is for the senses to make all experience exterior. In other words, there are two ways in which the mind may "wrong the season": the first is by denying any externality to the world; the second is by denying the external a mode of existence interior to the mind. "Tintern Abbey" addresses itself to the first wrong; stanzas 5–11 of the "Intimations Ode" largely to the second.

If "Tintern Abbey" is that timely utterance referred to in the ode, it clearly did not give "the thought relief," for after Wordsworth had written the first four stanzas of the ode, he laid it aside for "two years at least," he says, after which he returned to the poem to rationalize the experience. The final stanzas attempt to bring the thought of youth and of age, of life and death, together in some relationship more satisfactory to the intellect than "Tintern Abbey" or the first stanzas of the ode had done. For, as he indicates in the third stanza, the thoughts are together but not comprehensible: "The winds come to me from the fields of sleep, / And all the earth is gay." Though Wordsworth tends in such perplexed emotional states to look upon a tree or a prospect of nature, rather than an urn (or even a nightingale), he is really quite close to Keats in the section of the ode he laid aside. Those four stanzas compare to the movement in Keats's great odes, ending in a similar despondent questioning of illusion. These are the final lines of the fourth stanza, whose thought is enough to take us back to "Tintern Abbey" and to the question of self-illusion:

> —But there's a tree, of many, one,
> A single field which I have looked upon,
> Both of them speak of something that is gone:
> > The pansy at my feet
> > Doth the same tale repeat:
> Whither is fled the visionary gleam?
> Where is it now, the glory and the dream?

When Wordsworth realizes that blindness in himself, the effect is disastrous to his desire to write that great poem of the imagination, which in its conception seemed to give a prospect as grand as that of the *Divine Comedy*. With

Lyrical Ballads behind him, together with its important preface, he did turn to *The Prelude,* but he is scarcely able to return to *The Excursion,* started much earlier, and he is unable to bring form or completion to those three large segments to which *The Prelude* was to have been prologue, as Dante's *New Life* is prologue to the *Divine Comedy.* We now turn briefly toward some causes of this failure, examining him in the light of that great poet's poet whose shadow and whose light have most touched poets of our own day—Eliot, Pound, and a host of lesser men.

III

The Poet as Odysseus

DANTE'S LONG SHADOW

Eliot, "Dante"

> The attitude of Dante to the fundamental experience of the *Vita Nuova* can only be understood by accustoming ourselves to find meaning in *final causes* rather than in origins.

Eliot, *Burnt Norton*

> To be conscious is not to be in Time.

W. H. Auden, *The Dyer's Hand*

> Above all, do not write your autobiography, for your childhood is literally the whole of your capital.

Dante, so far as I can discover, is the first important imaginative writer in the western tradition who attempted to turn his personal life into a poetry of epic proportions. Virgil turned the more innocent wonder of Homer toward didactic ends. That is to say, he set out deliberately to dramatize his version of the *New Republic,* but Dante set out to dramatize *The New Life,* not of Florence, but of Dante Alighieri, a Florentine. Where Virgil was, at least in part, intent on turning all knowledge to the service of the political empire, Dante set out to turn all knowledge to the service of the spiritual state of the individual soul. It was a shift of science—knowledge—in the service of an art whose consequences we are concerned with in these essays, for it was a shift of the materials of art from the public toward the private. The shift itself carries in it a major cause of that difficulty with which Wordsworth was to concern himself so resolutely, the separation of the artist from his audience. Dante's approach to art is significantly different from Virgil's in this respect then: whereas both Virgil and Dante have the universal as art's end (Virgil the ideal state and Dante the ideal state of the soul), with Virgil the materials with which he fleshes that universal—the concrete materials—are not private in the way in which Dante's are. Furthermore, the legends and the history Virgil uses are not only general, they are capable of expression in terms of action in the world—actual journeys and battles. The ends toward which he focuses the significance of such details are themselves easily seen in terms of a social state in this world. On the other hand, though Dante makes use of the same kind of concrete elements of history and legend, the end toward which he focuses them is not one so easily accessible to the citizen's mind. For what he is attempting is to dramatize an ideal state of an individual being who cannot be content with the order of the earthly state as a final end. Order in the state may be used as a sign of that ordered being which is the individual soul. But Virgil's end is only partially Dante's. In other words, the allegory Dante is concerned with is one whose levels are finally suitable only to those who have ears to hear. That Homer's poems were orally performed and Virgil's read to a more limited audience by Virgil himself does not mean that Virgil was less accessible to the Roman as opposed to the ancient Greek citizen. The chauvinistic element of *The Aeneid* reached down toward social and political roots, even if the man in the street could not appreciate the flights of Virgil's similes. Dante's relationship to his audience in regard to his materials was somewhat different, as Eliot pointed out in an early essay. He had the advantage of that systematic development in the Church which had worked scholastic thought downward to the lower reaches of Dante's society. Dante and his audience did have the materials in common out of which he fashioned his art.

But Dante's art itself was peculiarly new in its conception. In attempting to express a desirable state of the soul's being through that art, Dante committed himself to a static image; static, that is, when we attempt to see it with the eyes as limited by this world. He attempted not simply to show the soul moving on toward an ideal state—the *Divine Comedy* is not a journey such as that conceived in *The Odyssey*— but to make the art object itself the very image of the soul at rest, which by definition in Dante's understanding was a *state* of being including in it all the stages of that becoming. It was an attempt to include the aspects of time, as they relate to the soul, *within* the timelessness of the soul. It was an attempt, one might say, to make of the *Divine Comedy* an image in its final simplicity analogous to that Divine Simplicity encountered in the final cantos of that poem. The poised balance of the parts within the whole of the great poem, which is of wondrous interest in explication, is more than structural. The poem itself is, one might say, an earthly manifestation of being, analogous to an ideal, complete state of being of the soul. The soul in turn is an existence analogous to, is an image of, that perfect existence which is ascribed to God, the source toward which the soul turns as rose to light.

Dante's conception of the poet's relation to his art, then,

is in terms of a conception of God's relation to the created soul. As we know, this analogy is one which has been most constantly called upon by the artist himself. It is an analogy, as we have already noted, which is in the unfolding of Stephen Dedalus' mind. But the deduction of the analogy from Dante's poetry requires our more careful consideration. To Dante, the object which is the poem, independent though it be of the individual mind, is nevertheless closely related to that mind, not only to the mind of its creator—the poet—but as well to the mind of its beholder—the reader. Its relation is that again of God to the soul. Though the beholder of that art be not its creator, when that art is supremely executed, hopefully he responds with a joyful recognition.

The problem of execution was an intense one for Dante. His concern with that execution was precisely the concern that Eliot was to make popular later in the phrase "objective correlative." The problem necessarily exists for each poet in any time, but it was complicated for Dante by the changed ends toward which he had shifted from Virgil. For in presenting the poem as an image of a state of being, he was automatically committed, in the interest of concrete materials, to the state of being of a *particular* being, that of the poet himself. He was put in a position which required him, in his thinking, to subdue himself to a higher concern: his art as a full tribute to his Creator. There is in Dante a humility which not only requires him to acknowledge his powers without false modesty (as when he ranks himself a sixth among those great intelligences he encounters in Limbo) but which also does not allow him to assume himself indeed a god, that temptation to which the artist, the "maker," of all men seems most susceptible.

The artist is so susceptible because he stands in a peculiar relation to his work which tempts him to think that work the final end, rather than to consider the perfection of himself through his gifts as artist as the final end. Very rarely does one find such an artist as Dante who can recognize at once not only that his art is not the final end of his being, but that the recognition does not thereby relieve him of the demands of perfection in the work of art as art. Dante could see, because of his humility, that he stood in a relationship to his art and his audience analogous to the position of God in relation to the created world and the individual soul. (This I think is part of the implication of Dante's attention to God's art as exhibited on Purgatory.) But the direct, full revelation of his own being, without the intermediary of his created world, would deny to the beholder that freedom of responsibility for his own whole state of being, a whole state which includes the eye's responsibility relative to aesthetics no less than the mind's to theology. To establish the proper objective correlative in the work of art was therefore a necessity in the interest of a freedom that would allow a free association of souls through the work of art itself. It required a transformation of the particularly personal to the universally personal. It required a figuring forth of *emotional becoming* from an object which was *unemotionally* a *being*. To accomplish such a work required as its immitigable circumstance a full awareness in its creator. Whereas *The Aeneid* or the *Eclogues* can have imposed upon them a later awareness, which adds the dimension of an allegory Virgil never intended (as when Aeneas is seen as a figure of Christ), Dante largely precluded such external imposition upon his poem. The work of art, he intended, must be larger than anecdote or exemplum in order to be protected from the imposition of false systems of thought upon it. Therefore he turned himself to the problem of full awareness.

I have suggested that the *Divine Comedy* is an image which in its complete simplicity is that of the soul at rest; the recognition of this completeness by the mind of the beholder releases that mind when it becomes equal to that state of rest. (One might describe this action of release as the spiritual catharsis appropriate to comedy as Dante defines comedy.) The figure we may borrow to make this argument clearer is Statius on Purgatory. Statius' soul is released to full awareness when its will corresponds to the

135

will of God, through the application of will to that high figuring of God's art which Dante describes as Purgatory Mountain. Such a conception of the reader's relation to the *Comedy* required, however, a preliminary releasing of the artist's mind through a perfection of awareness. The artist's awareness required the inclusion of the stages of a growing awareness within the full awareness. When Dante had reached this state of awareness, he set it down, working out the relations of full awareness to its intermediary states. That work is, of course, *The New Life.* If the *Divine Comedy* required of him the establishing of allegorical levels of meaning in an ascending order, each succeeding step including all else below it, *The New Life* as a prelude required an inclusive ordering whereby the full power of the poet's mind was revealed to itself.

It is inevitable that the history of Dante's relationship to Beatrice should force itself upon our attention; to the extent that it does, it obscures the real nature of *The New Life,* for Dante's central concern is with the figure of Beatrice as it is metamorphosed in the creative imagination. His attention is repeatedly to the relationship of the poet's awareness to the man's emotional experience. For the sake of clarity and convenience, I am here going to name the poet's full awareness as assumed in the poem "Dante the Poet." But the Poet Dante has as his materials his own history, preceding the present awareness from which he writes the final version of *The New Life;* he looks at himself as a particular man in time and place, a man developing toward the present awareness within which he writes. That figure of himself which the poet sees let us call "Dante the Pilgrim." It seems to me that *The New Life* is a deliberate dramatization of what Wordsworth was to call "emotion recollected in tranquility." A pattern is repeated by Dante the Poet in the sections of his work, each repetition dramatizing the enlarging awareness in the Pilgrim. In individual sections of the work, we are presented the circumstances that occasion the comment or the poem which is produced; these are the circumstances as remembered by the full awareness (Dante the Poet) of the limited awareness (the Pilgrim) in the particular stage of his journey presented. Sometimes the occasion is an actual encounter with Beatrice, sometimes a discussion of her with a friend, sometimes an encounter with mutual friends. Sometimes it is a recollection of an emotional state induced by contemplation; on one occasion it is an emotional state caused in part by physical illness; sometimes there is a dream in the midst of a sound sleep. Dante the Poet gives us an account of those circumstances, and usually recalls a deliberately conscious intention on the *Pilgrim's* part to write a poem: "I intended to write a ballad . . . / I resolved to take for my subject matter only the praise of this gentlest of women." After such information, often indicating a deliberate selection of materials from the experience for the sake of the poem, we are given the poem itself. Usually we are given a careful analysis of the structure of the poem in relation to the circumstances and to the conscious artistic intentions; Dante the Poet manages to impart a certain urgency to such literary concerns by his presenting the analysis after presenting the poem early in *The New Life,* then shifting the analysis to precede the poem later, finally abandoning analysis altogether at the end.

We notice in this procedure a larger pattern which keeps *The New Life* from being simply an anthology with commentary. The poetry becomes more spontaneous, though generally more complex as well, reaching a high point near the end, after which (following the fourth canzone) the poems become again a relatively simple expression of that vision of Beatrice which is to be fully expressed in the *Comedy.* Early in *The New Life,* we have occasions when the circumstances of the Pilgrim, relative to Beatrice, give rise to a poem immediately. Dante says in such instances that "the desire came upon me to write a poem." But there is a progression in which the mind of the Pilgrim increasingly asserts a control. Desire is not enough. When we come to the first considerable poem of *The New Life,* "The First Canzone," we have these circumstances given: while out

137

walking on a road beside a clear flowing stream, the desire to speak seized Dante.

> I began to consider what style I should adopt. I thought it would not be fitting to address her directly but to speak of her to ladies in the second person.... Then my tongue spoke as though moved by itself and said:
> Ladies whose understanding is of love.... I laid these words before my mind with the greatest joy, intending to use them as my beginning. Then I returned to the city and after pondering for some days began a canzone....

The inspiration, we notice, is submitted to the mind. The desire to write and the cause of the desire are interrogated. The question of technical concern—the point of view—is considered further. The whole problem is pondered "for some days" before the poem is written under the mind's control. Such is the nature of Dante's emotion recollected under the mind's firm determination to make of that emotion a work of art. The spontaneous overflow of powerful feeling which is the first cause of the poem is not allowed to be supreme. Emotion is the matter to which meter and rhyme and verse and stanza are the form. The result is a *posed* state of being within which the becoming composes itself. There is a double awareness of which the awareness of Dante the Pilgrim is the subject of Dante the Poet.

We notice the unity of *The New Life* then as one which incorporates through the medium of the creating mind—the poet's—the growth of that mind toward becoming such a medium. The poet Dante is to the man Dante (whose involvement as man is with Beatrice) as Virgil is to the character Dante in the *Divine Comedy*. And we might add that, just as both Virgil and Dante are enclosed by the awareness which creates the *Divine Comedy,* there is an enclosing awareness in *The New Life*. It is an awareness which Joyce's Stephen would call the disengaged artist. That is, we must ultimately name an awareness which *includes* the Pilgrim and the Poet. For the voice which speaks *The New Life* is one character, one agent, and the creature about whom he speaks, the Pilgrim, is another. The dramatic progression of the poem is toward the coincidence of full awareness of the Pilgrim with that of the assumed voice in the poem, the Poet.

Though both Joyce and Eliot (and Pound for that matter) have persuaded us of the necessity of the artist's disengaging himself from the work he makes, I should prefer to reject that word *disengage* because of its implications. For it is at precisely this point that Stephen Dedalus' analogy between the artist and God to their respective works breaks down. The full being, who is also an artist, must relate to his work in a way analogous to that in which God relates to his work. That is, one can not conceive of the maker as aloof, indifferent, paring his nails in grand indifference to his creation. Stephen's is a figure of the artist which in the light of our last essay must be called not God but Satan. And Dante's art, if misunderstood and imitated as misunderstood, will inevitably contribute to the separation not only of the artist from his audience, but of the artist himself from his work, so that, like that exhausted voluptuary whom Wordsworth describes to us in his "Preface" to *The Borderers,* the artist is pressed to sensations of form, to devices and tricks which become the end of his art rather than instruments of it.

We may note that even so powerful a mind as Joyce's comes finally to depend upon tricks and devices which become the end of his art. On these grounds, one raises objections to *Finnigans Wake,* as indeed Eliot among others did. A. Walton Litz, in calling attention to the centripetal control of Joyce's *Portrait* as it gives way to the centrifugal enlargement in *Ulysses* and *Finnegans Wake,* underscores Joyce's increasing interest "in formal—almost mechanical—designs." It is a concern for form which threatens to lose all anchor in substance, in fear of which Joyce becomes concerned with raw, natural detail of literal persons and places. Litz says at one point in his *Method and Design in Ulysses:*

> His obsessive concern with realistic detail reveals his desperate need for principles of order and authority. Deprived of social and religious order by his self-imposed exile, and acutely aware of the disintegrating forces in modern European society, Joyce turned to the concrete details of place and character as one stable base for his writing.... The details of Dublin life in 1904 were vastly important to Joyce during the making of *Ulysses....* In so far as they obscure the central concerns of the novel they represent the price Joyce had to pay for his personal decisions.

Joyce, too, was disturbed by recollections of the world as once inhabited, as was Wordsworth standing on the banks of the Wye. And it is with ironic pertinence that in his last struggles with his *Work in Progress* that he was more and more questioning whether he possessed imagination, or only that drapery of poetic genius, as Coleridge called it, fancy. Reading Coleridge's famous distinction, called forth by Wordsworth's definitions, Joyce could not but wonder at the achievement of that elaborate final work which is such a complicated display of "a mode of Memory emancipated from the order of time and space."

The attempted emancipation in Wordsworth's "spots of time" or in Eliot's pursuit of a still point is not through such an elaborate attempt as Joyce's to command all details of memory and details of place and character so as to disengage them from spatial and sequential limitations by considering the power of the poet absolute. Both Eliot and Wordsworth turn from that absolute egoism of the poet as creator that finally possessed Joyce. The centrifugal enlargement of a world dependent upon Joyce's mind finally depends too heavily upon the preliminary action of that same mind in dissolving all the world exterior to it into raw materials bearing no mark of mind, over which that mind assumes absolute authority through a language created for the occasion. But it is not a language created *ex nihilo,* any more than the external world which supplies particulars of place and character is created by that mind which borrows from it. Joyce both knows and does not know this. That is why such a shade of pathos falls across Joyce in his final phase. It inheres in those biographical evidences we come across in recollections by friends, in his letters, in his manuscripts. He writes home to an aunt asking her to determine whether "it is possible for an ordinary person [Bloom] to climb over the area railings of no 7 Eccles street, either from the path or the steps, lower himself down from the lowest part of the railings till his feet are within 2 feet or 3 of the ground and drop unhurt." In that letter he also asks Aunt Josephine, "Do you remember the cold February of 1893. . . . I want to know whether the canal was frozen and if there was any skating." Four days later he writes Robert McAlmon that he is about to send extracts from the Ithaca section to which Aunt Josephine's Zolaesque details are material, an episode he likes because it is "of a tranquilising spectrality."

We can but notice that in Joyce the mind of the creator has deliberately cut itself off from life. It may enjoy for a moment a "tranquilising spectrality," but it will very quickly reach out, in a terror, to grasp the most simple experience of the natural world, much as Wordsworth himself recalls doing in his younger days when in that terror occasioned by the mind's escaping the world of the body and nature he "grasped at a wall or tree to recall myself from this abyss of idealism to the reality." In such terror there is a loss of that power of harmony and joy whereby one sees into the life of things, leading repeatedly to the edge of that abyss from which spectrality will not long save one. Joyce's researches into whether the canal was frozen and whether there was skating would seem mechanically routine were it not for the source of his appeal, his Aunt Josephine. There is in such letters a quality of affection which manners alone will not account for, which says something to us of that pathos and loneliness in Joyce which the exiled Dante largely escaped.

Wordsworth's False Beatrice

FROM CIRCUMSPECTION, INFINITE DELAY

✿Wordsworth, *The Prelude*

> I felt the sentiment of Being spread
> Over all that moves and all that seemeth still;
> O'er all that, lost beyond the reach of thought
> And human knowledge, to the human eye
> Invisible, yet liveth to the heart. . . .
>
> If this be error and another faith
> Find easier access to the pious mind.

✿Wallace Stevens, "The Idea of Order at Key West"

> The ever-hooded, tragic-gestured sea
> Was merely a place by which she walked to sing.

✿Dylan Thomas, Letter to Bert Trick

> My own eye, I know, squints inwards. When, and if, I look at the exterior world I see nothing or me; I should like very much to say that I see *everything* through the inner eye, but all I see is darkness, naked and not very nice.

With this preliminary excursion into Dante and Joyce concerning the relations of the poet to his work, we return to Wordsworth, remembering along the way that we are considering Dante as the first great modern, as the first poet of consequence who deliberately attempted to turn personal, emotional, intellectual, and spiritual experiences to the service of poetry on a scale larger than the lyric. We can see something of Dante's transformation of the lyric source as follows: the Beloved of the Courtly Love tradition is pursued by the lover, whose intent is to turn the Beloved from her true master. Among those rules of Courtly Love prescribed by Capellanus, and specifically insisted upon, is that the Beloved's marriage to someone else is no excuse for not loving. In fact it becomes a condition of the definition of the Beloved. The lover's endeavor is to turn her affections from their proper object to the lover himself. But as Dante recognizes, such a separation constitutes adultery, whether or not any physical act occurs. Dante's concern is for the intellectual aspect of adultery since that aspect relates more closely to the soul and its turning to darkness. Neither in the affairs of men nor of art itself, so long as Christianity is professed, could such a subtle breach be tolerated. *The New Life* of course is replete with the old concepts of Courtly Love—a lover is always timid; his heart trembles at the sudden sight of his beloved; love seldom lasts after it is divulged; no one can love unless so compelled by Love itself. One can go down the rules set forth by Capellanus and see that Dante has that conception of Courtly Love in mind as he sets in dramatic motion the character we called Dante the Pilgrim as he is affected by that presence called Beatrice. What Dante does, however, is show a transubstantiation of that tradition so that love, springing out of the heart, becomes a separate personification (requiring an essay in the midst of *The New Life,* incidentally, in which Dante justifies such fanciful devices as personification) to the merging of that personification with Beatrice herself, to the eventual elevation of the concept in the person of Beatrice to the Courts of Heavenly Love following her earthly death. One of Capellanus' rules requires of the lover that he mourn the beloved at her death for "two years." But in section 29 of *The New Life*, Dante explains why he does not dwell upon the death of Beatrice, in a passage whose obscurity has caused debate reaching no conclusion. Dante says he does not dwell on her death because "it is not within the context of this book." He would be departing rather significantly from his declared intention, that is from the statement of theme in section one—the setting down of the book of memory. For what he is about is both the establishing of the nature of the poetic mind and the relating of that poetic mind to the Supreme Love. Beatrice is the figure through whom the concept of love is transubstantiated, and for Dante to dwell upon her worldly death so late in *The New Life* as section 29 would indeed be to turn aside from the major theme of his book. He would earn thereby precisely the kind of rebuke that Beatrice gives Dante the Pilgrim in that section of *The Purgatorio* where he exhibits a reluctance to give up Virgil (the light of the intellect), as he was reluctant earlier to give up the earthly Beatrice. She reminds him there, on the outskirts of the earthly Eden, that he had abandoned her when she changed states; that is, when she passed from the earthly Courts of Love to the Courts of Heavenly Love. For Dante to have dwelt upon her death in the world and upon his worldly sorrow in *The New Life*, the history of his conversion, would have constituted just such a turning. But the growth of the Pilgrim's mind by section 29 has already transcended such earthly concerns.

What the Beloved becomes for Dante at the close of *The New Life*, Nature becomes for Wordsworth in his *Prelude*, his setting down of his own book of memory, ostensibly for his philosophical friend, Coleridge. And even as Dante was interested in the characteristics of the poet's mind as that mind relates itself to all external to it, so was Wordsworth interested. Most particularly, Wordsworth was intent upon discovering the nature of mind, the principles of its reception of and adjustment to whatever in the physical or spiritual world came through the senses to be laid before the mind as possible materials of art. For art seemed not alone in being a thing projected by the mind. In some mysterious way, the mind participates in the making of that which it perceives. The being of things in the awareness is caused in part, he feels, by the awareness itself. Wordsworth records that impression in those serene lines of "Tintern Abbey" which conclude with the eye "made quiet by the power / Of harmony, and deep power of joy," whereby "we see into the life of things."

There is a more ecstatic figuring of that state in *The Prelude,* rising to an emotional pitch partly out of the particular remembrance of a moment when, though he made no open vows of dedication to poetry, vows were mysteriously made for him. There at the springtime of youth and of nature, the immediate world glows with benevolence.

> Magnificent
> The morning rose, in memorable pomp,
> Glorious as e'er I had beheld—in front
> The sea lay laughing at a distance; near,
> The solid mountains shone, bright as the clouds,
> Grain-tinctured, drenched in empyrean light.

There is in this recollection an affirmation of having been spoken to, from which the possibilities of a pathetic reading of the morning are excluded. Still the "memorable pomp" of the morning, the sea laughing, hint of an emotional excess beyond the justifications of thought. Wordsworth immediately supplies that thought. After concluding that he walked through the morning amphitheater of sea, mountains, and clouds "in thankful blessedness, which yet survives," he adds:

> Strange rendez-vous my mind was at that time,
> A parti-coloured show of grave and gay,
> Of inconsiderate habits and sedate,
> Consorting in one mansion unreproved.

It is a note of hesitation struck again and again, as when he follows the serene passage of "Tintern Abbey" with "If this / Be but a vain belief," or asserts in *The Prelude* a willingness to abandon his insight "If this be error, and another faith / Find easier access to the pious mind." The "plastic power" of mind, recollected from an earlier stage in the poet's growth of mind, is recognized as possibly an immature power, residing in an immature person who is sufficiently at distance from both the kind and nature so as to suggest an egotism which is to itself sublime. The principal protagonist of creation is the poet.

A series of epiphanies, and one worth dwelling upon, follows almost immediately that experience of dedication recorded in *The Prelude*. He sees a soldier in a "desolation, a simplicity, / To which the trappings of a gaudy world / Make a strange background." Here too is a figure at rest in nature, leaning against a stone. But while it is a form which "Kept the same awful steadiness" as the background, so that the very shadow at its feet is perfectly still, the effect is disturbing. There is sharp contrast between the innocent exhilaration of the poet in nature and the apparent misery of the figure he observes in that same natural world, a figure constant but with an "awful steadiness." It is the contrast Wordsworth will develop often, as with the old leech gatherer in "Resolution and Independence" and other spectral encounters in nature. These are arresting encounters in the bright morning of hope and expectation, analogous for our purposes to that encounter of Dante the Pilgrim in canto 1 of *The Inferno*. There, fleeing the dark wood of man's and nature's world toward the morning sun, the Pilgrim is suddenly confronted by those ambiguous creatures, the Leopard, the Lion, and the She-Wolf, hardly so propitious as Wordsworth's sea, mountains, and clouds. A difference is that Dante's encounters with these strange creatures of the natural world are ambiguous only to Dante the Pilgrim and do not continue ambiguous to him. But in Wordsworth, the ambiguity of such encounters is never confidently transcended when they are recreated by the mature mind and memory of the poet, the summoning of history to the reflection of the philosophic mind. For always there enters upon the reflection the specter of the mind's power itself, and the question of the legitimacy of its creation—whether it half creates or but distorts. "If this be but a vain belief" is an iterated chorus in Wordsworth. There is consequently a tension suitable to the necessities of lyric poetry, which accounts for striking passages in *The Prelude.* And those passages often carry a force comparable to epiphanies in the early Joyce and in later prose writers.

In relation to Wordsworth's encounter with his soldier, one thinks particularly of Stephen Crane's Henry Fleming and his encounter with the dead soldier in the temple of nature. Wordsworth does not flee from his soldier. He aids him, but also watches him as he walks painfully beside the poet "With an astonishment but ill-suppressed." Nor does the poet forgo painful questions which were "better spared" the old soldier, concerning the grief and misery the soldier has encountered in a long life. The old man's "strange half-absence" fascinates the young poet, who is bent upon satisfying his own emotional appetite by reading the stranger as he reads every neighbor, each of whom has a face "like a volume." Having seen the old man home, the poet departs:

> Back I cast a look,
> And lingered near the door a little space,
> Then sought with quiet heart my distant home.

The poet's departure is not so precipitous as Henry Fleming's from the temple on whose altar rests the still body of a dead soldier. But neither does one have the conviction that the encounter has left Wordsworth a sadder but wiser man. Although there is a feeling in the passage of a profound moment not unlike that recorded of the disciple on the road to Emmaus (which Eliot was to make dramatic use of in *The Waste Land*), one nevertheless has the impression that Wordsworth trembles on the verge of some recognition never fully consummated, leaving in him a necessity for repeated puzzling encounters with unresolved mystery.

If the turnings of experience in Wordsworth's philosophic mind leave us less satisfied as to a rational coherence than does Dante's *Vita Nuova,* they leave us as well less moved by aesthetic coherence. In contrast, Whitman's "Out of the Cradle Endlessly Rocking" carries a unity not entirely accounted for by virtue of its relative brevity. But most particularly, Wordsworth's re-creation of the growth of the poet's mind lacks a convincing immediacy. It does so largely because its center of interest is in the nature of the mind itself. For in spite of the uses of nature and rustic characters as a source of details, the primary burden of *The Prelude* is self-awareness. Wordsworth's fond desire for a reciprocity of mind and nature, the interaction through which each is at once active and passive, and his insistence upon a mediation in which thought and feeling become inseparable, make it inevitable that his words become memorials of states of existence in nature separate from those states themselves. In his poetry he comes to us with an address as of an ambassador from some far country of the mind to which words are finally inadequate transport. "I cannot paint / What then I was," he tells us, though he bravely attempts to do so, as does Prufrock, who also finds it impossible to say just what he means. Thus he becomes historian of moments of transport, recording what has been or what has seemed to be, with an anxious hope that it may be again. He is first and last, of course, a man speaking to men. In consequence he is concerned for his own experience of the mind as a universal, and yet he is somehow never fully convinced of a similitude of minds. He is continually torn between his desire that the land his mind knows be common to that land of other minds and the fear that it is private and separate, sometimes fearing awareness itself as illusional.

So it is that, as historian of those remembered states of being, Wordsworth records them not with that sense of probability which distinguishes the art of narrative or drama from history, but as the detailed search for a stasis in nature. Remembering instances which border on vision, suspicious of fancy's distorting powers which wrench perception and, through that perception, reality itself, he becomes a poet of degrees, not of metaphors. The auxiliary light of mind intensifies light in nature, bestowing new splendor on the setting sun. Similarly the midnight storm grows "darker in the presence of the eye." As we have seen, cliffs are "lofty," mountains are "solid," fields are "green." The emotional enthusiasm of recollection supplies a comparative degree to descriptive words even when they are positive in form. The comparison implied is "than they seemed *dark* or *lofty* or *green* or *solid* at other points in my awareness." One has only to recall the uses of imagery in Keats's poetry, such as in the odes or "The Eve of St. Agnes," to see how far removed from the possibility of sensuous immediacy Wordsworth's poetry tends to be, while remembering as well how anxious Wordsworth is to make the recollected experience impressive to his reader. Or one may turn to Wallace Stevens and his "Idea of Order at Key West," which is very much concerned with the transformational powers resident in the mind, to see a precise use of imagery to that end. Keats is given to the spontaneous engagement of the natural world through the senses, an action which he called at one point "negative capability," while Stevens is intellectually committed to the transformational powers of the imagination with a resoluteness of mind that refuses questions of illusion. But even as we point to such contrasts to Wordsworth, in whom "circumspection" breeds "infinite delay" as he acknowledges, we are by that contrast reminded that Wordsworth's struggles in part made possible the limited successes of Keats and Stevens. Thus "Tintern Abbey" anticipates, and in some degree is a cause of the "Ode to a Nightingale" and "The Idea of Order at Key West."

As we look at Wordsworth's version of *The New Life*, *The Prelude*, we begin to notice circumstances far more limiting to Wordsworth than Dante's to him. Wordsworth at the halfway house of the modern world, looks toward Nature as Dante toward Beatrice. He could not perceive

149

at that point in what respect his love poetry involved a divorcing of Nature from her true master, whether one take that master confidently to be God, as did Dante, or the individual mind's imaginative powers, as did Wallace Stevens. There were instances of instinctive fear of such separations in Wordsworth, both separations from God and from mind. Wordsworth, setting out to prove the proper home of a community of minds, the poet's and all men's, to be an abstract spirit, Nature, attempts the concrete particulars of nature, wishing to show man and his language at home in the world in order that other men might make themselves at peace in that world. But he was too honest a mind not to include misgivings. Thus in the process of writing his poetry, Wordsworth is at once pilgrim and poet. Both are dramatically present in his verses. Wordsworth writes his poem to become ready to write it. He has no position from which he may operate as detached and thereby *in-form* his journey of the mind. He writes a *history* of the journey toward poetry, where Dante is in a position to artfully create an imitation of that journey.

As if in a panic out of desperation, in spite of the joyfulness of the celebration sometimes present, Wordsworth turned to the things of Nature. Those words in "Tintern Abbey," "more like a man / Flying from something that he dreads, than one / Who sought the thing he loved," are appropriate to Wordsworth's mind more generally than his limiting them to that intermediary stage of his history. He turned toward the things of nature, even as Beatrice accuses Dante of having done when she quit her earthly state. Wordsworth, in his disappointment with mankind for not also turning toward Nature, like-minded with himself, failed at first to see how large a mote he carried in his own eye. On the level of art, as opposed to the spiritual level, Wordsworth began with an abstraction, Nature, out of his literal experiences; but he does not conceive of Nature as a personification as Dante does Love. He takes the abstraction as a breathing reality because he feels a very real presence in the world, a presence which as we have said Christian doctrine would agree to as the Life Giver, the Holy Spirit. But such abstractions, whether personifications or Persons, require both the rational intellect (which men have in common) and the artistic attempt at shadowing forth that intellect in an art object, the creation of a form through which that abstraction can be embodied in concrete detail. This is to say that Nature personified is insufficient to sustain the high comedy Wordsworth committed himself to in that projected work of three parts that was to follow *The Prelude*.

The result of Wordsworth's attempt is that he discovered himself fundamentally mistaken. Starting at a middle ground, himself halfway between the literal and the ideal, his conception of Love atrophies so that Nature becomes, in the sharpness of his disappointment, a prison house closing upon boy and man. Dante takes a person separate from himself, a concrete Beatrice, and his own relationship with her, and develops from that concrete toward the universal. He presents as action the figure of Beatrice—that is, the poetic figure of Beatrice as a term of that large metaphor constituted by his work—in a many-storied architecture of meaning. That meaning derives its appearance of action, its illusion of becoming, through the metamorphosis of love as centered in Beatrice. Love is centered in the figure of a man; it comes out of his heart, embodies itself in Beatrice, through whom it rises to Empyrean dimensions. It starts in the three-dimensional world of nature, which allows a geography within which the journey makes a significant pattern suitable both to dramatic art and to the requirements of the soul. That is, through the figure of Beatrice, Dante projects a work of art as a stasis of a mind, containing within it that multiplicity which he called the four levels of meaning.

We observe Milton starting with a conception of the transhistorical, the transnatural, in his *Paradise Lost* and working down to the imaginable beginning of time. Man's first disobedience is the culmination of his epic and not a beginning in medias res except by summary statement.

There is a fundamental difference, critically decisive, between beginning with the immediate problems of fallen man in A.D. 1300 and rarifying upward as it were, and in beginning before time and space but with the burden of time-space imagery as the necessary vehicle to present the Ineffable. Milton attempts to narrate what can only be briefly touched in a vision beyond articulation. In *Paradise Lost,* he is repeatedly forced to the paradoxical phrase, often an arresting phrase as in his *vast abrupt* or *palpable obscure.* He is so forced because of an inadequacy of narrative art to the transimaginative, in whose regions (as the mystics insist) contemplation and vision alone are adequate transport of our human inadequacies. The question becomes: under what conditions and in what parts of a work of art may one hope to bring art to an intersection with the transcendent? A sustained encounter seems impossible, such an encounter as Dante reserves to the brief falling away of vision in the final canto of the *Comedy.* Milton is forced by what he elects to narrate to reduce the Unsayable to the human level, yet at a point which the intellect affirms as prior to human existence itself. Thus Christ, before he has become man, must be charioted in his battle in Heaven. But he must not move, as would be allowable were he riding the donkey toward his crucifixion.

The requirement upon Milton's auditor is that he imagine a Nature counter to his experience of that Nature; he must operate in the mode of fancy rather than of the imagination, in Coleridge's terms. The effect, then, is not of one's having experienced an imitation of a vision, but of having been momently entertained by the fancy, through an engagement of one's wit by Milton the metaphysical poet. As seer, above poet, Milton feels repeatedly called to safeguard his reader from the cognitive illusions of literary metaphor, reminding him of the incommensurate dimension of one of his metaphorical terms. Hence the necessary proliferation of paradoxical phrases through which almost as much is taken away as is given (the *vast abrupt*) and sometimes more (God's descent to Adam and Eve in the garden or Raphael's cosmology in book 8). There is a brilliance in Milton's ingenuity such as Joyce also exhibits, particularly in *Finnigans Wake*—a struggling to make fancy substantial.

As for Wordsworth, his conception of Nature only vaguely relates to the possibility of multiplicity through which one approaches a transcendent state of being, that state which (in respect to the soul) allows the soul to look down upon time and multiplicity and up toward the timeless and unified from a still point. We notice in "Tintern Abbey" an attempt at such a stable position. Those "lofty cliffs" which the eye beholds are related to the general "wild secluded scene" and are a sort of intermediary between that scene and "the quiet of the sky." But the position of the poet is one disengaged from both Nature and the particulars of human involvements with nature, as we notice from his reflection that he stands under a "dark sycamore" when the rest of the world is bathed in sunlight. Dante the Pilgrim has Beatrice as intermediary to God, the Supreme Love. In Wordsworth's sequence, all the terms are objects of the natural world, related to each other and not to the mind on the one hand or to the transcendent world on the other, except through modifiers that reflect the separation of the reflecting mind from what it longs to be united to. The result is a vague hint of such relationships of mind to the world separate from it, hints of "something . . . deeply interfused." The hints out of the emotions have not been laid before a mind intense enough to transform those images through which the emotion must express itself—cliffs, sky, secluded scene. Wordsworth's thought is a thought which is not sufficiently aware of the mind's immediate relations to nature through which such vague connections have been aroused in that mind. There is vague Platonism quite other than that firm attention to detail and logic which is in Dante's initial Platonic figuring of Beatrice in *The New Life*. What sustains "Tintern Abbey" is mood, the coloring of words by the emotion in Wordsworth, rather than thought, the rational ordering of emotion in relation to circumstance—concepts in relation to images.

153

Saint Augustine argues that "each of God's creatures speaks to us in a kind of mystical code in order to stimulate our curiosity and to intimate an image of the Trinity every time we ask: Who made it? How? And Why?" But his is an approach to nature more amenable to the philosophical mind of Coleridge than to Wordsworth, who stands under his dark sycamore and puzzles a deep seclusion in nature which somehow connects the landscape with the quiet of the sky. The mood of "Tintern Abbey" is sustained by intimations to Wordsworth that metaphor is an instrument of mystical insight, intimations which submit to no rational articulation. There is the faint suggestion that nature is a living allegory; it trembles toward overt recognition in the poem through the multiple suggestions of "inland murmurs" of stream and thought, through the hidden correspondence of the river and human life, through the silent smoke that somehow speaks and lofty cliffs that reach toward a quiet being that contains all thinking things and all objects of all thought. Yet Wordsworth stands troubled in the shade, out of the sun's full light. What troubles him in "Tintern Abbey" equally troubles Eliot as he surveys the city landscape in his "Preludes": the fear that one may be "moved by fancies that are curled / Around these images and cling" as vaguely and inessentially as smoke on the hills. It is the fear that feeling is not inherent in nature but imposed upon images by the lonely awareness. Eliot's notion of some "infinitely gentle / Infinitely suffering thing" may be a notion only, a mirroring of the self and not a movement of communion with the Other. And lest that be so, Eliot's voice steps back into sardonic irony such as Wordsworth is incapable of:

Wipe your hand across your mouth, and laugh;
The worlds revolve like ancient women
Gathering fuel in vacant lots.

Wordsworth, hearing through his reflective thought the "still, sad music of humanity, / Nor harsh nor grating," views the external world more quietly than on those remembered occasions he summons to the present moment of the poem. He develops in those next few lines (102–11) a rhetorically persuasive argument for the interdependence of eye, ear, and the mighty world which the eye and ear both record and make. Yet at this high point in the poem he can affirm, in the ultimate phrase of his peroration, only that nature is the soul of all his "moral being." This is the point, three-fourths through the poem, at which he turns fervently to Dorothy, whose presence one has not suspected, to give her moral instruction on the uses of nature. That turning to Dorothy suggests itself a movement to escape the terror of the self as an illusion. It is a reaching outward to another person to affirm her mind as a mansion for all lovely forms as his has been. He sees in her eyes a proof of his memories of at least that experience five years earlier.

The fear of suicide through epistemological concerns, such as Prufrock executes, is more constant in Wordsworth than it was to be in Eliot. For Eliot will move with a confident leap of faith beyond that problem as he encounters it entangled in phenomenological philosophy. It is a leap Eliot makes with the aid of Saint Augustine, who says confidently that "without any illusion of image, fancy, or phantasm, I am certain that I am, that I know that I am, and that I love to be and know. . . . If they say, 'What if you are mistaken?'—well, if I am mistaken, I am. For if one does not exist, he can by no means be mistaken." Augustine's stillness—his assertion of knowing as a proof of being—was more steadying to Eliot than Descartes's process—thinking as a proof of being—with which Wordsworth was heavily burdened. It is closer to the possibilities of that still point which the later Eliot speaks of as constant than to the repeated "spots of time" which Wordsworth is continually pursuing as if those too were somehow caught in process.

Such a procedure as Wordsworth's must inevitably reflect back on the creatures of nature, those creatures thereby becoming more shadow than Plato's shadows. For there is for Wordsworth no significant line of travel beyond the limits of the world, and the effect of this handicap is to present as the central character of Wordsworth's poem, as we have said, not Wordsworth the Pilgrim but both Wordsworth the Pilgrim and Wordsworth the Poet. Hence one comes to what is in effect that cataloguing of incidents and images, the history of his encounter with the things of nature. It is this aspect of Wordsworth that one finds more obviously displayed in the catalogues of Walt Whitman. A Joyce, in contrast, though he rejects Dante's vision, nevertheless through the process of that rejection (and his book of memory, his *New Life,* is the *Portrait*) was provided by it with a structure of thought to his own art, a structure that gives it a precision of form that belies the endless wandering that it represents in its show of form. The thought of Aristotle and Aquinas is an effective element of the *Portrait,* as it is not of *Ulysses* and *Finnegans Wake,* works in the history of Joyce's mind analogous to Dante's *Comedy.*

Not of course that Wordsworth failed to recognize the problem. There are prefigurings of Joyce's concern for particularity such as those Joyce makes to Aunt Josephine back in Dublin, with a recognition that particularity is not enough. Powers of observation and description are indispensable, Wordsworth says. There must be in the poet "the ability to observe with accuracy things as they are in themselves, and with fidelity to describe them, unmodified by any passion or feeling existing in the mind of the describer." But this is detached statement, objective rendering in retrospect, and if it stands alone it overlooks the circumstance of accurate observation and description surcharged with the feeling of wonder and doubt that transforms the poet's "science" into poetry. Wordsworth's "matter-of-factness," his "laborious minuteness and fidelity in the representation of objects" for which Coleridge chides him, seem to Wordsworth to bear an intensity that justifies them. Still, the concern which was to be raised into the literary movement we call Naturalism, midwife to imagism in poetry, does not always bear the additional intensification through a wonder or doubt which Wordsworth thinks somehow present in the words. Often he confuses the wonder of details with magnitude or significance, as when he defends himself against Crabb Robinson's objection to the measuring of a muddy puddle in "The Thorn": "I've measured it from side to side / Tis three feet long, and two feet wide." Wordsworth's emphatic insistence that the lines "ought to be liked" is intelligible only when we see the center of his concern: the wonder of thought itself born out of perception. He would require of poetry that it enlarge human sensibility, the stimulation subtly and not violently induced. The dramatically spectacular has small place in that process. At the same time, the more subtle the procedure, the more fully developed a sensibility is required. What Wordsworth wishes to accomplish requires an already refined sensibility in the reader. In this respect he is much like Wallace Stevens, whose own subtle shifts in repetitions, as in "Sea Surface Full of Clouds," make much of what some readers consider Stevens's own measuring of a puddle. Nor are Stevens's devoted readers likely to be engaged by the refinements of "I Wandered Lonely as a Cloud." For Wordsworth's poem requires a sensibility more given to abstraction than Stevens's poem. Spectacle, in the form of imagery, carries Stevens's poem, where Wordsworth's is carried more by idea than by image.

The tendency of Wordsworth's imagery is to the generalized, the abstracted, however particular it may seem or be intended by the poet. One has only to set beside his images those from a poet such as Stevens or Keats to see how much he depends upon a recollection in the reader of an experience of the particular concrete he uses. Keats's "strenuous tongue" that bursts "Joy's grape" has a sensuous immediacy which is not present in Wordsworth's heart that "dances with the daffodils." Or compare the "sparkling waves" to that beaker in Keats with "beaded bubbles winking at the brim." Wordsworth is reluctant, finally, to allow the mind a surrender to nature; it opens itself to nature's "mighty stream / of tendency." It "watches and receives." This difference between Keats's inclination and Wordsworth's is what Keats recognizes when he speaks of the egotistical sublime in Wordsworth, a quality of Wordsworth's mind when it addresses itself to the Other which extends even to the particulars of measuring two-by-three puddles. From the advantage of age and the more general acceptance of his poetry, Wordsworth argues in 1827 that "sensible objects really existing, and felt to exist, are *imagery;* and they may form the materials of a descriptive poem, where objects are delineated as they are. Imagination is a subjective term: it deals with objects not as they are, but as they appear to the mind of the poet." Such a pronouncement seems, as Professor Heffernan says, "to license the most puerile kind of impressionism." But though it is qualified by setting it in the context of Wordsworth's other views of creative sensibility, as Professor Heffernan does, theoretical statement is still separate from poetic practice. In his practice, Wordsworth does slip into puerile impressionism, the answer to which is the multitude of parodies called forth by his poetry. Wordsworth does not always escape his own warning that the position which champions the appearance over the reality prepares "a world of delusion ... for the inexperienced." That imagination which is "the faculty which produces impressive effects out of simple elements" sometimes deludes the mind into accepting as impressive an attempt in which the disparity between those simple elements out of the external world and the effect the poet assumes accomplished through the agency of his imagination is so great as to make the line or the stanza or the poem banal. If a Wallace Stevens escapes that difficulty more often than Wordsworth, it is in large part because he very carefully restricts the range of his attempts in poetry.

The personification of man's history, and not the personification of nature, is the first step toward penetrating the world and enlarging that penetration in art of magnitude. But the figure must be elected by a mind fully aware. Wordsworth, realizing somewhat late that his own mind is the figure which is cast against the mystery of existence, laments not having recognized this innocent failure earlier. This new awareness of himself, an awareness of self-failure, makes a turning which is not so simply explained as when we ascribe it a result of his brother's drowning at sea, though that event was to make him publicly acknowledge and bewail having lived too long "at distance from the kind." There is a turning in Wordsworth by the time *Lyrical Ballads* is published, a turning marked by an increased attention to a history other than his own as an element of his poetry. He looks to the failures of the French Revolution and to the decay of English society, a phase of his development paralleled by Eliot's concern with history at the time of "Gerontion" on one side of Wordsworth and by Milton's concern with history at the time of "Lycidas" on the other. Beyond all three poets, in the prospect of time, is Dante and his *New Life,* in which Beatrice develops to a dramatic role of Christ, as the work makes explicitly plain. (It is in subsequent work by Milton, Wordsworth, and Eliot that the figure of Christ comes to occupy attention, in *Paradise Lost, The Excursion, Ash Wednesday.*)

What Wordsworth realized then, in effect, is that Nature cannot function as a figure of Christ in art or argument, as Beatrice can for Dante or perhaps even Tiresias in Eliot's dark night of the soul. It is some instance of "the kind," some figure of man, through whom we see mystery, the kind being most particularly in the image of God and so quite separate in this respect from Nature, man's awareness being the key to that difference.

The result of such a turning in Wordsworth was to give him a second lease on lyricism, on lyricism which is heavily rational and even heavily didactic, the best-known instances being his "Ode to Duty," "Elegiac Verses," the 1802 and 1803 sonnets, the "Intimations Ode." But Wordsworth after the awakening is never able to recover himself as journeyman in the world, recollect himself, with the profoundness necessary to sustain an *Excursion* or a *Wanderer.* The sense of personal failure is not to be overcome. "The light that never was on sea or land" with which he would have, in the innocent days, painted Peele Castle in a consecration of the poet's dream, had proved self-illusion—dream and not reality. He holds suspect "that blessed mood" praised in "Tintern Abbey" because it marks a time of peace uncomplicated by the necessity of thought. It was a mood

> In which the burthen of the mystery
> In which the heavy and the weary weight
> Of all this unintelligible world,
> Is lightened:—the serene and blessed mood,
> In which the affections gently lead us on,—
> Until, the breath of this corporeal frame
> And even the motion of our human blood
> Almost suspended, we are laid asleep
> In body, and become a living soul.

That blessed mood appears to Wordsworth's thinking after "Tintern Abbey" increasingly as a self-induced illusion through which the mind itself is laid asleep as much as is the body, thus losing that name of action which is peculiarly the soul's as Dante dramatizes it. We notice how often in Wordsworth's poetry after "Tintern Abbey" the *mind asleep* is lamented, and his best lyrics tend to be a dramatic presentation of an awakening to the fact of an illusion which has been induced by a deliberate exorcising of reality through a mood fed by emotion rather than examined by thought. "My Heart Leaps Up" requires the examination of the "Intimations Ode" (and compare this juxtaposition of epigraph to those poems so much the hallmark of Eliot's early poetry). Now it is "farewell, the heart that lives alone, / Housed in a dream." Wordsworth's new thinking can no longer accept dream as reality, nor can it ever hover over the possibility that the dream may be reality, as Keats does when he cannot go beyond his "Do I wake or sleep?" Shelley's skylark is too much like Wordsworth's own early birds, and finally will not suit the mind's needs. Here lies the cause of Wordsworth's disapproval of those young poets. Wordsworth has reached a point where he can look critically at the self-hypnotism of the mind accomplished through willed emotions, such exercises as that we see in Whitman's "Out of the Cradle Endlessly Rocking," or such as we may see by looking closely at Shelley's "Ode to the West Wind," or the attempts that led to spiritual failure in Keats's odes. It is a harder light Wordsworth sees by now, and out of that harder light comes one of his finest poems dealing with the spirit falsely lulled asleep:

> A slumber did my spirit seal;
>   I had no human fears;
> She seemed a thing that could not feel
>   The touch of earthly years.
>
> No motion has she now, no force;
>   She neither hears nor sees;
> Rolled round in earth's diurnal course,
>   With rocks, and stones, and trees.

Nature is changed for Wordsworth because Wordsworth is changed, but Lucy is not Beatrice. If she were, she would point out to Wordsworth that such a poem as this is a sign of failure in that attempt to transcend the lyric toward high comedy. If Lucy cannot be for Wordsworth a figure through which the mind transcends, it is because of a false courtship of the Beloved, a courtship engaged upon in innocence, which when so recognized leads only to a sternness of self-purpose that cannot transcend the self toward that old high innocence. Even with his new awareness, there could be for Wordsworth no gap sufficiently marked between Wordsworth the Pilgrim and Wordsworth the Poet to allow for that drama of becoming, the lyric transformed to a level of comedy whose end is the recovery of the soul through a vision achieved.

Wordsworth and the Ghost of the Mind

THE SEDUCTIONS OF METAPHOR

Rollo May, *Existence*

> The chief sources of modern Western man's anxiety and despair were, first, his loss of a sense of being, and secondly, his loss of his world.... Broadly speaking, the symptoms of isolation and alienation reflect the state of a person whose relation to the world has become broken.

Michael Polanyi, *The Study of Man*

> Man must try to discover knowledge that will stand up by itself objectively, but the moment he reflects on his knowledge he catches himself red-handed in the act of upholding his knowledge.

Wallace Stevens, "Notes toward a Supreme Fiction"

>   and yet so poisonous
> Are the ravishments of truth, so fatal to
> The truth itself, the first idea becomes
> The hermit in a poet's metaphors,
> Who comes and goes and comes and goes all day.

Wordsworth, as *The Prelude* repeatedly reminds us and as critics of Wordsworth's poetry keep saying, was born in the north of England, a remote region whose landscape was as yet untouched by the factory and its attendant squalor. *The Prelude* is full of attention to that scene, but as with "Tintern Abbey," the scene itself is vague. And for the same reason. "How shall I seek the origin? where find / Faith in the marvellous things which then I felt?" Such the question, and the difficulty of answer lies in "that the soul, / Remembering not, retains an obscure sense / Of possible sublimity." Thus the dogged pursuit of that presence that seems to shine forth from nature, not only from the fair scenes, but from the dark lowerings as well. Norman Lacey, after a close examination of Wordsworth's idea of nature (in *Wordsworth's View of Nature and Its Ethical Consequences*), summarizes the conception: "The universe is interfused throughout by an external creative spirit. It is a spirit of love which he sometimes speaks of as God, but more frequently as Nature. The physical universe is the pure signature of the Creator—the forms of Nature are 'types and symbols of eternity.' " But a delicate problem exists concerning the relationship of the beholder and the beheld, in which relationship there was added to nature's seeming glow an "auxiliary light" of the mind. It was a light which came from the poet's own mind to bestow new splendor "on the setting sun . . . : the melodious birds; / The fluttering breeze" and upon that continuing catalogue of vague details from the natural scene. Lacey's summary of Wordsworth's view of the external world is accurate, if we add to it that Wordsworth's expression of that view is constantly touched by an insistent tone that suggests uncertainty in Wordsworth. What Wordsworth is most concerned with is getting down in verse not the objects of that external world—there is little of the Hopkins or Pound or Amy Lowell in him—but that state of mind which is, to his recollection, a mystical experience in which his own mind was inhabited by the natural world. Yet before the reality of the external world can be accepted, the reality of consciousness must itself be ratified.

> what I saw
> Appeared like something in myself, a dream,
> A prospect of the mind.

The independent relation of language to the imagery born of the senses, and the individual mind's powers in making appropriate relationships of words to sensations, was a subject Wordsworth puzzled over from the beginning. Through the juxtaposition of given images, metaphor emerges, metaphor-making being in particular the poet's gift (as Wordsworth affirms in agreement with Aristotle). The poet is that man who has a way of seeing likeness in unlike things—"similitude in dissimilitude." But though Wordsworth is intent upon the "pleasures" of metaphor, *pleasure* being a word he has repeated recourse to, he is agitated by the metaphysical implications of metaphor. It is as if he wishes to affirm, without being convinced, that through metaphor's analogies the poet solved Plato's dilemma of the Many and the One. What prevents an exuberance in his pursuit of this old problem is the suspicion that the mind may not distinguish appearance from reality—that the "likeness in unlike things" may not reside in the things themselves but be conferred upon them by the mind misled by the senses. The poet, depending upon metaphor for his argument, cannot survive the rejection of his senses, as Plato would have the philosopher reject them. Image is the uncertain language of analogy, derived from the Shadow we call the real world in an attempt to name the Idea, or rather in an attempt to apply a name related in essence to the essence of the Idea, the true reality. Such is the direction the philosopher's metaphor takes, moving from analogy toward allegory. It is the direction Wordsworth would desire to move in, were it not that Platonic Idea seems to fade into illusion. Wordsworth reacts as if seduced by that which he would be won by.

The wonder that one finds constantly celebrated in Wordsworth is not, then, so much Wordsworth's response to external nature as it is his response to his own awareness. There can be little doubt that this focus upon the awareness itself robs his poetry of immediacy, that quality of melancholy in Keats's poetry or elevated joy in Hopkins's poetry which seems to present us with a present moment of awareness concurrent to our reading. With Wordsworth we are nearly always dealing with the past perfect, with a response at once hardened by the fact of its having been completed sometime since and the vividness of the response obscured by the wordy perusal of its memory. In spite of a concern for the significance of the past experience to the present moment, Wordsworth does not ask *do* I wake of sleep? He asks *did* I wake or sleep? The nightingale he might have been listening to is more remote from his reader than Keats's bird that loses itself in the hills just at hand. The dappled beauty of Hopkins's nature is an ominous beauty to Wordsworth. Basil Willey in his *Seventeenth-Century Background* looks at Wordsworth's problems as a poet, contrasting him to the eighteenth-century poet such as Thomson or Pope. Their "poetry exists to decorate, to render agreeable, a set of abstract notions; and these abstractions have been taken over, as truth, from the natural philosophers— from Descartes, Newton, Locke, or Leibnitz. Wordsworth's beliefs, on the other hand, were largely the formulation of his own dealings with 'substantial things'; they were held intellectually only because they had first been 'proved upon the pulses.' "

Yet this comparison does not quite tell all, since it makes Wordsworth more of a convinced empiric than he is. Wordsworth is constantly uncertain of the dependability of the pulses. As Professor Willey points out, the excesses of empirical science had separated mind and the external world, following Bacon's stated intention of "restoring or cultivating a just and legitimate familiarity between the mind and things." Wordsworth was undertaking precisely the same cultivation, except that in the interval between his day and

Bacon's the primacy of the mind had been reduced till it was required to be passive in relation to the empiric commands of the external world. A nice dilemma for a poet like Wordsworth, then: to reestablish the primacy of the mind while at the same time to endue the mind with a respect for and power over the external world that elevated the external above the merely mechanical. And complicating the problem was the basic question of whether what one *seemed* to see was a valid perception. There hovers behind Wordsworth's poetry a fear that consciousness itself may be illusion.

We must, then, qualify such readings of the romantic mind as Frank Kermode's *Romantic Image* in relation to Wordsworth, for Wordsworth is never quite comfortable with the belief "in the Image as a radiant truth out of space and time." Nor will he willingly admit "the necessary isolation or estrangement of men" (i.e., poets) who perceive images. Wordsworth, his mind "beset with images and haunted by itself" as he says, is repeatedly in that intellectual state that Saint Augustine recalls in praying, "I believe; help thou my unbelief." The self-haunted mind dwells in a constant fear that its abstractions from reality, through the agency of images, inevitably and insolubly imply isolation of that mind from anything but itself. Here lies one reason that Wordsworth is so dogged in his insistence that the poet is like other men and not a separate creature.

There does come to be in the literature of the nineteenth and twentieth centuries, as Kermode demonstrates in his *Romantic Image,* an increasingly high value placed "upon the image-making powers of the mind at the expense of the rational powers," an acceleration of modern poetry's opposition to science whose corollary in philosophy is existentialism's opposition to positivism. Wordsworth, too, was worried by science's threat to poetry, but he refused the premise of the poet as image *maker* precisely because implicit in it is the isolation of the poet from his fellow men. Wordsworth's appeal, in the "Preface" to *Lyrical Ballads,* that the poet precede and follow the man of science into new knowledge so as to provide to science the first and last of all knowledge is an attempt to prevent the poet's self-exile, the social suicide that has become a major state and theme of the poet since Wordsworth's day.

This is not, of course, to say that Wordsworth escaped the pains of estrangement. His early biography in particular shows otherwise. It is rather to call attention to that constant concern in him that mankind not cast off the poet, as it is always in the process of doing. When Wordsworth insists that the poet feels more than the ordinary man, rather than differently from him, and when he argues a skill in the poet which allows him to perceive likeness in unlike things, he is struggling against the threat of isolation thrust upon the poet by empiricism and the rise of science in the popular estimation. Science promises little solace to *feelings,* except for those worldly feelings Francis Bacon announced as the proper ends of knowledge: "the endowment of human life with new inventions and riches." The first and last cause of all knowledge, in that line of development, is called utility, not wisdom as Wordsworth would have it. It leads to that disturbing concern for "getting and spending" that cuts off man from significant life. Wordsworth argues against subjectivism as he must, subjectivism being a principal point of the empiricist's attack upon the poet, for he sees as the logical extension of subjectivism the breaking of all bonds between beholder and beheld. But his attack does not imply endorsement of empiricism. He affirms as his faith, in *The Prelude,* that "our puny boundaries are things / That we perceive, and not that we have made." Still, this affirmation is far more complicated than a casual reading of the bold statement makes it appear. He is haunted by a persuasiveness of eighteenth-century empiricism: man does not make those puny boundaries within which he must account for his existence—he perceives them. They are nevertheless *puny,* because of the limitations of the mind. When man reads the world of nature with Descartes's eyes and Bacon's ends he commits the mind to a passive acceptance of empirical knowledge. That is, the threat empiricism holds for the poet is that it limits and specializes the mind toward making it something of an IBM machine. Wordsworth is finally trapped. On the one hand he is beset by subjectivism, whose inevitable end is isolation and death to the poet, the particulars of which Kermode expounds. On the other he is confronted by those louder callings of an objective empiricism, whose inevitable conclusion is a conception of the universe as a closed mechanical system, untouched by any transcendent cause, within which the mind of man must be accounted for in terms of that closed system. Descartes and Locke had already provided the foundations upon which the doctrine of Progress would rise, with its optimistic extensions of a future community of men moving toward a perfect society in nature's storehouse. And the Industrial Revolution was already exhibiting some products of Bacon's dreams of human comfort. But Wordsworth, by the accidents of his history, as for instance his involvement in and disillusionment with the French Revolution and his awareness of the factory, which reduced man toward machine, could find little cause for optimism in his role as poet. There was already much talk of the great society to come, not only on the part of the French revolutionaries but of the English imperialists as well. Bacon's "new inventions and riches" were already enlarging to include the "new man," perfected in due time. But Wordsworth saw that new spirit in operation politically on the continent and economically in England. It was devoted to setting aside the old, as in the replacement of monarchs by popular governments on the continent or of the old nobility by the emerging industrialists in England. These are the activist extensions of Bacon's and Descartes's having set aside the accomplishments of the ancients in favor of the moderns in science and philosophy, a point of some importance to the argument of the unfinished *Excursion*. The new thought, one must consider, necessarily emphasizes *unlikeness* in nature and society, past and present, as preliminary to a belief in an infinite progress in history. That necessary emphasis, at the heart of the new doctrine of history growing out of the eighteenth century, strikes at the very heart of Wordsworth's confidence in metaphor. For likeness in unlike things, embodied in language, allows a sense of continuity of mind in time and a community of mind in place such as is necessary to buttress one's fellowship with "the kind." (One notices, in considering Yeats in this line of thought, the struggle he makes toward reestablishing the possibilities of metaphor. It is a principal comfort to him afforded by his *Vision*. And one notices in his friend and rival, Ezra Pound, an emphasis on image making and a deep suspicion of metaphor as obscuring the unlikeness of images yoked by metaphor.)

Wordsworth found himself attempting to hold mankind together through his calling as a poet at a time when empiricism had advanced, through Newtonian physics, to a point that suggested ordinary perception of the world by the senses to be an illusion. But he was also at a point in history in which it was undeniable that Plato's Idealism, the ascendant metaphysics of Protestantism, had always held the world of the senses illusional without providing an accommodation to that world acceptable to science. Wordsworth finds himself in an age increasingly skeptical of any realm of existence transcending the puny boundaries declared by empirical thought. As he insists upon the poet's legitimate brotherhood with the man of science, so too he insists on a brotherhood with the man of ideas, the philosopher. The possible meeting of a philosopher and scientist he concludes to lie in that figure of the child celebrated in the "Intimations Ode," the child being metaphysical empiricist and therefore "best Philosopher." But the conclusion is asserted through the child image at a time when Wordsworth is uneasily concerned with being at distance from the kind, whether child or peasant. He is still very much engaged with establishing an anchor for his purest thoughts sufficient to assure him that those thoughts are substantial and not illusional. The possibilities of becoming as a little child seem forever flown; he worries that problem aloud, as if speaking to the child, in his most famous ode. (Wordsworth attempted the office of poet and priest at once, as the characters in *The Recluse* indicate, in the face of science's effects in discrediting both. Since 1900 science has attempted more particularly, in the interest of the doctrine of Progress, to substitute the psychiatrist for priest and sociologist for bard—a state of affairs not lost upon some writers, as witness the plays of T. S. Eliot and Harold Pinter and the fiction of Flannery O'Connor.) The diction of those stanzas of the "Intimations Ode" following the first four, which were written in despair and put aside for some time before the poem was finished, is more deliberately archaic and in the tradition of the literary pastoral than one expects from the precepts of that "Preface" to *Lyrical Ballads.* The stanzaic form, the venerable abstractions that are more directly out of Platonic thought than the Platonisms of "Tintern Abbey," are signs of that fundamental problem that I have introduced and with which I want now to deal with a more specific attention to Wordsworth's metaphor. For the difficulty he faces is to prove the validity of his awareness "upon the pulses" in relation to external nature. But more importantly he must prove the validity of his own "immaterial nature" as in some acceptable way an image of a supernatural existence capable of enlarging the significance of those puny boundaries man perceives.

Wordsworth tells us, in his late note to the "Intimations Ode," of his childhood inability "to admit the notion of death as a state applicable to my own being." He insists that it is not a fear of death that he describes. It is rather an inability to believe fully in the substantiality of things on the one hand or the reality of thought—idea inhabiting awareness—on the other: "I was often unable to think of external things as having external existence, and I communed with all that I saw as something not apart from, but inherent in, my own immaterial nature. Many times while going to school have I grasped at a wall or tree to recall myself from this abyss of idealism to the reality." The phrase "abyss of idealism" should give pause to anyone who would take Wordsworth's poetry as serene. It is a frightening abyss, nowhere more evident than in the "Intimations Ode" itself, in which there is an insistence tinged with desperation in those final stanzas. Wordsworth insists that the universe is interfused by a creative spirit, the physical world itself a signature of the Creator, but that "abyss of idealism" continues a threat to serenity long after Wordsworth's childhood. It leads him to a constantly reiterated insistence on the validity of the "immaterial nature" of his being, statements in which there is an unsettled note of ambiguity. Such a passage as the following, from the "Preface" to *The Excursion,* carries just such a note of unresolved wonder as to the mind's credentials.

> From deep analogies by thought supplied,
> Or consciousness not to be subdued,
> To every natural form, rock, fruit or flower,
> Even the loose stones. . . .
> I gave a moral life, I *saw* them feel,
> Or link'd them to some feeling; the great mass
> Lay bedded in a quickening soul, and all
> That I beheld respired with inward meaning.

Wordsworth's insistent italics (*saw*) climax the battle between the external existence and the consciousness which refuses to be subdued by the external.

Through a surge of will on the part of the consciousness, a moral life is infused into the material world, or is said to be infused, an important qualification. The strong insistence seems undercut by an element of doubt: Wordsworth protests too much with the italics of "I *saw* them feel," as if he were a watcher in the night attempting to convince his reader and himself of having encountered an apparition. The passage, upon examination, becomes quite ambiguous. Whose is the "consciousness not to be subdued"? Is it the poet's or a consciousness underlying all "things" including the poet? Whose then is the "thought" that supplies the "deep analogies"? If the "great mass" lies bedded in a "quickening soul" (that is, a soul coming alive), whose soul can it be but the poet's, the aliveness of which is

171

testified to by the insistence that it *"saw"* things "feel"? *Consciousness* and *thought* emerge as two powers which the soul recognizes in itself, leading to the recognition of a third, but unsettling, power: the *imagination*. It is the imagination which is capable of confusing self-awareness with an independently existing awareness subsuming all "things." Through the imagination, the soul confuses its own awareness with an existing God or an existing soul in nature. The imagination may subversively lead the self to suppose that it sees things feel, and the subversiveness is unsettling.

> A plastic power
> Abode with me, a forming hand, at times
> Rebellious, acting in a devious mood,
> A local spirit of his own, at war
> With the general tendency.

Such a rebellious spirit may well seize the mind's experience with "rock, fruit, or flower" and force upon them a "moral life." Recognizing the possibility of such illusion, the soul comes upon doubt: has imagination indeed led the soul to create a world in its own image? What if that rebellious "creative" power be intent upon making the soul its own Heaven, thus removing itself from all else except itself? Wordsworth's refusal to ignore such a possibility, while a tribute to his honesty, is also a cause of his uncertainty about the dependability of his own mind. Consequently, he cannot *will* life into the world about him with a constancy sufficient to sustain the long flights of poetry he attempts in *The Prelude* and *The Excursion* but rather succumbs to the kind of vacillation Keats was generally wise enough to confine to the ode.

The passage from *The Excursion* in which the poet argues that he sees things feel and the passage calling the imagination into question might well take us back to those powerful lines written by Wordsworth's chief mentor, John Milton. Milton puts directly rebellious words into the mouth of an agent intent upon sustaining an illusion through a powerful, though evil, will. "What though the field be lost?" asks Satan in book 1 of *Paradise Lost.* "All is not lost." And so Milton's "foul Fiend" sets about building a private world out of the materials of darkness, the antithesis of the "All" that he has indeed lost. The "plastic power" of the imagination in Milton's antihero is clearly subversive in Milton's understanding of it. Wordsworth speaks often of that power which, as he says in the famous "Preface" to *Lyrical Ballads,* compels the poet "to create [volitions and passions in the Universe] where he does not find them." But he is no Don Juan or Faust. Though he argues for such a primacy of the imagination, he lacks the audacity necessary to such creation; he lacks the arrogance necessary to declare that "The mind is its own place, and in itself / Can make a heaven of hell, a hell of heaven." Still pursuing his long argument with Coleridge over the meaning of imagination, he defines it in explicit contradiction to one William Taylor's definition included in *English Synonymes Discriminated* (1813). Wordsworth argues, in his "Preface" to the 1815 *Poems,* that, where Taylor's use of *imagination* would have it the faculty of the mind through which a poet "can distinctly copy in idea the impressions of sense," the imagination is rather the faculty of the mind that can shatter the inclination to merely depict and thereby rise through the mind's power to a new synthesis of images out of the order of nature. (At such points he is prophetic of Wallace Stevens.) Metaphor becomes supernatural. Imagination confers upon image aspects which are, in effect, the mind's playing of tricks upon the senses. He cites Milton's figure describing Satan appearing as when a fleet of ships "*Hangs* in the clouds" (Wordsworth's italics). But when Wordsworth cites this particular metaphor from *Paradise Lost,* he does not consider it within the context of the poem's action and the poet's perspective upon that action. The passage is in book 2 and Milton is describing "the flying Fiend" as he sets out from Hell, after committing himself to his own mind, to corrupt the world. The metaphor is an action of the mind in this passage, Wordsworth says, "for its own gratification," but his argument carries none of the awareness of the irony implicit in such "pleasure" of the mind as Satan is launched upon. He goes on to say that the imagination is that power of the mind which is used to the mind's pleasure through "conferring," "abstracting," "modifying" whatever the senses behold. It redistributes nature to its own pleasure, and in such redistribution lies the poet's powers as creator. In pursuit of this delineation, Wordsworth cites lines from his own "Resolution and Independence" to compare to Milton's passage, those lines beginning "As a huge Stone is sometimes seen to lie." The images involved in the lines—stone, sea-beast, cloud—are all related to the passive old man being described. Wordsworth writes:

> The Stone is endowed with something of the power of life to approximate it to the Sea-beast; and the Sea-beast stripped of some of its vital qualities to assimilate it to the stone; which intermediary image is thus treated for the purpose of bringing the original image, that of the stone, to a nearer resemblance to the figure and condition of the aged Man; who is divested of so much of the indications of life and motion as to bring him to the point where the two objects unite and coalesce in just comparison.

So much for the "endowing and modifying" power of the imagination, says Wordsworth. But the imagination also *creates* (Wordsworth's italics). At which point he returns to the passage in *Paradise Lost,* book 2, in which we see Satan far off in relation to images I take to be heavy with a Keatsean suggestiveness of the worldly:

> As when far off at Sea a Fleet descried
> Hangs in the clouds, by equinoxial winds
> Close sailing from Bengala or the Isles
> Of Ternate or Tydore, whence Merchants bring
> Their spicy drugs . . .
> > so seem'd
> Far off the flying Fiend.

There is, we now notice, a rather distinct difference between Milton's extended metaphor here and Wordsworth's which he quotes and analyzes out of "Resolution and Independence." Milton is dealing with an agent whose essential nature he has carefully defined for himself; his agent is the Prince of Seeming, who has elected to oppose the Prince of Being, Christ. The last thing Milton would have his reader do is mistake the power of evil to dissimulate, to seem other than it is, for it is the very power of dissimulation which corrupts the intellect in Milton's view of the matter. If the power of the poet is, as Aristotle says and Wordsworth affirms, that he sees "similitude in dissimilitude," the danger of that power is that the unlikeness of those objects which are likened to each other by images will be ignored or destroyed. Images are at best distantly related to the objects they attempt to picture to the senses so that when too much credence is given image, the effect will be to destroy the mind's orderliness, which in turn will mean that "old chaos" is indeed come again. No matter how wishfully one might call such chaos the "All," as if confirming a unity without division (by the agency of the mind as its own place), All is indeed lost. If anyone wished a reason for the voluminous prose work Milton expended himself upon, I think it would lie precisely here: his prose is to control, guard against, the deceptions of the mind's "plastic power," the imagination. It is the scholastic side of his being. Wordsworth, on the other hand, is committed to the imagination as he defines it, without always being sufficiently aware of the dangers of that commitment to him. In his analysis of his figuring of the old man in "Resolution and Independence" (and note the title here and argument of the poem) he is juxtaposing surfaces—images of things not seen in their essences, which essences would require an awareness of dissimilitude. It is the same mistake that leads him to ignore the context and the agent involved in Milton's metaphor describing Satan. The appearance of the old man is allowed to seduce the reason, through Wordsworth's easy sympathy, so that reason accepts the appearance as the reality. Coleridge would no doubt insist that here one has not imagination but fancy, for as he says (book 13 of the *Biographia*), "Fancy ... has no other counters to play with, but fixities and definites. The fancy is indeed no other than a mode of memory emancipated from the order of time and space."

When Wordsworth says "Such seemed this Man," he allows himself to be taken in by surface similitudes unprobed for the essences of their dissimilitudes, and being taken in by his metaphor, he expects his reader to accept it. Milton, on the other hand, when he says "so seem'd / Far off the flying Fiend," expects his reader to be put on his guard. Satan is, after all, setting out for Eden to destroy it by dissimulation, in his form and argument. "So ye shall die perhaps, by putting off / Human, to put on Gods." Thus that temptation to Eve to become "creator" of her own world, whose only antidote is Christ's putting on the "Human."

Thus it is that Wordsworth, endowing his stone "with something of the power of life," confuses (1) that power of the imagination to distort things out of their nature with (2) a valid insight into the "life of things." So long as the focus of his mind as critic is upon the analysis of figures, such analysis as we have seen him making in his "Preface" to the 1815 *Poems,* or so long as the poem he is writing is focused upon an old woman or old man or a child, he dwells upon the surface of things with a sad tranquility. But he becomes agitated, and often distraught, when the focus becomes his own mind. It is so in "Tintern Abbey," in *The Prelude* and *The Excursion.* For it is in these examinations of his awareness that he begins to have his faith in the holiness of the imagination shaken. It is in these works that we have Wordsworth puzzling the loss of Eden, that overwhelming part of his memory which he attempts to explain in the "Intimations Ode."

What I am suggesting is that Wordsworth, when he looked closely at his own mind, began to realize that the imagination of the poet is inevitably subversive. When it

176

makes use of the "aggressive and associative" powers of fancy by "shaping and modifying" in order to "idealize and unify" (in Coleridge's phrases), it may indeed build such an imposing edifice as that beside the dark lake in Milton's Hell or where Alph the sacred river ran. And, when the poet commits himself to such a power as that of the imagination, he risks those excesses that call forth tragic effects. Even Milton must guard against Satan's persuasiveness, for the possibilities of hubris can never be far removed from the creative process. (In depicting Heaven, piety is some safeguard to a Milton or Dante; but piety is a restriction upon the imagination. Satan had to get out of Heaven to build Hell's shadows. That, I suspect, accounts for the more powerful, or at least more arresting effect upon the modern mind of Dante's and Milton's Hells over their Heavens. To appreciate those upper regions in either requires a piety peculiar to the world since the birth of Christ. In the absence of piety, we treasure the realities of Hell and suspect the artificiality of Heaven, an indication of our intellectual kinship to Huck Finn.)

Wordsworth did not attempt the possibilities of tragedy, presenting the poet's mind as it descends into the world of the self, as Baudelaire chose to attempt. Nor does he create a narrative presentation of that struggle of the mind with the world, such as one has in Satan or in Goethe's *Faust*. Yet he was at the same time aware that he lived in a world where the self had become so cut off that a descent into the self was necessary to any restoration. Instead of the kind of distancing from his history that Browning attempts through the figure of Sordello, Wordsworth is consumed by a mask. That is, he forgets his present moment by concentrating on the past perfect images of the self, as in *The Prelude*, writing a cumulative memoir of his quest that led to no grail. In contrast, we recall that Dante's own "plastic power" results not in statement but in poems which are presented for inspection, poems which represent the interplay between the awareness of his Pilgrim and the involving milieu. Wordsworth's failure is largely because his gift was not sufficient to overcome the conditions imposed upon poetry by his age, conditions out of the teachings of those natural philosophers on the one hand and the Protestant reformation on the other. For empiricism had established a realm of objective universals to be assumed in one's thinking about the external world; and the Protestant revolution had succeeded for the moment in separating spiritual affairs from the external realm, partly as a revolt against medieval and Renaissance worldliness and partly as revolt against the worldliness of the new science of which Bacon is harbinger. Wordsworth was left in a position requiring him to bring those two realms together, particularly since he wished to function as prophet to a world he thought in dissolution. The inner spiritual world and the outer natural world had seemingly suffered an unhealing breach.

In Wordsworth's address to his audience, one notices an awareness that it is a secular, worldly intelligence that requires his primary address. It is partly this concern in him which prevents his examining with any nicety the question of paganism in his view of nature. Better the sensibility of the pagan than no sensibility at all. What he must do is not convert the intelligentsia to Christianity but justify that burdensome consciousness which is his gift to an age heavily empirical in its faith. First things first, and the first thing is to examine that consciousness as scientifically as possible, on the grounds of its particular experiences. He writes *The Prelude* not for Dorothy nor for Coleridge, but for an increasingly skeptical age, of which we must conclude him, finally, a very prominent member.

Around the Prickly Pear

ELIOT ON COLERIDGE ON SIR JOHN DAVIES

⁂Samuel Taylor Coleridge, Letter Dated April 1798

I devote myself to such works as encroach not on the antisocial passions—in poetry, to elevate the imagination and set the affections in right tune by the beauty of the inanimate impregnated as with a living soul by the presence of life—in prose to the seeking with patience and a slow, very slow mind . . . what our faculties are and what they are capable of becoming.

⁂Eliot, "Wordsworth and Coleridge"

In Wordsworth and Coleridge we find not merely a variety of interests, even of passionate interests; it is all one passion expressed through them all: poetry was for them the expression of a totality of unified interests.

⁂Eliot, "Sir John Davies"

Davies is much more mediaeval; his capacity for belief is greater. . . . There is only one parallel to *Nosce Teipsum,* and, though it is a daring one, it is not unfair to Davies. It is the several passages of exposition of the nature of the soul which occur in the middle of the *Purgatorio.*

At this point, we may allow ourselves an aside concerning Coleridge and his relation to Wordsworth, and especially Eliot's late reading of that relationship. By 1933 Eliot could say that, whereas he was "intoxicated by Shelley's poetry at the age of fifteen," he can look into that poet now "only with some special reason for reference." But as for Wordsworth's poetry, "I enjoy it more than when I first read it." Coleridge he reads for the greatness of a mind failing to achieve great poetry. For Coleridge, Eliot says, was rather fearfully haunted by the muse, as evidenced in the *Biographia Literaria*. He came to the depressing realization "that the little poetry he had written was worth more than all he could do with the rest of his life." In contrast, Wordsworth "had no ghostly shadows at his back, no Eumenides to pursue him," and so "went droning on the still sad music of infirmity to the verge of the grave." We have argued to the contrary that Wordsworth, too, was haunted. He does not burn with that intensity of concern that one finds in Coleridge, but it is not quite right to say of him that his "inspiration [had never] been of that sudden, fitful and terrifying kind that visited Coleridge." Wordsworth on occasions found himself in terror looking suddenly into the abyss. He too worries the question of the mind's distortion of reality, a problem Coleridge is increasingly concerned with as he turns the uses of imagination and fancy toward Christian orthodoxy, toward problems of the Word within the word. Coleridge laments, in dejection, that through "abstruse research" he has stolen

> From my own nature all the natural man—
> This was my soul resource, my only plan;
> Till that which suits a part infects the whole,
> And now is almost grown the habit of my soul.

The difference between his struggle with the mystery of the mind and its several faculties and Wordsworth's is that Wordsworth did not consciously and deliberately abstract all "natural man" from his own nature in the manner of a philosopher, but rather set about discovering himself in the whole, in the Other. The initial impulse in him leads of course to contemplation of the problem and its dangers; in Coleridge it is rather the other way around: the reflection and analysis through philosophical and psychological discursiveness seem necessary to arouse impulse, or at least to check it until ratified by reason. The division of labors in *Lyrical Ballads* as originally planned is an indication to my point. There is also Coleridge's distinction between the purpose of Wordsworth's "Preface" and his own intention in *Biographia Literaria:* "It was Mr. Wordsworth's purpose to consider the influences of fancy and imagination as they are manifested in poetry, and from different effects to conclude their diversity in kind; while it is my object to investigate the seminal principle, and then from the kind to deduce the degree." Wordsworth's concentration is on "branches with their fruitage," while Coleridge's is to be upon the "trunk, even the roots as far as they lift themselves above ground, and are visible to the naked eye of our common consciousness." But given this difference of approach, we need not conclude Wordsworth unconcerned as to whether he may have been innocently duped through his feelings into assuming that "that which suits a part" by extension is the whole.

It is because both poets, Coleridge and Wordsworth, attempt to solve the problem of the part's relation to the whole in terms of that most intimate part of the world, individual consciousness, and try to solve it in terms of the imagination that we call them philosophical poets. We add at once that Coleridge is more nearly the philosopher. And so we may here introduce that much discussed problem which Coleridge is credited with having burdened criticism with, the distinction between the fancy and imagination. The terms were of fundamental concern to each poet, a problem Coleridge himself never considered resolved. In chapter 13 of the *Biographia Literaria* occur words which we know almost by heart from their constant repetition in our criticism. The text may nevertheless be helpful:

> The IMAGINATION then, I consider either as primary, or secondary. The primary IMAGINATION I hold to be the living Power and prime Agent of all human Perception, and as a repetition in the finite mind of the eternal act of creation in the infinite I AM. The secondary Imagination I consider as an echo of the former, coexisting with the conscious will, yet still as identical with the primary in the *kind* of its agency, and differing only in *degree,* and in the *mode* of its operation. It dissolves, diffuses, dissipates, in order to recreate: or where this process is rendered impossible, yet still at all events it struggles to idealize and to unify. It is essentially *vital,* even as all its objects (as objects) are essentially fixed and dead.
>
> FANCY, on the contrary, has no other counters to play with, but fixities and definites. The Fancy is indeed no other than a mode of Memory emancipated from the order of time and space; while it is blended with, and modified by that empirical phenomenon of the will, which we express by the word CHOICE. But equally with the ordinary memory the Fancy must receive all its materials ready made from the law of association.

In his argument, Coleridge is wrestling with the complications which eighteenth-century science and philosophy have imposed upon the old distinction Milton made between the intuitive and discursive intellect, both of which are present in Coleridge's version of the finite mind under the aspects of the primary and secondary Imagination. His argument is also in part an attempt to rescue the Imagination from an old Platonic charge against it and from a Platonist error as well. Coleridge is surely influenced by the Cambridge Platonists, but not enslaved to them. The Platonic charge against the poet, as old as *The Republic,* is precisely that the poet's powers are those which Coleridge describes under the title "Fancy," and consequently of no validity in the pursuit of the truth about existence. Coleridge makes "choice" stand for a willful distortion of reality in his definition, through which the drapery of reality (independent of the form draped) is taken for the reality. It may become daydream built of ideas and images removed from the continuum of existence, derived from the same law of association under which imagination operates, but emancipated "from the order of time and space."

The specter that Coleridge is engaged against is one haunting English poetry, at least from Sir Philip Sidney's attempt to exorcise it in his *Apology*, through Shelley's *Defense* and on to the continuing justifications in academy and the proliferation of little magazines: the haunting suspicion of poetry's irrelevance to Platonic Idealism. That the daemon is not laid is apparent most spectacularly, I suspect, in one almost universal characteristic of the disaffected youth who plague us: they are poets, primitive poets, but blatantly so, as if possessing an instinct for the outrageous. Plato's argument that empathy is madness, that art itself is inevitably a distortion of the shadow world of nature—itself a distortion of the ideal reality—is deep-rooted in English and American thinking. Perhaps it is so because Plato was historically more influential upon us in consequence of the Reformation than was Aristotle. Whatever the causes, Plato's "ancient quarrel between philosophy and poetry" persists. It underwent a sea change in moving west across the channel, but an even more marked change when it crossed the Atlantic Ocean. When Platonism turned Puritanism, the shadow world turned a harder proof of the transcendent than generally proves comfortable to the poet. Progressively he found himself alienated by that worldly Platonism which gave birth to the materialistic, secular world of the American Dream. (Wordsworth, we remember, says harsh things about this side of our culture in *The Excursion*.) One notices how haunted and perplexed Hawthorne is by the problem, torn between his disaffection with Puritanism and that inclination to allegory whose justification lies in the Platonic roots of Puritanism. Jonathan Edwards's insistence in 1734 that the "spiritual and divine light does not consist in any impression made upon the imagination" succeeded in calling the credentials of imaginative writing into question in America before there were imaginative writers. One notices James's struggle with "romance" versus "realism," his version of Coleridge's Fancy and Imagination. One notices as well the emergence of a strong attempt at a refutation of that charge of poetry's "impracticality" in a conspicuous assertion of masculinity by our imaginative writers at the turn of this century and through its first quarter. Pound, for instance, is full of a declaration of his virility in his early poetry; the chief article of his faith, that the poet is the wisest king, is an attempt to seize by force the Platonic principle of the philosopher king. In a far simpler instance, Hemingway's paraded masculinity is an extension out of James's attempt to culture the robust American. (James is a far more important antecedent of Hemingway than Mark Twain, and not simply in matters stylistic.)

Coleridge's distinction between the Fancy and the Imagination is an important attempt to rescue art from new forces released out of empiricism and Platonism, which is why so many moderns have recourse to Coleridge. For he was very well aware that Sir Isaac Newton's description of poetry as "ingenius fiddle-faddle" was a position generally held. He is quite specific about the audience which responded to his and Wordsworth's attempt to rescue poetry for the general welfare. Wordsworth's admirers, he says, are found "chiefly among young men of strong sensibility and meditative minds" whose admiration is distinguished "by its intensity, I might almost say, by its religious fervor." In countering the Platonic and Puritan attempt to cast the poet into outer darkness, Coleridge also counters the similar error of an antithetic movement, conspicuously represented by Newton's attitude. Those materialists who were everywhere increasing about Coleridge shared with the strict Platonist a determinism in respect to knowledge, though the two are in radical disagreement on the source of and process of knowledge in the finite mind. As he was influenced by the Cambridge Platonists then, so was Coleridge influenced by determinism emerging in eighteenth-century philosophy. But

184

he is dissatisfied by both, and on epistemological grounds. In his distinction between fancy and imagination, he has moved a considerable distance from the school of Hartley, which in 1794 was so attractive to him that he could declare, "I am a compleat Necessitarian . . . but I go further than Hartley and believe in the corporeality of *thought,*—namely, that it is motion." It is an inevitable consequence of analogy that its figurative mode be superseded by a literal: to describe the movement of mind or will in terms of movements sensually perceived must lead eventually to the possibility that the mind's movement involves a "corporeality of thought." But Coleridge is a poet, not a mechanist, and he is not long at ease with Hartley, once the imaginative appeal of Hartleyan psychology fades to allow an examination by the reason and new emotions. Then, too, there is always in Coleridge's mind, I believe, an influence underlying all his positions, an influence more fundamentally corrective than the intermediary influences along the way: it is an inclination toward an orthodoxy which would justify individuality, relate it to the created world, then both to a transcendent I Am. James Boyer's "wise and sound" response to Coleridge's youthful atheism left an impression considerably more long lasting than the birch rod he administered to drive out Coleridge's devil. He could never go all the way with the Cambridge Platonists, nor with the Necessitarians, nor with the vagueness of the Transcendentalists. If he could say that the Hebrew poets were writers with the power of imagination, in contrast to the Greek poets who wrote with the power of fancy, it was because he was attempting precisely these distinctions. In the Hebrew poets, he says, "Each Thing has a Life of its own, and yet they are all one Life. In God they move and live, and *have* their Being—not had, as the cold system of Newtonian Theology represents—but *have*."

Coleridge is maintaining that the Hebrew poet combines both Matthew Arnold's "spontaneity of consciousness" and "strictness of conscience," which Arnold separated as Hellenistic and Hebraistic. The "corporeality of *thought*" of

1794 has undergone considerable change. There is still motion, but it is the spiritual motion of being in relation to first cause. Nor should we mistake in Coleridge a pantheistic understanding of nature. That is another of the heresies he is careful to withdraw from. "An IDEA," he says, in discussing the secondary Imagination, "in the highest sense of the word cannot be conveyed but by a symbol." And in a real way, living nature is a symbol of the mind of God, but it is not identical.

The contemporary influences upon Coleridge, then, were not so pervasive of his thought as his investigation of them has subsequently led us to suppose. He reminds us that "All great discoveries bear the stamp of the age in which they are made," talking specifically of discoveries in poetry. The discovery that he is bent upon is a way of reconciling new knowledge to an old perspective which he believes abiding and fundamental. Both he and Wordsworth are pressed to find an intellectually tenable accommodation of valid discoveries about the mind and nature to the unity of the soul, to find some tenable accounting for that medieval conception of the soul with its vegetative, animal, and rational modes. Wordsworth seems aware of that old system which E. M. W. Tillyard calls our attention to in his *Elizabethan World Picture.* In "Tintern Abbey," for instance, memory feeds sweet sensations "Felt in the blood,...along the *heart;* and passing even into my purer *mind.*" Tillyard turns Sir John Davies's *Orchestra* to impressive account in revealing the Renaissance indebtedness to the Middle Ages. But Coleridge before him turns Davies's philosophical justification of the soul's existence, its unity and immortality, directly to bear upon his definition of the imagination. That Davies was impressive to him, particularly through this philosophical poem, is witnessed by Coleridge's quotations and references to him. That medieval chain of being, with the order and harmony so much sought by Coleridge and embodied in Davies's cosmic dance, is rich with those correspondences which bound outer and inner, the macrocosm and microcosm. Empiricism was rapidly claiming the everyday world of nature for its own, under the generous auspices of Hobbes, Newton, Locke. The senses had been reduced to subjective apprehension of matter in motion, with the mind an accidental medium—graph paper recording that motion. Coleridge set about rescuing mind from such enslavement to the materialist universe. In the light of modern science and philosophy, how reconcile once more mind to the universe, as it had been reconciled by the scholastics? Moral consciousness is more, Coleridge believes, than the net effect of mind as compendium of sensation. It is no accident that Coleridge turns to the most didactic of the Elizabethans and to his most didactic poem worthy the title "poem."

Sir John Davies lacks, in the quatrains of his *Nosce Teipsum,* the adaptable art of Pope's couplets, though he shares with him an ability to make rhetorical and metrical form coincide. We read Pope's *Essay on Man;* we encounter the title of Davies's poem in footnotes. But it was of more considerable importance to Coleridge than to us, and consequently of more importance to us than we might at first suppose. To Coleridge, Pope's verse is prose thought too ineffectively translated by meter and artificial diction. It is not poetry, but something more nearly derived from "the custom of writing Latin verse, and the importance attached to these experiences in [the] public schools" but added to the bad influence of the eighteenth-century poet. Even Wordsworth did not escape that influence, as *Descriptive Sketches* has been shown to demonstrate. Relatively late (in 1815) Coleridge writes Wordsworth praise for having escaped that influence, for having taken "the human race in the concrete" to explode "the absurd notion of Pope's 'Essay on Man,' Darwin, and all the countless believers even (strange to say) among Christians of man's having progressed from an ourang-outang state . . . to have affirmed a Fall in some sense, as a fact, the possibility of which cannot be understood apart from the the nature of the will." Pope sounds too much like an irritated, almost cynical, Polonius for Coleridge, as Erasmus Darwin's evolutionary ideas were too narrow a concept to explain man. Long before the 1815 letter, Coleridge had gone behind the eighteenth century, back to Davies for substance, to Shakespeare for passion.

Nosce Teipsum argues for an essential unity of the soul such as Eliot felt himself struggling to reject in "Tradition and the Individual Talent." It is an intermediary argument between formal scholastic order and harmony and Coleridge's revised version of it. Through it one gains a clue to that movement of mind which materialism cannot explain, but which is a progressive movement larger than a Platonic recovery of a prior state. (There is too little sense of growth, of becoming, in Platonic epistemology to be satisfactory.) Coleridge then moves closer to Aristotle and Aquinas than to Plato and Saint Augustine in this respect. The false alternative to Platonism in the intellectual milieu—Hobbes, Locke, Newton—is rejected. As Coleridge says in a letter: "Newton was a mere materialist—Mind in his system is always passive—a lazy *looker-on* on an external World. If the mind be not *passive,* if it be indeed made in God's Image, and that, too, in the sublimest sense—the Image of the Creator—there is ground for suspicion, that any system built on the passiveness of the mind must be false as a system." There is implied a rejection of Platonism's turning away from the world of nature, from the body and its senses, as well as the explicit rejection of the materialist position.

If we read Davies's poem, we discover that there is more than a passing likeness between his "Wit" and "Fantasy" and Coleridge's "Imagination"; between his "Will" and Coleridge's "conscious will." The soul, with the aid of its "Intellectual Powers" (the title of a section treating wit and will), aspires to eternity "with the motions of both Wit and Will." The process involves that inward sense of "absent things," the memory, which receives responses of the senses to the contemporaneous world, and transmits both the impression of present things and of absent things to a "higher region" where Fantasy, "near handmaid to the mind," reconciles them by compounding and comparing. In its powers Davies's Fantasy bears resemblance to Coleridge's secondary Imagination which "dissolves, diffuses, dissipates, in order to recreate," as we see in "Apprehension: Fantasy: Memory." There Fantasy

> Sits and beholds, and doth discern them all:
> Compounds in one thing divers in their kind;
> Compares the black and white, the great and small.

The Fantasy also makes preliminary value judgment, deciding the bad, the good, the neutral. And in a passage particularly suggesting that Davies's is a part of Coleridge's conscious present, we learn that Fantasy, this "busy power"

> is working day and night;
> For when the outward senses rest do take,
> A thousand dreams, fantastical and light,
> With fluttering wings do keep her still awake.

Davies's concerns are close to the concerns in Wordsworth's "Tintern Abbey" and in Coleridge's "Ancient Mariner: A Poet's Reverie," to the concerns both of the "meditative and feeling mind" of the one and "the dramatic truth of such emotions, as would naturally accompany such supernatural situations" of the other. More particularly one may notice an analogy between Fantasy's presiding over the active "Apprehension" and the passive "Memory" in Sir John Davies, and in Coleridge the Imagination's presiding over two powers, "active and passive," at work in the mind. Those two powers are combined in their operations, but "this is not possible without an intermediate faculty, which is at once both active and passive. (In philosophical language, we must denominate this intermediate faculty in all its degrees and determinations, the IMAGINATION.)" There is a danger that the Fantasy may disengage wit from its proper office of reconciling disparities. (We may keep in mind that Coleridge, subsequent to the passage above, describes imagination as tripartite, yet one: primary Imagination, secondary Imagination, and Fancy.) Fantasy, the mental apprehension of the objects of perception stored in memory and

189

currently supplied by the senses, can become dislocated by frenzy and become too fantastical and light. The soul may become victim to a deluded imagination, as for instance in the Greek poets Coleridge opposes to the Hebrew. In such circumstances, it becomes, in Coleridge's term, Fancy, "a mode of Memory emancipated from the order of time and space," so that its "fixities and certainties" (shared with the secondary Imagination) can be but dead excisions of a living creation.

We may notice in summary two excerpts from Sir John Davies's long explication of the proper way whereby the soul may know itself. The first describes the healthy state of the imagination, the second its unhealthy state, corresponding to Coleridge's description of secondary Imagination and Fancy. The first from "Intellectual Memory":

> The quickening power [vegetative soul] would be,
> and so would rest;
> The sense would not be only, but be well;
> But Wit's ambition longeth to be best,
> For it desires in endless bliss to dwell.
> Yet these three powers are not three souls, but one,
> As one and two are both contain'd in three,
> Three being one number by itself alone;
> A shadow of the blessed Trinity.

Davies's mind is Coleridge's "Image of the *Creator*." One need only look into J. Robert Barth's recent *Coleridge and Christian Doctrine* to see what a heavy concern Coleridge, too, has with the doctrine of the Trinity, to see how intimately that concern is related to his understanding of the creative mind, throughout his intellectual development, as a "shadow of the blessed Trinity."

Wit, common sense (to which we compare Coleridge's "*good sense*"), may "show false forms."

> . . . if a frenzy do possess the brain,
> It so disturbs and blots the forms of things
> As Fantasy proves altogether vain,
> And to the Wit no true relation brings.

Then doth the Wit, admitting all for true,
Build fond conclusions on those idle grounds;
Then doth it fly the good, and ill pursue,
Believing all that this false spy propounds.

These defects in the Senses' organs be
Not in the soul or in her working might;
She cannot lose her perfect power to see,
Though mists and clouds do choke her window light.

It is not the natural world, Plato's shadow, which is deceptive; it is the senses themselves, the "five wits," which have escaped the control of wit and will, building "fond conclusions on those idle grounds," Coleridge's "fixities and definites." Davies is saying, as does Coleridge, that forms of the world of sense and memory may become emancipated from the order of time and space.

The inclusive soul, which is organically one and as such an image of its creator, casts its own reality in the form of the organic poem. The good poem reconciles those materials, received "ready made from the law of association," to Memory. Davies's description of that process is the description of the soul's coming to the fullness of its potential wholeness in words which, says Coleridge, as he quotes them, "may with slight alteration be applied, and even more appropriately, to the poetic IMAGINATION." Having quoted the lines he concludes: "GOOD SENSE is the BODY of poetic genius, FANCY its DRAPERY, MOTION its LIFE, and IMAGINATION the SOUL that is everywhere, and in each; and forms all into one graceful and intelligent whole."

We may now dwell somewhat upon Coleridge's secondary Imagination as distinguished from the primary, since it is of importance not only to the creative act of the soul but because it is also the principle mode in the finite mind whereby the finite is reconciled through its creative act to the "eternal act of creation in the infinite I AM." The secondary Imagination as Coleridge defines it in book 13 is close to what Wordsworth means by the imagination in 1815, with this important distinction: Coleridge would have

191

the primary Imagination establish limits to the secondary. Wordsworth admits, in his 1815 "Preface," that the imagination's operation "upon those objects, and processes of creation or of composition" is "governed by certain fixed laws," but he does not pursue the nature of those fixed laws within the finite mind as does Coleridge. What Wordsworth seems most intent upon is a freedom for the imagination that would make valid a capriciousness that one ordinarily associates with fancy. And we may notice that he allows his "Poems of the Fancy" an honorable place in his collected poems. One might add that Wordsworth is immediately concerned with the act of poetic composition while Coleridge is concerned more largely with poetic composition as a concrete center of his metaphysical system. Given Coleridge's distinction, one deduces the creative act of writing poetry, but Coleridge is more concerned with the existence of finite mind in nature than with either.

Coleridge, in distinguishing between the primary and secondary Imagination, is attempting to rescue the poet from the dilemma of his position as creator of that thing, the poem, of which he is not an absolute first cause. It is almost as if he is attempting to rescue a Wordsworth from the dangers of the egotistical sublime, for he recognizes the hubris implicit in humanism which may lead the poet to take the secondary as the primary. It is a mistake which Joyce suspects himself to have made, particularly in *Finnegans Wake*. Joyce, we remember, read Coleridge's distinction with a disturbed concern as to whether he, Joyce, was not after all a writer of fancy rather than imagination. He had in effect ironically presented Stephen's inclination in that direction in the *Portrait*. But by *Finnegans Wake* he has lost that distance between himself and his agents which would allow the question to be ironically present in the work. Thence his fear that he is taken in by, absorbed by, his own devices.

One may shift that early humanist position that "nothing human is alien to me" to read "nothing is alien to me," and by a metamorphosis elevate oneself while obscuring the essential distinction between the human and nonhuman, between the Self and the Other. The hubris of such a seeming elevation makes one initially suppose man equal to the gods. The final effect however, may be to destroy distinctions by the mind, and thereby destroy the distinctiveness of mind itself. The final victim is individuality. The mind is left in a state of uncomfortable awareness: it is aware of its particular existence but is not able to explain or justify it. That is, one becomes an awareness alienated from all else except self-awareness.

Eliot, in his discussion of Coleridge's distinction, misses the profundity of the problem Coleridge is dealing with. He says, "If, as I have already suggested, the difference between imagination and fancy amounts in practice to no more than the difference between good and bad poetry, have we done more than take a turn around Robin Hood's barn?" We have done more, if we consider Coleridge's two imaginations in relation to his Fancy, which Eliot does not do. In faulting Coleridge's definition of Imagination for omitting "memory from the account" of it altogether, while making Fancy a mode of memory emancipated from the order of space and time, Eliot wanders from the center. In point of fact, Coleridge does not omit memory altogether: "ordinary memory" is explicitly juxtaposed to Fancy's moods. Coleridge means that Fancy is an *aberrant* mode of memory in contrast to the "ordinary" memory which the secondary Imagination healthfully operates. The primary Imagination is "a repetition in the finite mind of the eternal act of creation in the infinite I Am." The primary Imagination then, as Coleridge sees it, partakes remotely of the definition of memory such as that advanced by Socrates in accounting for knowledge in the *Phaedo*. But Coleridge does not consider such a passive account consistent with an action of the mind which cannot be simply ascribed to will: the action of becoming which must be larger than predetermined, more novel through its development than recollection of past knowledge allows. Indeed, the primary Imagination is that limit to individual existence which implies the human mind

193

itself to be "the Image of the Creator." The movement of primary Imagination is a true enactment of the eternal, and as such a direct present reminder of the ultimate source of all being, and most particularly of the finite mind itself. It is the constant measure by the unchanged, such as Wordsworth ascribes to "something" deeply interfused in nature. To Coleridge it is a mode of mind against which the secondary Imagination, the specific power of the finite maker of things, the gift of person, measures itself. It measures itself through dissolving, diffusing, dissipating in a movement toward wholeness of understanding, toward becoming right-minded. That is why Coleridge says that the secondary Imagination "struggles to idealize and to unify," through its coexistent aid, the "conscious will."

Having found Coleridge at fault in the most famous part of his definition of imagination and fancy, Eliot goes on to praise him for an almost equally famous passage. It is a passage in which that unity which the secondary Imagination struggles toward is described as process, whose evidence is the poem. The complete context of the description is as follows:

> the balance or reconciliation of opposite or discordant qualities; or sameness, with difference; of the general, with the concrete; the idea, with the image, the individual, with the representative; the sense of novelty and freshness, with old and familiar objects; a more than usual state of emotion, with more than usual order; judgment ever awake and steady self-possession, with enthusiasm and feeling profound or vehement; and while it blends and harmonizes the material and the artificial, still subordinates art to nature; the manner to the matter; and our admiration of the poet to our sympathy with the poetry.

What the poet does, Coleridge says at the beginning of the paragraph in which this passage occurs, is to bring

> the whole soul of man into activity, with the subordination of its faculties to each other according to their relative worth and dignity. He diffuses a tone and spirit of unity, that blends,

and (as it were) *fuses,* each into each, by that synthetical and magic power, to which I would exclusively appropriate the name of Imagination.

This power, "first put in action by the will and understanding" and subsequently under their control, leads to such a reconciliation of opposites as described.

What is being described by Coleridge is his version of the operation of what Eliot calls the "classicist, or adult mind," a mind Eliot praises as "thoroughly realist—without illusions, without daydreams, without hope, without bitterness, and with an abundance of resignation." Both Coleridge and Eliot are talking about the mind's address to reality, Coleridge's discussion made concrete by a concern for the nature and uses of poetry. Their concerns are larger than the creative act which results in the poem. Both are talking ultimately about a perfection of being in which the will and the understanding are in accord with reality. Eliot's version of the passage is, he tells us, "in the form in which Mr. Richards has abbreviated it." And Richards, we may remember, is at pains in his abbreviation to avoid, as he says, "part of the fate which befell Coleridge," so that Richards's account "will be devoid of theological implications." Richards charges Coleridge with that most heinous modern literary sin: he introduces "value considerations" into his criticism. In 1933 Eliot is not yet at ease with value considerations in criticism and poetry, yet it is precisely in this region of discourse that he feels most attracted to Wordsworth and Coleridge. He is in marked sympathy with Coleridge, whom he describes as having gone through a dark night of the soul, as having been haunted by the muse. For Coleridge, in *Dejection, an Ode,* has also experienced April as the cruelest month. Though the word *joy* is the dominant one in his poem, still the emotional import justifies Eliot's remark that (at this point at least) Coleridge "was condemned to know that the little poetry he had written was worth more than all he could do with the rest of his life."

It is very much to Coleridge's point, and cannot be re-moved from his consideration as Richards does without changing Coleridge to someone else, that at the close of that second most famous passage about the reconciliation of opposites by the imagination he makes occasion to quote those three stanzas of Sir John Davies on the soul as it finds itself in the world. Coleridge rejects thought as "real-ity's dark dream" in his moment of dejection, but in that later version of those thoughts, in an emotional mood as-sured by intellect, he affirms Sir John Davies's words on the operation of the soul. "Finally, Good Sense is the Body of poetic genius, Fancy its Drapery, Motion its Life, and Imagination the Soul that is everywhere, and in each; and forms all into one graceful and intelligent whole." Such a peroration recalls once more that poetic genius is in Cole-ridge's view a particular gift in one finite mind, that its exercise is properly toward higher ends than poetry for its own sake, whose immediate purpose even so "must be the communication of truths." In short, to Coleridge poetry and poet are impossible of separation from "theological implica-tions." For the work of art is an image of the movement of its creative mind. Its seemingly static nature, maintained by the abstractions of aesthetic discussion, is but an illusion of motionlessness, of stasis. That is, it may be spoken of as static only so long as we do not engage our mind directly in its enactment. Eliot, in his generous praise of Coleridge and Wordsworth, gives evidence of the truth of his state-ment in 1928 that "intellectual freedom is earlier and easier than complete spiritual freedom," that to "put the senti-ments in order is a later and an immensely difficult task." It requires no less than that complete surrender of the *Quar-tets,* in which one may come at last to see that the words, the poems, did not matter in quite the same way they seemed to matter, that they were steps toward an enlargement of the mind and soul to the harmony and unity of which the good poem is a reflection.

Dante has argued a similar position in the person of Statius on Purgatory Mountain, a figure at once of the poet and of the saved soul. Statius demonstrates and explains to the pilgrim Dante that joyful condition of the classical-Christian soul, in which the will and the understanding are in such accord with reality that, as Statius demonstrates, it rises to the presence of that infinite I AM, the avowed end of the journeying of both Coleridge and Eliot. Another and more general way of saying the idea which underlies this complex concern in Coleridge, through which we may see how high is that concern, is that the finite mind will have accomplished its potential when its harmony and unity are capable of that harmony and unity in its sign, the poem. The accordance of the finite will to the transcendent will, which Statius witnesses for Dante, is the theological summary of Coleridge's argument for an accord between the secondary Imagination and the primary Imagination. It is a summary which Eliot will make in *The Rock,* a year after his argument in praise of Coleridge and Wordsworth, when he describes the creative process from which the poem emerges as a sign of the soul's movement toward its proper end:

> Out of the sea of sound and the life of music,
> Out of the slimy mud of words, out of the sleet and hail of
>   verbal imprecisions,
> Approximate thoughts and feelings, words that have taken the
>   place of thoughts and feelings,
> There springs the perfect order of speech, and the beauty of
>   incantation.

The Wandering Poet

Wordsworth, *The Prelude*

> Hard task, vain hope, to analyse the mind,
> If each most obvious and particular thought, . . .
> . . . in the words of Reason, deeply weighed,
> Hath no beginning.

Eliot, *Burnt Norton*

> Words strain,
> Crack and sometimes break, under the burden,
> Under the tension, slip, slide, perish,
> Decay with imprecision, will not stay in place,
> Will not stay still.

Coleridge is formally addressed by *The Prelude,* and in that address is an acknowledgment of common assumptions as well as differences about the powers of mind in the poet Wordsworth and the philosophical critic Coleridge. The philosophical critic, so adept at making precise distinctions, knows already the weaknesses in science as science is abused. Wordsworth knows that to Coleridge,

> Science appears but what in truth she is,
> Not as our glory and our absolute boast,
> But as succedaneum, and a prop
> To our infirmity. No officious slave
> Art thou of that false secondary power
> By which we multiply distinctions, then
> Deem that our puny boundaries are things
> That we perceive, and not that we have made.

The Prelude is written not so much to Coleridge as to an increasingly skeptical age caught in the very act of distorting perception and exaggerating its power to create, the eternal dangers to poet or scientist.

But Wordsworth keeps discovering, in spite of such resolute statement to Coleridge, that he himself is of a decidedly divided mind. Thus the necessity of a search into the nature of things external to the mind in order to demonstrate to the skeptical mind (his own included) that the search is a valid experience.

> I had an eye
> Which in my strongest workings, evermore
> Was looking for the shades of difference
> As they lie hid in all exterior forms,
> Near or remote, minute or vast, an eye
> Which from stone, a tree, a wither'd leaf,
> To the broad ocean and the azure heavens,
> Spangled with kindred multitudes of stars,
> Could find no surface where its powers might sleep,
> Which spake perpetual logic to my soul.

The pursuit in this passage of *The Prelude* is of a distinctiveness in things; it expresses that attempt to see into the life of things without the "consciousness" being forced to "subdue" those things. But it is an attempt which fails. A Hopkins can approach the "inscape" of things; Wordsworth's poetry presents one inscape only—that of his own mind. This sad conclusion, to which he returns again and again, is very discouraging to him, for what it means is that he cannot be assured of the similitude of his own consciousness to that of other men. There must be a dissimilitude for separate consciousnesses. If separate consciousnesses exist, poetry itself is valid beyond the personal. So Wordsworth looks into things, attempting to establish dissimilitude. Wallace Stevens, long after Wordsworth, will continue Wordsworth's argument for *correspondence,* against identity, having the advantage of the quest for a valid modern poetry begun by Wordsworth, extended by Baudelaire, and aided by the new "sciences" of the mind. Stevens will insist on a likeness in unlike things which gives rise to a third thing, none of the three things being identical, therefore each being distinguishable in that supreme fiction which is poetry. But Wordsworth isn't sure. The "shades of difference" have a discomforting way of dissolving within the consciousness, thus destroying any assurance that they are aspects of those universal principles of the empirical naturalists, who cannot quite be ignored. Such a tendency to dissolution in the mind makes difficult as well the acceptance of that older orthodoxy of individuality, which the medieval thinkers had established as perceptible to the mind in their answering Plato's dilemma of the Many and the One. Still Wordsworth, though he cannot solve the problem, continues the struggle:

> I looked for universal things; perused
> The common countenance of earth and sky. . . .
> Or turning the mind in upon herself
> Pored, watched, expected, listened.

Always there is the turning back of the mind upon itself, and the attempt to make valid that condition of the mind as if it were a universal. The constant threat to his poetry is that he will be reduced to a valid audience of one—himself. That is why he seizes upon the moral intent of poetry and attempts so doggedly to make it a part of the empirical intent of revealing the poet's mind to the world. For to him the reaction of the self to the world must be valid in two respects. First, the recollection of the self's encounter with the world must be presented in terms of a cause-effect relationship that is empirically acceptable and establishes the validity of the self. Hence that aspect of *The Prelude* as case history. Second, it must be valid in that the established state of mind, in relation to the external world, must be harmonious with that world, not rebellious; thus a proper moral relationship of the consciousness to the rest of existence will have been established. We see the two aspects of his intention brought together in his statement to Lady Beaumont: "There is scarcely one of my poems which does not aim to direct attention to some moral sentiment, or to some general principle, or law of thought, or of our intellectual consititution."

The center of that "moral sentiment" in his private history is the period of his uncomplicated relationship to the external world, before the disillusionment with the French Revolution. The intrusion of thought itself, and finally of that rebellious "plastic power," the imagination, with its insistence on a primacy over fancy, led to the withdrawal into the self. Love as we have seen it set forth in Dante's *New Life* begins in the heart of the Pilgrim, springs free of the Pilgrim as a separate existence, and finally melts into the being which is Beatrice. But Wordsworth, a child of the new age, having little firm anchor in the thought of the medieval world which established Love as external to the self in its ultimate aspect, nevertheless *felt* that it must be external. As an act of faith, Wordsworth affirmed Love as external. Love comes to dwell within the heart, making the heart love itself. But Wordsworth says it comes out of Nature, whom he addresses in *The Prelude:*

> 'Twas thy power
> That rais'd the first complacency in me,
> And noticeable kindliness of heart
> Love human to the Creature in himself
> As he appear'd, a stranger in my path,
> Before my eye a Brother of this world.

To see an old man coming down out of the mountains, to encounter a beggar woman, to approach any seemingly separate person was to involve Wordsworth in a projection of that "Creature in himself" upon that figure; or more accurately to draw that figure into the self as an *identity* (in Wallace Stevens's sense of the term) with the self. That is, the separate individual was destroyed and only the self of the poet remained. However high the intention, however moving the psychological relationship, one still has finally a pattern of self-love. The causes of this internalizing were not all from high intention. To some extent, surely, what Wordsworth was doing was burying personal failures. His relationship to John Wordsworth and to Annette Vallon allow a burdening of himself with their misery as a substitute for action on their behalf. Out of self-torture no doubt comes his treatment of the woman in "The Thorn" and "Ruth" and the "Forsaken Indian Woman" as well as the more overt grief over John's death. Wordsworth knew the danger to his poetry, knew that to maintain such a relation to the world was in effect to live at "distance from the kind," and we must recognize that aspect of his poetry. The minute attention he directs to his self-awareness, or his insistence upon it as a joyful awareness, should not obscure from us the fact that his fascination is touched by a sharp disappointment with the self.

In pursuing that question of where he might once more find "faith in the marvellous things which then I felt?" he is attempting to discover wherein he failed. The impression that *The Prelude* as a whole leaves with one is of the failure of a mind whose powers have come to less than it thinks they should have. As in that earlier stage of the poet's development, when all nature seemed a prospect of the mind that beheld it, all stages of the poet's mind in *The Prelude* seem a prospect of the reflecting mind—the present awareness of the poet. There is the conscious attempt to make these stages so. Now *The Prelude*, in its attempt at an exploration of consciousness, bears close comparison to Dante's *New Life*, as I have suggested. But the comparison must look closely to a difference in that consciousness in Wordsworth within which past states are assembled for examination, as if they too were as particular as "natural form," having in themselves a "moral life." Dante speaks from a point of assurance that the stages have been a growth toward "Beatrice in glory." He remembers her "in the order of time's passing" (40). But, again, it is a remembrance that transcends time to such a degree that the consciousness of Dante's poem can look with particular scorn upon failures in the Pilgrim's progress, failures which were the result of a wavering from the true way. For instance, the Pilgrim in Dante mistook as intimations of immortality the sensual appeal of the "lady of the window." Wordsworth cannot see Annette so, and lacking power of transforming Annette into a Beatrice or of accepting her as a distraction, he turns with some desperation to Dorothy, the child of simplicity, who accentuates the memory of that old freedom of his own mind before it became troubled by Annette or the French cause itself. Coleridge attempted to help Wordsworth at this point of his distress. But the "lady of the window" or Annette Vallon are better suited to the poetic pursuit of the relation of the senses to thought than the teachings of David Hartley: Hartley's sensationalism could give Wordsworth no transcendent prospect from which to view his own mind's growth. He does make an attempt at a stasis of mind; he tries to establish a steady prospect upon the past, but it proves to be a false attempt to recover that old condition which Dorothy is celebrated as possessing in "Tintern Abbey." Where Dante asks and answers the question "How did I get to this point?" by defining the point, Wordsworth asks the question without being confident of having arrived at any point that is at all tenable. I have at the moment little concern for whether Dante's vision was true. I believe it to embody truth, but the point here has rather to do with the degree of control each poet is able to exercise in his art to give form to it.

So Wordsworth's version of *The New Life*—*The Prelude*—turns out to be no collection of metaphysical poems annotated by the poet in regard to the order of their composition so that the ordering establishes a journey of the mind. Even Wordsworth's notes to the poems, dictated at the close of his life, still have that same quality of recollection of circumstances which are not yet fully assimilated. Dante's recollection is not complete until he has, in addition to having given the history of the poem as related to the poet's life, indicated the art object that results, and given attention to the process of composition—concerns that have the effect of cutting the poem loose from the life of the poet. The next-to-last poem of *The New Life* contains in its commentary an indication of what I mean. It is an anniversary poem, a recollection of Beatrice's new power in him, and the poet looks out on pilgrims passing through the city to Rome, pilgrims who have not found their true country but are seeking it, in contrast to the poet himself. It is a situation, clearly, in which the poet is engaged both as Poet and as Pilgrim on a very high plane. Having repented of his deviation from the true journey by dallying with the lady of the window, Dante has now put from him such self-concern as his own pleasure with that lady. In consequence of these circumstances, he is in a position that presents a relationship to the pilgrims that allows in a poem complexities in which a John Donne would have delighted—though it is Dante who most convincingly unites the "Jack" of Donne's love poems and the sobered, intense priest of the *Meditations* and *Sermons*. Dante's pilgrims are on their way to see the handkerchief of Saint Veronica. As Saint Veronica is to the pilgrims in respect to Christ, Dante the Poet is to the Pilgrim in respect to Beatrice. Saint Veronica looks down upon such pilgrims from Heaven as Dante literally does from his window above the street. The whole course of Dante's pilgrimage has been toward an association of Beatrice with Christ. She is the cause of Dante's right-mindedness, and we do not forget that she descended into Hell to raise him up in the *Divine Comedy*. The transubstantiation of earthly love into Heavenly love is now complete in *The New Life.* Dante says of the incident: "These pilgrims were walking, it seemed to me, in a very reflective manner. Thinking of them, I said to myself: 'These pilgrims seem to come from a distant country, and I do not believe they could have heard of that lady.' " The process of his reflections continues until "I said to myself: 'If I could detain them a little I would make them weep as well before they left this city, because I would say words which would make any weep who heard them.' " I have not exhausted the relationships of the principals in this event which provides the materials for the twenty-fourth sonnet of *The New Life,* relationships extending from Christ down to the pilgrims in the streets of Florence. The whole section (41) is more complicated I suspect and more commanding of the mind than Donne's "Canonization." What I have prepared for is to point out that, the complications aside, Dante returns us to the mind's relation to art. The deliberate manipulation of the materials is such that the poem pretends to do what the man Dante did not in fact do: "To make it even more appealing, I decided to write [the sonnet] as though I had spoken to them [the pilgrims]." Dante always comes to the necessity of "making it more appealing." That is, he always comes to the necessities of art as being of a separate order of concern. He can do so because he has done what the poet must; he has come to terms with history, whether his own personal history or the broad span that lies behind his immediate culture. It is precisely this failure that I find in Wordsworth, who continued too much puzzled over the nature of the numinous he detected in the external world and in his own mind to control it effectively in art. Dante isn't puzzled about that light in Beatrice's face to the point that he cannot order his puzzlement. (His *New Life* as a whole, we might say, is Beatrice's Veronica.) In the period following Wordsworth's return from the two-year stay in France, he became concerned with a history larger than the personal, but he does not rise above it, or rather he is not able to put history in a perspective relative to that light he senses to be dwelling in

>   the light of setting suns,
>   And the round ocean and the living air,
>   And the blue sky, and in the mind of man.

His difficulty in large part was that he could not see his own relation to the past or to the external world with a steady enough conviction that his seeing was more than illusion. That is to say, he could not rest assured of the validity of his own awareness, so that metaphor, no matter how strongly he insisted upon its indebtedness to the imagination's power or a sign of transcendent reality, seemed tainted by the ghostly presence of illusion.

Wordsworth without History

THE FASCINATION OF YEWS

Wordsworth, *The Excursion*

> . . . through improvidence or want of love
> For ancient worth and honourable things,
> The spear and shield are vanished, which the Knight
> Hung in his rustic hall.

Eliot, *Little Gidding*

> A people without history
> Is not redeemed from time, for history is a pattern
> Of timeless moments. . . .
> History is now and England.

If Wordsworth, in that period ending with the publication of *Lyrical Ballads,* could not satisfactorily unravel the mind's strange world, he could for relief turn back toward his childhood when the world seemed less complicated to the mind. He and Dorothy moved to Grasmere, and he began to look more closely into a history removed from his personal encounters with man at Cambridge and on the continent. Grasmere in Wordsworth's day, as he recalls it in the prose note to *The Excursion,* was still sufficiently removed from that world whose center was London so that if it were necessary for a man to get away from civil troubles, he could go there and be reasonably safe. Occasionally, there were even bands of outlaws among the hills. It was a region where independence and self-sufficiency were still respected. Yet it was not given over to chaos as both London and France seemed to be. Indeed here was a region with a history that gave some measure of orderliness to that independence which was a heritage from the Middle Ages. Such indeed had been the reasons for Wordsworth's choosing that country as background for *The Borderers,* as he tells us.

The Tudors, one must recall, heralded a breakthrough into a secular society which became increasingly devoted to the world that was too much with Wordsworth's England. And in the interest of political expediency, they not only tolerated but encouraged the fiercely traditionalist spirit of the north, that spirit Shakespeare has captured for us in the persons of Hotspur and Westmoreland. For Tudor expediency was clever enough to recognize that, while the fierce spirit of a Hotspur was to some extent a danger to London's peace of mind, it nevertheless made the northern lords and their vassals an admirable buffer to the "termagant Scot," allowing London to expand its empire and develop its new middle-class mind. In the north of England the idealistic conception of hierarchy continued to function, far longer than in London, Wordsworth himself pointing out the continuance of the institution of primogeniture as an instance. While the nobility, in whom the ideal hierarchy found its center, declined rapidly elsewhere, its decline was

somewhat slower in those counties about Grasmere. I do
not believe that Wordsworth was aware of the details of
the political and economic causes of the shift of power from
the nobility to the middle class, the shift which Prof. Lawrence Stone has treated exhaustively in *The Crisis of the
Aristocracy, 1558–1640.* Wordsworth's uncomplicated praise
of Milton suggests that he did not. But there can be no
doubt that he was uneasily aware of its effects. The truth
is that his awareness is that of a mind long accustomed
to a lyrical relation of itself to its immediate world, an
awareness suddenly entangled with the larger world that
had, of course, been about him all his life. The separate,
lyrical awareness is in the heart of "Tintern Abbey" in spite
of its attempted enlargement toward echoing the still, sad
music of humanity. His flowing awareness yet clings close
to its riverbed as if a stay from the implications of beginning
and end, the implication that inland murmurs terminate in
the large anonymous ocean. Much later Wordsworth will
have his Solitary revisit a stream of his youth and appreciate
the murmurs of inland waters as echoing still the sad music
of his own humanity. But the music will be a more desperate
one, including a larger and more particular history of man
in nature than implied by the earlier, more innocent revisiting of the Wye. For the Wye of "Tintern Abbey" rather
limits its correspondences to the course of that particular
awareness reflecting upon it, a mind which associates the
literal murmuring of inland waters with recollections of
its own past. The movement implied separates that awareness from the history of the kind, until almost with shock
it turns to address its kindred spirit, Dorothy. One recalls
Spenser's Thames, Pope's Thames, Eliot's. Each of these
engages the history of a people and, taken chronologically,
in an increasingly inclusive scope. From Spenser's early optimism, at a period when London was anticipating itself the
future capital of creation, to Pope's orderly assurance of
that accomplishment, to Eliot's reflections upon the failure
of that national optimist, which he casts through allusions
to Spenser and Pope in *The Waste Land.*

Not the river, Thames or Wye, was to be Wordsworth's metaphor for the enlargement of historical awareness, but the yew. In 1795 Wordsworth writes from the "circling bower" of a lonely yew, which speaks of one man who was no "common soul." He writes of the prospect of nature as seen by that man withdrawn from humanity, sympathizing with the man but condemning his withdrawal. But the context within which this early version of the Solitary is rebuked leads to the assurance that

> True dignity abides with him alone
> Who, in the silent hour of inward thought,
> Can still suspect, and still revere himself,
> In lowliness of heart.

The separation from the kind is more nearly a withdrawal from nature itself in this poem in which humanity and prospects of nature are hardly distinguished. The yew tree is a place of "gloomy boughs" from which the solitary man cannot escape beyond remembrance of his own history.

That the Solitary of *The Excursion* is in some respects William Wordsworth is suggested by a much more impressive poem written in 1803, a poem which also deals with yew trees' gloomy boughs, but with a skill of suggestiveness not general in Wordsworth. "Yew-Trees" has to do with history, England's and that of the race. One first sees a yew "single, in the midst / Of its own darkness." The poet establishes its continuity through English history, moving from the present moment back into that period of England's emergence as a nation when the yew was

> Not loth to furnish weapons for the bands
> Of Umfraville or Percy ere they marched
> To Scotland's heaths; or those that crossed the sea
> And drew their sounding bows at Azincour,
> Perhaps at earlier Crecy, or Poictiers.

But there are more impressive yews, specifically those "fraternal Four of Borrowdale," which incorporate a history larger, more ancient, more inclusive than the lone yew first observed. Together they form a chapel within which man moves beyond time and place. With an orchestration of sound in a heavily Latinized diction, richly suggestive through ambiguities, the poem rises to its conclusion.

> Huge trunks! and each particular trunk a growth
> Of intertwisted fibers serpentine
> Up-coiling, and inveterately convolved;
> Nor uninformed with Phantasy, and looks
> That threaten the profane;—a pillared shade,
> Upon whose grassless floor of red-brown hue,
> By sheddings from the pining umbrage tinged
> Perennially—beneath whose sabled roof
> Of boughs, as if for the festal purpose decked
> With unrejoicing berries—ghostly Shapes
> May meet at noontide; Fear and trembling Hope,
> Silence and Foresight; Death the Skeleton
> And Time the Shadow;—there to celebrate,
> As in a natural temple scattered o'er
> With altars undisturbed of mossy stone,
> United worship; or in mute repose
> To lie, and listen to the mountain flood
> Murmuring from Glaramara's inmost caves.

It is a fitting tribute to Milton's powers, but it largely escapes those bad influences upon subsequent poets which Eliot charged Milton with exercising. It does so because there is a very real trembling upon the threshold of vision here. Wordsworth, because of an emotional proximity to vision, manages to rescue the commonplace metaphor. The lone yew as it attaches to history, presented in the early lines, is hardly impressive. The "fraternal Four," however, suggesting such an immediate surface likeness to "a natural temple" somehow don't allow the easy pleasures of literary metaphor. There is the pillared shade, the floor, the roof,

211

altar stones—such correspondences to the temple in this natural phenomenon as to tempt the fancy. But working against
that easy playfulness with language is a very disturbing
quality. The trunks are growths of "intertwisted fibers ser-
pentine / Up-coiling." Is it temple to the God of Light
or to darker powers? And as it threatens the profane, which
worship is profane? Here is an object in nature, subject
to nature's laws, which seemingly escapes those laws, being
more durable than marble or gilded monuments. Its floor
is paved with dead needles, the intercaused shadows of the
four holding back the sun and so the grass. A phrase like
"Pining umbrage" is such as one might expect to meet with
in a metaphysical poet, as also the paradoxical decoration
of this temple to the unknown in nature—the boughs
"decked / With *unrejoicing* berries." How strangely awful,
this temple in nature, but perhaps not of nature, built
through centuries out of English soil, but with a tacit acceptance through forebearance by many generations of
Englishmen.

For the grove is a constant upon which settles the reflections of succeeding generations of the sons of man, each
in the midst of his own inconstancies and decay. Thus it
is that one in this moment of reflection upon that temple
may meet at noontide those "ghostly Shapes" that haunt
the mind under the shadow of time: Fear, trembling Hope,
Silence, Foresight, Death the Skeleton, Time the Shadow.
These brought together by reflection upon the continuing
yews, so ambiguous in their import; brought together either
by the mind's "United worship" or in the noontide moment
of "mute repose" while the sun stands still and time itself
seems overcome. The murmuring waters, an image to which
Wordsworth is repeatedly drawn in his poetry, is surely
much more suggestive than those "inland murmurs" of
"Tintern Abbey," though it is as difficult still to make their
language specific. What seems to me remarkable is a tone
in the poem, an enthusiasm of expectation, a trembling upon
vision, without knowing whether it will be beatific or
demonic. Metaphor which is literary seems suddenly to trans-

form itself toward an insight, tempting the poet so far as personification, but not so far as allegory. For allegory requires a penetration of emotional intimations by the intellect.

To put it another way, the long struggle we see in Eliot, as for instance in his own attention to the English yew, leads finally to his seeing beyond the yew in the garden. Eliot walks long between the violet and the violet, between "the various ranks of green," before he sees that

> silent sister veiled in white and blue
> Between the yews, behind the garden god,
>
> Whose flute is breathless.

In "Yew-Trees" it is as if Wordsworth has also returned to a place from which he started, to almost see it for the first time. That feeling about the experience and about the poem lingers in him. It leads him very wisely to strike out a banal conclusion, eight lines in which he instructs the reader upon piety in the presence of the yews as historical monument, quite undercutting the qualities of the concluding lines as we have them. Later, in a note on the poem, he is still fascinated. He describes an even more ancient yew fallen in decay, one so huge that its trunk is "like the entrance of a cave." It must be, he concludes, "as old as the Christian era." What is most striking to him, however, is "the number of shrubs and young plants . . . which had found a bed upon the decayed trunk and grew to no inconsiderable height." In the poem and in the note, Wordsworth exhibits an interest larger than that which

> the Historian's pen so much delights
> To blazen—power and energy detached
> From moral purpose.

But Wordsworth's 1803 version of the yew tree, to which we compare Eliot's more subtly allusive use in *Ash Wednesday*, is relatively late. Before he comes to it he at-

213

tempts to recall, in *The Prelude,* the early state of innocence as he enjoyed it upon coming down to Cambridge:

> Unknown, unthought of, yet I was most rich;
> I had a world about me; 'twas my own,
> I made it; for it only liv'd to me.
> And to the God who look'd into my mind.

The effect of the larger world's intrusion upon this private world was not to make him the thorough recluse he sympathizes with in the earlier "Lines Left upon a Seat in a Yewtree," that man of genius who, similarly baffled by the outside world, "turned himself away / And with the food of pride sustained his soul / In solitude." Instead of such a complete withdrawal into himself and to the private pleasures of nature, Wordsworth turned his desires and interest toward becoming a bard. Whether under any circumstance Wordsworth could have been an effective bard, an English Laureate whose station was of immediate consequence beyond a hollow title, is highly doubtful. The times little allowed a singer the position of that man who sang *Roland* to William's men at the Battle of Hastings. Besides which, Wordsworth's own gift, that talent which he strove mightily not to hide, made him more a Lucretius of the mind's workings than a Homer or Virgil. But the fact remains that he did set out to be a bard anyway, and in doing so he became deeply involved in that problem chief among those confronting the English poet since Shakespeare: the relation of the poet to his audience. That concern is the principal cause of most of the poetry of *Lyrical Ballads* and of the "Preface" to that volume and its "Appendix" and other prose writing, including those late notes intended for the collected poems.

In the interest of clarifying the somewhat confused desire in Wordsworth to be bard to England, it seems appropriate to suggest a modification of argument in James A. W. Heffernan's impressive study of the development of Wordsworth's mind, *Wordsworth's Theory of Poetry: The Trans-*

forming Imagination (1969). It is a correction necessary to a rather general confusion about Wordsworth's audience as he envisioned it in relation to the materials of poetry he early elects to treat. "Gradually," Professor Heffernan says, "Wordsworth's fondness for the rustic reader disappears, and he acquired in its place a preference for the student of poetry." But Wordsworth wrote *of* Goody Blake and the leech-gatherer, not *for* them. With somewhat nervous expectation, he looked to the equivalent of our own university quarterlies to see how his poems would be received, from the beginning. If one emphasizes as a primary thrust in the "Preface" of 1800 and the first books of *The Prelude* a denunciation of art in favor of elementary feelings, one may overlook the real object of Wordsworth's attention, namely a hostile, educated audience which has already accepted the separation of both poet and poetry from society. His secondary emphasis, or rather complaint, is that sensibility has been dissociated. It is secondary only relatively and is indeed a part of the first concern. Wordsworth is arguing for a hearing and attempting to educate disaffected or indifferent intellectuals whom as an idealist he believes responsible for the cultural decline that is larger than a decay of poetic sensibility. Later he does shift emphasis, as Professor Heffernan shows, to the virtues of meditative emotion; but the shift is in part because of a growing reception of his poetry. Analogously, Eliot's winning of a twentieth-century audience comparable to the one Wordsworth sought made possible his *Four Quartets,* Eliot's vehicle of meditative emotion.

From the beginning, however confusing or confused Wordsworth may be on some points, he does not confuse the purity of the rustic life as it appears to him and the culturally decayed sensibility he addresses or the restored sensibility he argues necessary to appreciate its celebration in elevated speech. Even John Wordsworth was aware of the distinction, writing Mary Hutchinson in praise of Wordsworth's poetry at the same time he lamented its not selling so that he and Wordsworth might invest the proceeds in commercial speculation in the Far East. "The fact is," John wrote in 1801, "there are not a great many that will be pleased with the poems but those that are pleased will be pleased in a high degree." He adds emphatically, "they *will be people of sense* this will have weight—& people who neither understand or wish to understand will buy & praise them." A little later, again to Mary (whom it must have seemed to him in retrospect he wooed for brother William), "I do not think that Wms poetry will become popular for some time to come it certainly does not suit the present taste."

Wordsworth's famous "Preface" is an attempt at both moral and aesthetic suasion, assuming a relationship between the two. It is directed against and for what he would soon himself characterize (in a letter to John Wilson, 1802), as an audience of "false refinements, wayward and artificial desires, false criticisms, effeminate habits of thinking and feeling." These are the signs of a decayed sensibility in those representatives of altar, sword, and pen whom Wordsworth denounces so forcefully in the sonnets, his formal bid for position of authority as bard to England. Wordsworth's position is nevertheless confused. His audience requires a severe address to move it out of its bad taste, sloth, indifference to old values. He is forced to sing to an audience, not for it, having at the same time to correct its sensibilities. His approach is not so subtly efficient as Eliot's was to be. For Eliot's stratagem of critical essays, seemingly directed away from immediate concern with his own poetry, prepared us to read his poetry. Eliot can say later, the task largely behind him, that his criticism is a by-product of his poetry. But Wordsworth, like Pound, takes a more direct approach, even if he is not prepared to assert as categorically as Pound, "Quite simply: I want a new civilization."

Another source of cloudiness in Wordsworth's position is his concern with the process of creation of the poem, a concern so modern as to support magazines and journals devoted to it in our day. That concern somewhat confused his address to an audience. The poet's "habit of meditation" prepared the mind to engage the event—the composition of the poem—in such a way as to insure (hopefully) a control where otherwise there might simply be an automatic flow of emotion in easy words. What is implied in this process is a deliberate intention to art, in which the concentration is on the made thing, the poem. (Wordsworth in his concern is not so far removed from the New Critic as we are accustomed to suppose.) While a large part of Wordsworth's concern remains the wooing of an audience with a rhetorical address intended to persuade it of the virtues of aesthetic language, he does not content himself with an address to a "fit" audience. Thus at points in his discourse he is aware of the attention of such minds as Coleridge's, at others of the attention of semisophisticated, even semiliterate pretenders to cultural authority. The clouded nature of his audience must lead him inevitably to that bitter complaint against his readers, expressed in a letter in 1807: he writes of "the Public" who "either are, or are striving to make themselves, people of consideration in society." What is suggested is not so much a change in attitude or ends on Wordsworth's part so much as a fuller understanding of how difficult a task it was to be an English bard at the turn of the nineteenth century. John Wordsworth, as tedious and unlettered as his letters appear, nevertheless clarified the problem and expectation. For *Lyrical Ballads* was and continues to be an appeal "to people of sense" who can distinguish achievements within the larger context of its failures, people capable of sympathies larger than the aesthetic, who recognize a heroic attempt on Wordsworth's part in the midst of his own threatening wasteland.

The problem of the modern poet as bard is a peculiar one perhaps in Wordsworth's day and since. In the literature of English history through Shakespeare, as it survives to us and to Wordsworth, the center is primarily upon the agents who are members of the nobility; secondly one finds the serf treated. Seldom does one find in imaginative literature a presentation of agents from that middle section of the medieval social structure who emerged as the dominant force of society by Shakespeare's day. The *chanson de geste* such as *The Song of Roland* is concerned with the highest of the high. The folk ballad, which was such an influence on Wordsworth, treats the noble and, less often, the serf. It is the "Elfin Knight" or "Lord Randal" or "Lady Isabel" that predominates in Child's collection. Even Robin Hood, when he has worked himself to some eminence, has a case made for him as having sprung from the nobility. Chaucer is remarkable in the *Canterbury Tales* in that he fills in the interior of that social spectrum that stretches from the Knight to the Plowman, which two characters it is well to note are among the few fully "worthy" pilgrims we meet. And it is also Chaucer who calls our attention to the change whereby the journey is becoming its own end rather than a means to the soul's good health, a race without a goal.

It was with the background of the medieval social structure and (most important) its chivalric code that the ballad singer or the bard sang human nature, fallen, but hopeful of restoration. Wordsworth was, however, in no position to sing to England as either the bard or the ballad maker insofar as those singers' traditional audience is concerned. His awareness of handicaps leads him at first to that form one notices as regularly emerging in a predominantly middle-class society—the drama. *The Borderers* was attempted, he tells us, in order "to preserve in my distinct remembrance [and this purpose indicates the bard in him] what I had observed of tradition in character, and the reflections I had been led to make during the time I was a witness of the changes through which the French Revolution passed." Why that border country at the time of Henry III? "As to the scene and period of action, little more was required for my purpose than the absence of established law and government; so that the agents might be at liberty to act on their own impulse." But the choice, we note in reading the play, was such as to allow as a measure of a character's villainy that ideal order that lies behind *The Song of Roland* or *Macbeth*. Wordsworth's Iago is dragged off to his execution as Ganelon is. That old order is one most markedly decayed

at the turning of the nineteenth century because the myth
which had established that order had been abandoned. Given
a different quality of mind, Wordsworth on viewing that
decay might have written a version of *Reflections upon the
French Revolution* on the one hand or *For Lancelot Andrews*
on the other, depending upon whether he centered upon
political or spiritual anarchy. The two concerns are present
but dissipated in *The Excursion*. That he held scant sympathy with the religious dissenter is indicated by the portrait
he draws of such a person in *The Excursion* and by the
words he gives us on the literal source of that character
in his "Preface." The Solitary of *The Excursion* is a version
of his Iago from *The Borderers,* not a man engaged in
active evil, except insofar as he insists upon the complete
corruption of man. The Solitary has as a part of his "quandam position," Wordsworth says, a number of dissenters
encountered in those days when revolution was the center
of Wordsworth's attention.

> The chief of these was, one may now say, a Mr. Faw-
> cett, ... an able and eloquent man.... But his Christianity
> was probably never deeply rooted; and, like many others in
> those times of like showy talents, he had not strength of
> character to withstand the effects of the French Revolution,
> and of the wild and lax opinions which had done so much
> toward producing it, and far more in carrying it forward
> in its extremes.... There were many like him at that time,
> which the world will never be without.

The passage from Wordsworth's introduction to *The Excursion* is very reminiscent of Edmund Burke's excoriating
analysis of such dissenters which is the beginning of his
famous letter of reflection on the French Revolution, and
it is worth remembering that Wordsworth praises Burke
specifically in *The Prelude,* having personally measured the
sordid spectacle of the French Revolution against its principles of disengagement from history.

In *The Excursion* the Poet is accompanied by the Wanderer and they encounter the Solitary and a Priest, the four

engaging in a debate of man's place in the world as illustrated by the experience of each and in particular by the balanced presentation of the human condition argued by Wordsworth's Priest, who serves, along with the Wanderer, as the Poet's Virgil. That deliberation which had led Wordsworth in his first attempt to cast the present against the past in *The Borderers* has given way to a version of man's wandering in the wasteland of the present. But in shifting from the time of Henry III, he does not abandon that world. The Wanderer is a figure of the knight-errant, and the parallel is specifically drawn; the Priest is related to the ancient fathers of the Church in contrast to the dissenters, and with approval. Old modes of society and rituals of the spiritual world are recalled and rescued in esteem. Thereby the effects of decay of the ancient order are pointed to in the modern world, as when the Priest defends the sacraments and the Wanderer gives an account of the effects of the "manufacturing spirit" upon England, "chiefly as it has affected the humbler classes." That spirit has affected those on the land no less than those in the city hovels, as the Wanderer makes clear. He pursues these concerns at tedious length in that education of the Poet as Wanderer in *The Excursion*. Such considerations as these are involved in Wordsworth's concern—heroic concern—for the decay of the language of those "earliest poets" who were immediately engaged in events about which they sang. It is a decay brought about by false poets, disengaged poets who wish merely the name of poet and not the office of bard. But among those false poets is Wordworth as he was in those early attempts at finding himself in nature, those attempts in which he was at "distance from the kind." For the growth of the poet's mind, as he intends to present it, is not finished when *The Prelude* is completed; it is to be continued through the large works which follow.

What one has in those incomplete works then is not the education of the soul toward beatitude as in the *Divine Comedy,* but a continuation of the mind's education toward being a poet. In other words, Wordsworth never finished his *New Life.* The wandering poet never reaches a point from which he may look down upon his wandering and dramatize it. That prose quality of *The Prelude* which seems to me very closely related to those prose passages of *The New Life* in which the circumstances of particular poems are enumerated by Dante, continues into *The Recluse* and *The Excursion,* becoming more pronounced.

There continues in Wordsworth the strong element of naive innocence which, suitable in the lyric poet, dooms larger attempts. Wordsworth could not come to a sufficiently satisfying accommodation of his own history to England's past to allow him a position of address to his time so effective as Eliot's address to his age. Self-disappointment assails him, a sense of futility prompts him once more to prolonged self-analysis, in consequence of which his elegiac address to a busy and indifferent audience prevents that practical effectiveness he largely intends. The audience he would affect, in his desire to change the course of human events, was not the committed traditionalist, nor the peasant whose life and language interested him so heavily; it was rather those men of power, wielding scepter, sword, and pen. He hoped to persuade them to a recovery of ancient virtues; he ultimately succeeded in convincing a Browning, no mean traditionalist himself, that he had sold out "Just for a handful of silver."

Stranger in a Strange Land

WORDSWORTH CIRCA 1802

&Chaucer, *Prologue of the Nun's Priest's Tale*

> Whereas a man may have noon audience,
> Noght helpeth it to tellen his sentence.

&Eliot, *The Waste Land*

> "Speak to me. Why do you never speak. Speak.
>   What are you thinking of? What thinking? What?"

> I think we are in rats' alley
> Where the dead men lost their bones.

As I have suggested, the shock of John Wordsworth's death to William goes much deeper than the surface indications of a betrayal by nature. It reaches into the uneasy and tangled regions of betrayal by human nature and involves the possibility of violation of those bonds of nature and those special bonds of love that mark the significant division of Dante's upper and lower Hell. Wordsworth could not be innocent of the special sacrifice John made on his behalf by engaging the sordid world any more than he could be oblivious of the more spectacular incidents (within the family's knowledge) of the circumstance of his having won Mary Hutchinson as bride the month after visiting Annette and their daughter Caroline at Calais after those years of neglect. As for the betrayal by the forces in the natural world, those "Elegiac Stanzas" to John which focus attention on a painting of Peele Castle beset by storm are not Wordsworth's first expression of something unsettling in nature. In "Tintern Abbey" he says emphatically that "Nature never did betray / The heart that loved her," but he has said in the same poem that nature's joys are accompanied by that sad music whose powers are ample to "chasten and subdue." There is also the famous passage in the first book of *The Prelude* in which the ominous threat of nature is everywhere about the boy Wordsworth in his stolen boat. Furthermore, the disillusionment expressed in "Elegiac Stanzas" and in the "Ode to Duty" is with himself more than with nature, and that as we have seen is an old disappointment. The disappointment is in part for having placed his trust in the French Revolution, but it is also for having been so shocked as a result of the failure of that cause that in consequence he had been tempted to a retreat from mankind into nature to recover. One sees that he does not praise the man he memorializes in "Lines Left upon a Seat in a Yew-tree" for having become embittered with mankind. Nor does he later approve of a similar figure in *The Recluse*. The messengers of that French cause, such as his dissenter in *The Excursion* and Rousseau, proved false. In retreat, Wordsworth felt compelled to make some accounting of that falseness. The revolution had failed to call forth any voice that could command both the heart and the mind. As he looked toward France in puzzlement, he could not forget that his own heart and mind had been attracted and repulsed at once. Why no great voice? Those five sonnets written in London in 1802 display his confusion, reflecting a turmoil in Wordsworth which gives them an immediacy *The Prelude* lacks.

These poems have an immediacy precisely because they are not premeditated, not recollected by a memory thoroughly chastened and subdued. They spring from an unresolved conflict, the terms of which we have already introduced but which are specifically keyed for us by Wordsworth's late note. That note, we see, has as its primary intention an apology for a rebelliousness, an angry spirit, that intrudes into the poems.

> This was written immediately after my return from France to London, when I could not but be struck, as here described, with the vanity and parade of our country, especially in great towns and cities, as contrasted with the quiet and I may say the desolation, that the revolution had produced in France. This must be borne in mind, or else the reader may think that in this and the succeeding Sonnets I have exaggerated the mischief engendered and fostered among us by undisturbed wealth. It could not be easy to conceive with what depth of feeling I entered into the struggle carried on by the Spaniards for their deliverance from the usurped power of the French.

Wordsworth, then, is in a confused state somewhat like that experienced by those idealists of the 1930s who engaged themselves in the Spanish Civil War, whose symbol of despair is Lorca senselessly slain. Neither Loyalists nor Republicans could finally command heart and mind. What Lorca is to these disillusioned, Annette Vallon became to Wordsworth. At Orleans, he had found himself engaged in rebuking Royalists who would thwart the revolution, but at the same time he was involved with Annette, whose family was of Royalist sympathies. To further confuse matters, his friend Michael Beaupuis, though a dedicated Republican, was by nature more nearly one of King Charles's Cavaliers than Cromwell's Roundheads. Looking at the situation on the continent, Wordsworth could recall, as he does in *The Prelude,* that he was from a region where no one "Was vested with attention or respect / Through claims of wealth or blood."

But the saying did not make it so. There was his own family's relations with Sir James Lowther to the contrary. The question of Royalist versus Republican proved complicated indeed. Under family pressure and in confusion, he deserted both Annette and Beaupuis, returning to England. But at Racedown neither nature nor Dorothy's understanding nor Coleridge's enlivening mind could heal his spirit. He came to see that England's opposition to the French was not out of Royalist sympathies. Rather, England is reprehensible to him precisely because it has abused the "Royalist" heritage in pursuit of materialism.

> To think that now our life is only drest
> For show; mean handy-work of craftsman, cook,
> Or groom; . . .
> The wealthiest man among us is the best:
> > Rapine, avarice, expense,
> This is idolatry;
> Plain living and high thinking are no more:
> The homely beauty of the good old cause
> Is gone; our peace, our fearful innocence,
> And pure religion breathing household laws.

And if Milton is a true figure of the holy revolution called forth by revolution—the hero of the good old cause—how comes it that the revolution in France is both sterile and imperialistic, calling forth no champion to set it right? What indeed is the good old cause? And why no effect of virtue in the French?

France, 'tis strange,
Hath brought forth no such souls as we had then.
Perpetual emptiness! unceasing change!
No single volume paramount, no code,
No master spirit, no determined road;
But equally a want of books and men!

The revolution showed traits of that change in the west
which Chesterton was to embody in a figure setting our
world off from Chaucer's. Up to a certain time in history,
says Chesterton, life was considered a dance, after which
it came to be considered a race. And we have added: a
race without goal, a journey in which the journey is its
own end, resulting only in perpetual emptiness and unceasing change. Wordsworth came to consider that English opposition to the revolution did not finally reside in any fundamental principle. Both countries were dedicated to exploitation, and the conflict concerned the means to that end.

Wordsworth, in the next sonnet of the five, says, "We
must be free or die, who speak the tongue / That Shakespeare spake; the faith and morals hold / Which Milton
held." Still, Wordsworth seems little aware that Shakespeare's language is less self-consciously concerned with "unceasing change" than Milton's and that Milton's faith and
morals are antique and reactionary, though expediently desirable as instruments to the unceasing political change that
involved a shift of political power in the sixteenth and seventeenth centuries. Eliot complains of Milton that he "writes
English like a dead language." But Milton does so not simply because he is engaged in a tortuous style dictated by
a disunion of feeling and thought. The dissociation is more
complex than being the result of "the hypertrophy of the
auditory," as Eliot has it. Milton, too, is torn between the
claims of order that are so deeply rooted in him by his
training and temperament on the one hand and on the other
by the swiftness of the change under way in church and
state, change which threatens chaos. Revolution is anarchy
if there is no clear sense of a new order to take the place

of the old. The heavy transfer of Latin vocabulary and syntax that marks Milton's prose and verse is deliberate and not without parallel in the deliberate style one remarks in Eliot's own prose. With deliberateness Milton chose English as his medium, he says in *Reason of Church Government,* reflecting that he intended to do for England what the ancients had done for their own native soil,

> not caring to be once named abroad, though perhaps I could attain to that, but content with these British islands as my world, whose fortune hath hitherto been, that if the Athenians, as some say, made their small deeds great and renowned by their eloquent writers, England hath had her noble achievements made small by the unskilled handling of monks and mechanics.

But the circumstances were not propitious. Eliot observes, in regard to Dante: "The poet can deal with philosophic ideas, not as matter for argument, but as matter for inspection." We must add: provided he is in a position such as Dante was, a position requiring no justification of philosophy. Milton cannot devote himself to England's noble achievements any more than Wordsworth can or than Eliot can, for those achievements are rooted in a world Milton has been called upon to attack because of his political and religious commitment. King Arthur is not suitable material for Milton. He must turn to the courts of Heaven to show how far fallen are the courts of men. He must finally justify the execution of a king, not with the passion of a Rousseau or Tom Paine, but with that careful argument that owes far more to the church fathers who grounded the system Milton engaged than to revolutionary emotions. A poet can treat philosophical ideas "as matter for inspection" when they are generally acceptable. The strange position Milton finds himself in then is that of being at once revolutionary and reactionary. That is why one feels about *Paradise Lost* that it is not of a time or place. Milton's championing of manners and morals in *Paradise Lost* is medieval in its myth, but the myth requires a disengagement from Holy Rome. I think that Eliot is exactly right when he suggests that "our mythology was . . . impoverished by the divorce from Rome." Eliot observes also that "one remarks about the Puritan's mythology an historical thinness." It is for these reasons—and not simply because Milton's ear became dominant as his eyes went literally dark—that Milton's "celestial and infernal regions are large but insufficiently furnished apartments filled by heavy conversation." (Though Eliot cites Henry James's style in contrast to Milton as evidence that the "tortuous style" is not necessarily a dead one, what he says of Milton here applies equally to James, whose "celestial and infernal regions" turn out to be the English or French or Italian drawing rooms of a decayed society, decayed because its myth and history are rejected.)

The "tongue that Shakespeare spake" had already done for England's past what Milton wished to do, for Shakespeare had been content with those British isles and England's greatness in a way Milton or Eliot could never be. He had not had to *elect* the English tongue, or choose a role as bard-mediator of society. That is, he did not have first to recover or establish a language as a means of making an audience. The history of his myth was in his blood so deeply that Holinshed or Plutarch were English clay in his hands. His telling of all the pretty kings of England is, of course, in large part a picturing of the decay of medievalism and the rise of a less admirable spirit, two poles that order the texture of his plays. The rise of Bolingbroke and his spiritual kinsman Worcester stand before us; and before them, Henry v. Behind them all is that rich tapestry of the medieval world to remind us of a most final dimension to history.

Actually Wordsworth, in his London Sonnets, looks behind Milton and Shakespeare and the sixteenth and seventeenth centuries. We see evidence that he does so in some of the imagery, as he regrets the loss of that "ancient English dower / Of inward happiness." It is lost because "men change swords for ledgers, and desert / The student's bower for gold." Though "In everything we are sprung / Of Earth's first blood, have titles manifold," the homely beauty of the good old cause is represented by empty symbols. "In our halls is hung / Armory of the invincible Knights of old." But hall and armory alike are deserted by the spirit, leaving them at best time's natural museum and museum piece. Wordsworth's election of Milton and "others who called Milton friend" as the figure he imagines ideally as inhabiting "the student's bower" and his election of Shakespeare as the figure who endowed the language with that strength toward action does not show Wordsworth fully conscious of that world wherein their virtues lie. The Clerk of Oxenford and the Knight inhabit the world Wordsworth looks backward to, but not fully into. For between Wordsworth and the subtlety of Chaucer loom the figures of Shakespeare and Milton, giants themselves intent upon an honoring of what Wordsworth laments as lost—"manners, virtue, freedom, power."

Wordsworth then is a traditionalist seeking a tradition, one who analyzes his own day and attempts to maintain the value he discovers in it, attempting as well to restore whatever of abiding worth he may from the past. But the unfortunate truth is that his vision is weak in precisely the respect that Eliot finds Milton's weak. One remarks about his mythology, as about the mythology of so many nineteenth-century romantics who dream of the good old days, "an historical thinness." His delving into the past was less thorough than Milton's—whose chief sources were the scholastics, those rationalists of myth. Compared to Milton, Wordsworth is an uneducated man, and part of his uneasiness is from the realization that he deliberately chose to avoid a systematic training of the mind. His inconsistency of thought, which Coleridge is quick to chide him about, leads him initially to such expediency for joy as to suppose society's salvation to lie within nature, and a return of society's foundations to nature, as the French Revolution seemed at first dedicated to. But the virtues ascribed to the common man proved illusional. Wordsworth discovers that it is in truth the uncommon man upon whom the responsibilities of society devolve—such men as the Wanderer, the Pastor, the Poet of *The Excursion.* He had turned first, of course, to the simple rural folk he knew, among whom there is always a strongly conservative bent which expresses itself in a language of ancient origin and through an inclination to direct action. Yet Wordsworth gives little evidence of ever being close to the rural folk he turns to. In his poetry they are less kinsmen than objects to which he attempts to relate himself. He is no tapestry maker capable of seeing at once their world and their way of seeing the world, and so he comes slowly to know the limitations of the imagination.

So it is that there is always about Wordsworth's argument on poetics and in his poetic practice as well, either an element of rebellious dissent or the bemused wonder of the alien, sometimes hidden by the melancholy tone that accompanies hindsight, as in *The Prelude.* He comes slowly to discover himself of no country, but with strong intimations of a country that should have belonged to him and to England. His sympathy for the lowly, before he is himself "betrayed" by nature, is more conjured sympathy than real, despite his sincerity. While he chides himself for having been "at distance from the Kind," he can no more overcome that distance than a Milton could socialize with the common Roundhead. Intellectually he is moved by Platonism, but emotionally by his separateness, not so much from the Ideal, as from rural England itself—not nature, but the society which was of interest to the "earliest poets." When he is not decrying the destruction of the world's body by industrialism, as in "The World Is Too Much with Us," he is expressing himself as if he were a wanderer returned to a land he recognizes as his but in which he cannot quite freely immerse himself. This separateness is reflected in the tone of "Tintern Abbey," in *The Prelude,* in the "Intimations Ode," and in the awkwardness of his attempts to present the peasants he wishes so much to represent. It leads him to a leech gatherer who can say, "And hark! how blithe the throstle sings!" Or "Yet still persevere and find them [leeches] where I may." But while this uneasiness, this separateness from those he is attracted to, is the source of the bathos in so much of Wordsworth's treatment of the English peasant, it is also the source of that which is powerful in his poetry and sound in his poetics.

For with such uneasiness constantly in his spirit he saw, while lamenting England's fall from the old high ways, the necessity of a new start on old foundations, not only in regard to poetry's subject matter and techniques, but more important to him, for society itself. Though he starts out in his famous "Preface" to *Lyrical Ballads* with a concern for the language really spoken by men, that concern soon gives way to one for the proper voice in himself. His concern ultimately is with autobiographical fiction reflected in a language not really spoken by the common men but rather a language peculiar to William Wordsworth in his private quest. Hence his great poetry—"Tintern Abbey," the "Intimations Ode," some of the sonnets, *The Prelude*. The concern for establishing his own identity in an alien world, and the necessity of a poetics suitable to it, lead him to discoveries and statements about the possibilities of poetry in the modern world. He set out to treat the common in an uncommon way, to make legitimate to the art of words a subject that has become the burden of modern song and story: the insignificant individual as a substitute for Oedipus or Prometheus. He set out, in other words, to replace the burden of the song of the "ancient poets," addressed by them to the elite in the interest of their glory, with the burden of those folk ballads which treat of the lowly with a concern for their oppression and abuse.

Yet he addressed an audience presumed to be the elite. It is here that Wordsworth is most revolutionary; his "Preface" is in part an apology to that elite audience for the materials of his poetry. He does not sing to the peasant in his bower but to the immediate inheritors of the heroic halls whom he feels to have failed in their responsibilities as temporal lords of England. He intends above all to make his poetry immediately relevant to life by a directness of language that reveals the poet's engagement in such a way as to restore him to that honored place in the lord's esteem, poets themselves having lost that place through a failure to engage themselves in the life of man. There is an ambiguity about his position similar to that of Milton. Can he do the work of an Aeschylus by placing himself in the position of Homer? Or of Shakespeare from the position of a Chaucer? The solution to the poet's ambiguous position in the modern world has not, of course, been solved. Assuming the post of Latin secretary in a revolutionary cause was not fully suited to the needs of a Milton: in our own day assuming the role of literary secretary, the academy's "poet in residence," seems no better solution. Establishing a kingdom that continues revolutionary, as Pound did, leads back finally to the concerns for order as in Sophocles, and destroys the revolutionary. Perhaps Eliot's is finally the better solution in that he grows painfully toward an audience by reuniting poetry to life as Dante was able to do, requiring no programs of action, no crusades, but requiring only a development of the mind's self toward selflessness. The reader will have become aware long since that my own thought accords with this view of the poet's role in the modern world, given the nature of that world. But Eliot's is a position he comes to, not one he sets out from; he comes to it by reflecting upon the role of "the earliest poets of all nations" as compared to his own position, no less than did Wordsworth. It is an ironic reflection upon our own general attitudes toward Wordsworth, caught from the early Eliot and from Pound's many reflections upon "olde shepe Wordsworth," that in his day Wordsworth's fit audience, though few, was exactly analogous to Eliot's and Pound's in the 1920s; the bright, sophisticated young men. As we have said, Coleridge notices and remarks the fact in his *Biographia Literaria:* Wordsworth's admirers were found "not in the lower classes of the reading public, but chiefly among young men of strong sensibility and meditative minds; and their admiration (inflamed perhaps in some degree by opposition) was distinguished by its intensity, I might almost say, by its religious fervour."

IV

Wordsworth, Eliot, and the Personal Heresy

Wordsworth, *The Prelude*

>   I warred against myself—
> A bigot to a new idolatry—
> Like a cowled monk who hath foresworn the world.
> . . . so could I unsoul
> As readily by syllogistic words
> Those mysteries of being which have made . . .
> Of the whole human race one brotherhood.

Eliot, *Little Gidding*

> Since our concern was speech, and speech impelled us
>   To purify the dialect of the tribe
>   And urge the mind to aftersight and foresight.

There are some sentences in the "Appendix" which Wordsworth attached to the 1802 republication of his original
"Preface," sentences which it is well to recall in a consideration of Wordsworth's influence upon twentieth-century
criticism and poetry:

> The earliest poets of all nations generally wrote from passion
> excited by real events; they wrote naturally, and as men: feel-
> ing powerfully as they did, their language was daring, and
> figurative. In succeeding times, Poets, and Men ambitious of
> the fame of Poets, perceiving the same effect without being
> animated by the same passion, set themselves to a mechanical
> adoption of these figures of speech, and made use of them,
> sometimes with propriety, but much more frequently applied
> them to feelings and thoughts with which they had no natural
> connection whatsoever. A language was thus insensibly pro-
> duced, differing materially from the real language of men
> in *any situation*. The Reader or Hearer of this distorted
> language found himself in a perturbed and unusual state of
> mind: when affected by the genuine language of passion he
> had been in a perturbed and unusual state of mind also:
> in both cases he was willing that his common judgment and
> understanding should be laid asleep, and he had no instinctive
> and infallible perception of the true to make him reject the
> false; the one served as a passport for the other. The emotion
> was in both cases delightful, and no wonder if he confounded
> the one with the other, and believed them both to be produced
> by the same or similar causes.

The passage is likely to be overlooked. Coleridge's "willing
suspension of disbelief" is more economical than Wordsworth's Reader or Hearer who is "willing that his common
judgment and understanding should be laid asleep." Nor
does Wordsworth's prose suit the modern ear. It plods, and
worst of all, it preaches, either of which heresies confounds
Wordsworth to the popular critical current. It is a current
swollen since Eliot's and Pound's critical influence, one
which looks to Coleridge's definitions of a poem rather than
to Wordsworth's: "If the definition sought for be that of
a *legitimate* poem, I answer, it must be one, the parts of

which mutually support and explain each other; all in their proportion harmonizing with, and supporting the purpose and known influences of metrical arrangement." Here is a definition one can make use of in explication, in dealing with the poem as an independent existence, sustained within itself and unanchored in poet or the life of man. It provides an approach suited to Dante or Poe. But for Wordsworth, while the definition was not antithetical to his view, it was incomplete. As the passage quoted from the "Appendix" indicates, Wordsworth would have the poem anchored in the heart as well as the mind of man. The passage contains within it these concerns which are of considerable relevance to the aesthetics that Eliot grows to a hundred years and more after Coleridge and Wordsworth.

For purposes of comparison, we might once more take as a point of departure Eliot's essay "Tradition and the Individual Talent" in which his concern is with a refutation of that conception of the poet he takes Wordsworth to hold—the conception of the poet as personality. It is worth noting that C. S. Lewis, attacking the "personal heresy" in that famous exchange with E. M. W. Tillyard, presents Eliot's criticism as involving the personal heresy. Professor Tillyard was quick to respond to the charge by citation from Eliot's essay. But I think it can be shown that Eliot, in the fervor of his attack upon the personal heresy of the romantic—and he clearly has Wordsworth in mind, though he is reluctant to name him—really succeeds in establishing a more subtle version of that heresy. The new version makes the significance of the poet lie, not in the emotional and intellectual quality of his response to the world, but in the intensity of his art, an art whose peculiar instrument is his unique *feeling* rather than his *emotion*. These are terms Eliot distinguishes in his attempt to free poetry from the clutches of the romantic such as Wordsworth. It is an approach which lends itself to a conception of the poet which Wordsworth was combating above all else in the "Preface," a conception of the poet as *essentially* unlike other men. Eliot, finally, will not agree to this essential difference, but his early criticism contributes to a climate of belief which Lewis characterizes as widespread in the 1930s: "There is a . . . belief that the poet is a man who habitually sees things in a special way, and that his metaphor and other technique are simply *means* by which he admits us to share for a moment what is normal with him." By the time Eliot comes to write his introduction to Pound's *Selected Poems* in 1928, he will see this belief as a romantic one and will at once admit to an inclination to such romanticism while defending Pound's vast body of work, most of which is of a lower level of achievement than those limited times when he rises to the peak of his powers.

Eliot, in avoiding that suspected romantic word *emotion* which Wordsworth used unabashed, sets up *feeling* against it. We "give a name to some of our feelings . . . love, hate, envy and admiration." He speaks of "feelings inhering for the writer in particular words or phrases or images." The tone of his argument, no less than the attempted distinction of feeling from emotion, suggests a confidence in Eliot that feelings are intellectually accessible and consequently of some objective validity; feeling is a quality "inhering" in the word or phrase or image, thus allowing limits to and control of the emotional response to those elements through composition. He is talking about what he was to characterize in a famous phrase that was subsequently to haunt him, the "objective correlative." For he is not sufficiently aware that an imprecision in the objective correlative inevitably results, since after all we "give a name" to our feelings. Feelings inhere "for the writer," and are not necessarily in the word or image. But Eliot, along with Pound, is seeking at this early stage of his career to purify the language of the tribe, to remove the stains of romanticism by discovering and using a control of the aesthetic response lest Wordsworthian "emotions" cloud the mind.

Thus in the "Prufrock" period, the measure of the poet's achievement lies for Eliot in an intensity whereby the personal is removed. The critical concern is whether, in the poem, there is a mutual support of the parts within "the purpose and known influences of metrical arrangement." The result of Eliot's argument was a general shift of critical attention from the poet to the poem, a most desirable shift at that stage of our letters. But it was a shift that had inherent in it a new type of the personal heresy. For in spite of Eliot's insistence that the poet's vision was of integral concern to the poetry (as in his essay on "Dante") the relevance of vision (except as part of the materials of art as opposed to its relation to the general human condition) was largely discarded. The critic focused his attention upon the peculiar characteristics of a poem or a body of poetry, in effect making a new definition of *Dante* or *Donne*.

As C. S. Lewis contended, though he did not present his objection clearly in the initial essay of *The Personal Heresy,* Eliot, while attacking a conception of poetry as a reflection of emotional personality of the poet (a concept Lewis attacks himself) was substituting for it a concept of poetry as a reflection of the intellectual personality of the poet. He quotes from Eliot's essay on Dante (1920): "The rage of Dante . . . the deep surge of Shakespeare's general cynicism and disillusionment, are *merely* gigantic attempts to metamorphose private failures and disappointments." Eliot's statement is such as to be genially received into an atmosphere already alive with those thoughts of Freud concerning the artist. But what Lewis wants to know is "Metamorphoses *into what?*" The emphatic *merely* cuts the poem loose on the one side, relative to the poet's "traumatic experience," that is, cuts it loose from concerns with the natural estate of the poet, but the vagueness of *metamorphoses* leaves the relevance of vision to poetry indecisive. Lewis does not pursue these questions, though he insists on leaving them suspended for investigation, for he is about a literary question and not at the moment a metaphysical one. He continues: "It concerns our present purpose more to notice the assumed, and concealed, major premise that the cynicism and disillusionment put into the mouths of some Shakespearian characters are Shakespeare's. Even dramatic poetry is tacitly assumed to be the expression of

239

the poet's personality." In spite of Tillyard's rejoinder, Lewis has a point; that he does is indicated by Eliot's "Three Voices of Poetry," or at least that Eliot thinks him to have a point is so indicated. What seems likely about the passage Lewis quotes against Eliot is that Eliot is engaged in that self-concern which unsympathetic critics have objected to as being his primary interest in his prose work, an apology for his own poetry. For it is true to a considerable extent that his prose is a continuous pursuit of a suitable poetics, conceived by Eliot as desirably separated from his poetry. That separation does not imply that the prose is either unrelated "pure criticism" or subversively related fifth-column work in the interest of his poetry, as Karl Shapiro would have it. One of Eliot's principal concerns was his poetry, and he was from the beginning engaged upon an examination of himself. Still, his self-examination has more fundamental concern than its appearance as merely literary criticism or poetics suggests. For already in that early criticism, which is so carefully objective on its surface, there is the presence of those pursuing furies that bring Eliot finally to bay, that require him finally to confront those questions that we left suspended in Lewis's quotation from the "Dante" essay: Eliot finally concerns himself with the relation of the vision of poetry to life itself, the spiritual life of the poet and of men in general.

Eliot is not as "romantically" open as Wordsworth, but one need not from that difference suspect him of a diabolical plot, as Shapiro does. Still, there is considerable truth to Shapiro's charge that *The Waste Land* became "the sacred cow of modern poetry and the object of more pious literary nonsense." We recall that Eliot, in his essay on Milton, considers the bad influence of Milton on English literature as resulting not necessarily from badness in Milton. A certain failure of capacity in those poets influenced by Milton makes them the causes of their own failure, not Milton. The enthusiasm with which critical minds seized upon a new dissociation of sensibilities out of Eliot's prose—the new personal heresy we have defined—and the eagerness with which they applied it to such vulnerable vehicles as *The Waste Land* leads to a "pious literary nonsense," as Shapiro says, where it might better lead to pious sense which can include the literary. But it is an illusionary giant step as well to move from such effects of Eliot's poetry and criticism to insist that "Eliot created a literary situation deliberately; he and his 'situation' are fabrications, and very plausible fabrications at that. In other words, Eliot invented a Modern World which exists only in his version of it; this world is populated by Eliot's followers and is not a reality.... Eliot exists only on paper." Karl Shapiro's essay, which wildly attacks Eliot's influence while insisting that "no poet with so great a name has ever had less influence on poetry," is not without its value in making us look more closely at Eliot. It is not only possible, but inevitable, that a poet's concern for finding his own voice will involve him in certain blindnesses, whether that poet be Eliot or Karl Shapiro, whose own Dante is Whitman and who can consequently charge Eliot with intellectual pretension while asserting that by definition "a poet of religion" is second- or third-rate. Involved in his possible blindness, insofar as Eliot himself is eventually concerned, is that conception of man's nature which led Eliot finally to declare himself a High Church Tory, the real objection Shapiro has to him. Eliot's was not a conception which absolutely protected him from arrogance. In fact it called especial attention to that possibility, rather than deliberately redefining arrogance in terms of blood-knowledge or spontaneous engagement through strong and unexamined feelings. For Whitman, Lawrence, or Rimbaud would require action to be the inevitable uninhibited pulsing of the self outward which admits of no characterization as arrogance. That position allows such a display as Shapiro's essay and for a conception of poetry in which the poem and the poet are indistinguishable.

One must note in fairness to Eliot that he is an honorable man who will take neither knowledge nor ignorance as defenses against hubris. He takes a position to examine the relation of his prose to his poetry less excitedly than Shapiro is capable of doing. The objective stance in Eliot's early criticism is a mask assumed to guard against his own inclination to illusion, the danger being that those emotions attendant upon the pursuit of poetics will lead to hidden, untenable premises that cannot be supported, such as that cited by Lewis in his comment on the "Dante" passage. Eliot's pose also is, I believe, intended as a protection of the reader. If his prose style strikes one as *ex cathedra,* as it does Shapiro, it nevertheless carries as a formal part of its rhetoric a reminder to the reader that the words are those of a fallible man. *Perhaps, one might suppose, this point suggests*—such words and phrases are constantly evident as reminders of the reader's obligation to examine the argument closely. (Shapiro points to Eliot's "famous humility" as evidence of his "uneasiness in the face of overwhelming success," which a few sentences earlier has been denied: "No poet with so great a name has ever had less influence on poetry.") An additional purpose of Eliot's very formal prose style is to encourage men to treat literature with high seriousness. The style is a part of his reaction to that element of American culture which has generously entertained the literary man so long as he considers literature an entertainment. Cooper is more tolerable than Hawthorne, Twain than James, Poe than Pound—each preference involving false grounds in Eliot's eyes. The conditions under which Eliot worked out his own poetics were such as not to preclude excesses in him, either in his prose or poetry. But those excesses he was quite willing to modify, as in his attempt to establish the relation of the poet to the voice of poetry in "The Three Voices of Poetry" and in his remarks about the footnotes to *The Waste Land* in "The Frontiers of Criticism."

Every American English major knows that Eliot repudiated those footnotes to *The Waste Land* as window dressing, book padding. It was an acknowledgment on Eliot's part which shocked some of his followers who had devoted themselves as disciples of the new personal heresy, the poem disengaged from poet's mind but subtly reanchored in the critic's. It was one acknowledgment in a sequence of seeming betrayals. There was, for instance, Eliot's public assertion of political and religious affiliation which seemed to move poetry back toward a relationship with the poet from whom it had been liberated. In "Thoughts after Lambeth," Eliot seemed to ascribe some relevance to the poet's intentions, our current inexcusable fallacy: "I dislike the word 'generation.' When I wrote a poem called *The Waste Land* some of my more approving critics said that I had expresssed 'the disillusionment of a generation,' which is nonsense. I may have expressed for them their own illusion of being disillusioned, but that did not form part of my intention." Later, in his essays and in the *Four Quartets,* Eliot's early concern for an objectively inhering *feeling* in words that calls forth a controlled emotional response is replaced by a larger concern for *meaning* beyond the reach of words, a meaning necessarily approached through the reach of words: the Word within the word. In "The Music of Poetry" (1942) he is prepared to argue that "a poem may appear to mean very different things to different readers, and all of these meanings may be different from what the author thought he meant." Unlike his friend Pound, who steadfastly maintained the word as bearing limits of meaning through the virtually infallible control of the poet, leading to an inevitably precise effect in the reader, Eliot comes to acknowledge as more important the growth of the mind of the poet and reader alike through the poem, in consequence of which he comes to say, in "East Coker," "The poetry does not matter / It was not . . . what one had expected."

Let us consider, in order to see Eliot's poetics in relation to Wordsworth's, that it is possible after all that the old may see some things better than the young. There is no law of nature, of the blood, which requires true sight in age or the absence of true sight in youth. Is it not also possible that one's view may change without that change being decay? "Just for a handful of silver he left us" is after all the cry of blind youth intent on describing difference as evidence of betrayal. At least the proposition is worth considering that Eliot's later views are not necessarily softer views, any more than that his early view is untainted vision. The necessity of revised opinion may indicate a worthy mind's growth, which does not require the repudiation of all past opinion so much as it requires a purification of it so that it may be assimilated in a larger awareness. This indeed is a part of F. H. Bradley's legacy to Eliot. As each new masterpiece makes its place by reordering the body of masterpieces (Eliot's argument) so that it becomes an integral part of the mind's tradition; even so does each new addition to a particular mind's awareness reorder its knowledge. I pursue the subject in this manner lest I be misunderstood as encouraging a rejection of "Tradition and the Individual Talent" as superseded by later essays from Eliot's pen. That essay is irrevocably a part of what Eliot knows as he writes later essays, and it is as well a part of what we know; and what we must do, as Eliot did, is reach an accommodation with its thought, not dismiss it.

I think it is possible to argue reasonably that Eliot is both wrong in his understanding of Wordsworth as that understanding is a part of "Tradition and the Individual Talent" and that subsequently he came to a position much closer to Wordsworth's argument of the 1800 "Preface" and the 1802 "Appendix." Though both Eliot and Wordsworth were in their early thirties at the publication of the principal essays here recalled, Eliot was in one sense far younger in his understanding than Wordsworth. He moves closer to Wordsworth, refining particular elements of Wordsworth's poetics as he moves. We may see this if we look at Wordsworth's argument concerning the relation of the poet to his language and to the private experiences and emotions which are the poem's germ and then detail Eliot's own development of that subject over a period of years; an undertaking I have made in *T. S. Eliot: An Essay on the American Magus*. For the present we may reflect upon kinships hinted at by two statements in which Eliot's indebtedness to Wordsworth are reflected. They are statements by Eliot in which are inherent just such a refinement of points made by Wordsworth as I have suggested we will find. I think we should do Wordsworth an injustice to suppose those refinements the result solely of Coleridge's influence on Eliot, an influence generally acknowledged by Eliot and his critics. In 1945 Eliot remarked, "A poet must take as his material his own language as it is actually spoken around him." When this statement was recalled to him by an interviewer not long before his death, he added, "The music of poetry . . . will be a music latent in the common speech of his time." Finally, we recall words from his essay "The Music of Poetry," in which he speaks of the "law that poetry must not stray too far from the ordinary everyday language which we use and hear. . . . Whether poetry is accentual or syllabic, rhymed or rhymeless, formal or free, it cannot afford to lose its contact with the changing language of common intercourse." Eliot both echoes Wordsworth here and modifies him, recognizing "common intercourse" and "ordinary everyday language" as more dynamic than Wordsworth does in his famous prefaces.

Keats's Journey Homeward to Habitual Self

Psalm 139

> I am fearfully and wonderfully made.

Sir John Davies, *Nosce Teipsum*

> The quickening power would be, and so would rest;
> The Sense would not be only, but be well;
> But Wit's ambition longeth to be best,
> For it desires in endless bliss to dwell.

Eliot, *Little Gidding*

> When the last of earth left to discover
> Is that which was the beginning;
> At the source of the longest river
> The voice of the hidden waterfall
> And the children in the apple-tree . . .
> . . . heard, half-heard, in the stillness
> Between two waves of the sea.

The problem Keats concerns himself with, late and soon, under the eventual rubric of "negative capability," is the universal problem of the mind in nature, the problem of the mind's peculiar distinction from nature whereby thought itself seems symptom of the supernatural. It is the enduring problem of the poet, who attempts to reconcile the concrete present with the universal timelesss and both with the very awareness wrestling with the problem—whether that poet write a *Divine Comedy,* or "Dejection: An Ode," "Yew-Trees," *Ash Wednesday,* or "Ode on a Grecian Urn." Keats, because he is a poet and dedicated to poetry, feels himself pressed to justify an agitated disinterestedness as the wellspring of immediacy in poetry; that is, in order that emotion, though controlled by art, may seem spontaneous, the poet must dwell among uncertainties. We have seen the same concern as dramatized in Dante, in Wordsworth, in Eliot, but with development quite unlike Keats's.

The engaging aspect of Keats's mind is his particular reading of mind in nature, in which a battle rages between his desire for certainty and his fear that certainty is the death of wonder. For, considering himself a poet, he yet fears the poet's uncertainty as the death of the self. He can admire that "Wordsworthian or egotistical sublime" quality in "Tintern Abbey" and the "Intimations Ode," yet speak his admiration with the tone of one happily escaped the cold breath upon poetry of such a mind as Wordsworth's. "The burden of the mystery," a key phrase in "Tintern Abbey," is often repeated in his letters. He suffers that burden in some pain, but does not wish it laid aside. We nevertheless see him desiring intellectual scope, some assurance of a metaphysical system. He writes Reynolds in 1818: "An extensive knowledge is needful to thinking people—it takes away the heat and fever; and helps by widening speculation, to ease the Burden of the Mystery." But to think is to be full of sorrow and leaden-eyed despair. Is "Milton's apparently less anxiety for Humanity" an appearance to us only because we see him at greater distance than we see Wordsworth? He recognizes as desirable some union between Ariel and Prospero for peace of soul, but how accommodate Caliban? We hear Crazy Jane rebuke the Bishop, without solving the paradoxical burden, in the following outpouring:

> Here is the old plague spot; the pestilence, the raw scrofula. I mean that there is nothing disgraces me in my own eyes so much as being one of a race of eyes nose and mouth beings in a planet call'd the earth who from Plato to Wesley have always mingled goatish winnyish lustful love with the abstract adoration of the deity.... Has Plato separated these loves? Ha! I see how they endeavor to divide—but there appears to be a horrid relationship.

A horrid relationship, whose beauty shines in "The Eve of St. Agnes." A relationship fed and inflamed in the interest of poetry by what appears at times a self-induced infatuation for Fanny Brawne for the sake of poetry. For the whole conduct of that romanticized affair has an air about it very much like that famous fictional transformation of an Irish boy into a would-be Irish poet: Stephen Dedalus infatuated by his first love, finds a consummation in the pale morning, in the languid orgasm of a villanelle to the girl, a tender compassion for the temptress while in an emotional state reduced from action or desire:

> Are you not weary of ardent ways,
> Lure of the fallen seraphim?
> Tell no more of enchanted days.

Similarly Keats writes of passions which are asleep "from my having slumbered till nearly eleven and weakened the animal fiber all over me to a delightful sensation about three degrees this side of faintness—if I had teeth of pearl and the breath of lilies I should call it languor." It is the emotional state displayed in "Ode on Indolence," in which the specters of Love, Ambition, and Poesy tempt to an action which is finally rejected. It is not a state precisely like Stephen's, upon which Joyce shines an ironic light such as we do not have in Keats's poem, except as we may ourselves supply it. But neither is it that high state Wordsworth describes in which "we are laid asleep / In body, and become a living soul."

While tempted by it, Keats suspects Wordsworthian introspection of the soul, suspects thought's peace with the body, as disastrous to the chameleon chemistry of the poet. It leads to such false poetry as Wordsworth's "Gipsies," of which Keats observes in a much quoted passage, "I should judge it to have been written in one of the most comfortable Moods of his Life—it is a kind of sketchy intellectual Landscape—not a search after Truth." The languid dream of peace, in which Love, Ambition, and Poesy appear so enticingly, is also too comfortable a mood, too much a "state of effeminacy" in which "the fibers of the brain are relaxed in common with the rest of the body, and to such a happy degree that pleasure has no show of enticement and pain no bearable frown." Thus his prose version of the rejection of indolence, whom the poem commands to "vanish...from my idle sight."

What is immediately obvious is that in castigating Wordsworth for succumbing to a comfortable mood in a pleasant intellectual landscape that he might avoid the "search after Truth," Keats is characterizing his own most constant temptation. He, too, is drawn by Prufrock's mermaids as his sonnet "On the Sea" tellingly shows. He is again and again hopeful of discovering young Stephen Dedalus' place of green roses, as when he insists that "in the midst of this wide quietness [for which one may read "intellectual Landscape"] / A rosy sanctuary will I dress." Thus his response to a truth he sometimes makes painfully explicit: "The point at which Man may arrive is as far as the paral[l]el state in inanimate nature and no further—For instance suppose a rose to have sensation, it blooms on a beautiful morning it enjoys itself—but there comes a cold wind, a hot sun—it cannot escape it, it cannot destroy its annoyances—they are as native to the world as itself." But still the "green remote Cockagne" (of *Endymion*) calls.

The ode "To Psyche" is a most deliberate response, a mental landscape constructed by the will as a refuge from nature. It is nature denatured, into whose regions, deep within the mind, neither cold science nor natural philosophy may enter. The mind is hopefully posited as a mansion for such select forms, but hardly with that extrinsically inevitable way Wordsworth considers. Fancy then landscapes the "fane" raised to Psyche; the soul is created and enshrined. The "wreath'd trellis of a working brain" is supplied by "the gardner Fancy" with buds, bells, and stars. It is a statement of imaginative powers such as Wallace Stevens more firmly maintains. But in a metaphor anticipating Henry James's own use of it to distinguish romance from realism, Keats remarks the limits: "for at the cable's length / Man feels the gentle anchor pull and gladdens in its strength" ("Lines Written in the Highlands"). Keats's gladness, however, cannot be convincing, since he can never embrace or reconcile the paradox of "pied beauty" with joy or understanding.

One may conclude that Keats becomes firmly grounded in the realities of the natural world, as many sympathetic readers do; but one might better conclude, as the tone of the great odes reminds us, that he rather becomes on occasion resigned to those realities. "Do you not see," he insists, "how necessary a World of Pains and troubles is to school an Intelligence and make it a Soul?" But this is finally but a step on that road whereby the self-made soul, freed of the burdens of science and metaphysics, transmutes its awareness—its "Intelligence"—to Fancy's slow-burning greenness. The burden of the mystery, the dreamed greenness under the pressure of time, transmutes his words sometimes to simple coal, sometimes (and happily so for us) to rare diamonds. But soul to Keats is, finally, the smoldering poet John Keats who must insist with a more private concern than Wordsworth that "every mental pursuit takes its reality and worth from the ardour of the pursuer—being in itself a nothing." The loneliness implicit here is not one a Fanny Brawne can assuage nor a Benjamin Bailey explain.

Not that the active engagement of the mind in the world

leads to a truth comprehended and embraced, but that poetry is the consequence of its pursuit. It is poetry of an action in which Stephen Dedalus' enchanted days are still to be pursued, still to be enjoyed. The ideal land of mind, the lotus land which Keats pursues, must above all not be realized, as Wordsworth would realize his. Keats is never so miserable as when there seems nothing to be miserable about. How engaging then, his faith in the power of the imagination as a supreme god, restlessly capable of forming "greater things...than our Creator himself made!" The Garden of Eden was the grand earthly creation but will not suffice the poet. Having written the great odes, he yet dreams of creating "some great Poem." And always before him, beyond the possible grand poem should he manage it, is his "greatest ambition," to write "a few fine Plays."

Though his is a faith in the imagination as resident in the mind whereby it makes possible "greater things" than God Himself created, curiously there is an absence of that intellectual arrogance that would seem a necessary accompaniment to the attitude. Keats is no Stephen Dedalus in this respect. For the ambition to make great works, the faith in the powers of imagination, is everywhere accompanied by a marked humility about the "personal" role of the poet in such a making. It is a humility so pervasive that, given our distance from him, the pugnacious, virile personality in the memoirs of him and in his letters is continually surprising. The experience of late sleep which leads to his "Ode on Indolence" follows a vigorous game of cricket, from which he emerged with a severe black eye to which a leech must be applied. Whatever faults as man or poet we may charge Keats with, then, one of them is not that creative arrogance which is so often an irritant in Shelley or Joyce or Pound, or as Keats sometimes felt, in Wordsworth.

Keats's humility bears directly upon his pursuit of impersonality as a poet, a pursuit which the more sophisticated Joyce and Eliot adumbrate in argument and practice in such a way as to make it a principal concern to poet and novelist

for over a half a century. (I have deliberately not linked
Eliot with the arrogant poets, though he impressed many
as arrogant. The evidence seems sufficient, from personal
testimony by acquaintances and from the Eliot letters we
have, to make it more certain that he was shy and deferen-
tial, qualities all too easily taken or seized upon as aloofness
and condescension.) It is notable that Keats's pursuit of
impersonality as a poet is to be found largely in his poetry,
and to an extent in his letters. We have no three volumes
of formal prose from Keats as from Wordsworth, or the
eight or ten from Eliot, a circumstance which no doubt
makes *Hyperion* and *Endymion* more richly attractive to
speculation. (One writing on Keats is almost tempted to
borrow Eliot's statement as he begins his essay on the *Vita
Nuova:* "I mean to restrict my comments to the unprovable
and the irrefutable.") Still, there are aids more dependable
than simply subjective assertion as we examine the poet
Keats in relation to our own minds. Thus he writes Richard
Woodhouse about ideas we have seen Eliot discuss in a
formal essay. The "poetic Character," he says, "is not
itself—it has no self—it is every thing and nothing—It
has no character. . . . It has as much delight in conceiving
an Iago as an Imogen. What shocks the virtuous philosopher, delights the chameleon Poet." This is a statement
which defines a marked difference from Wordsworth's concern with poetry as a moral force in human affairs, and
Keats is thinking particularly about a difference he sees between himself and Wordsworth. His is an attitude more
compatible to Eliot's, particularly to the early Eliot's, so
long as we remember that Eliot's kinship to Keats and his
interest in him lies in the limited region of poetics. As
with Joyce, poetics is Keats's lifeblood, which fact leads
Eliot to say of him, "He was occupied only with the highest
use of poetry." The tendency of his whole energy is to
be the poet, and it is not until relatively late in his short
career that he becomes disturbed as to whether that is a
high enough expectation of life. We see the distinction between Eliot and Keats in Eliot's words of praise, for the

252

letters Keats has left us. They are, Eliot says, "the most notable and most important ever written by an English poet."

To the orthodox Bailey, who has attempted to persuade Keats into the larger influence of Dante such as Eliot was to experience, Keats writes, "A Poet is the most unpoetical of any thing in existence; because he has no Identity." Having escaped thought and personality, the chameleon poet "is capable of being in uncertainties, Mysteries, doubts, without any irritable reaching after facts & reason." In the light of such an elected burden it is no wonder that the question of Keats's limited perspective must be raised concerning the final achievement of his poetry. We see as a symptom of restriction his fascination with that variety of influences extending from Leigh Hunt downward to obscure contemporaries, whose names are remembered because Keats remembered them and overpraised them. Keats too easily mistook as great men both those for whom thought was tedious and also those who lacked that capacity for the negative capability which may serve the lyric poet on rare occasions and with limited sustenance in the absence of powers of thought. How often Keats suffers from the local coloring he assumes—the influence of immediate friends and immediate books. Which is not to say that his suffering is always in vain. It is to say that, lacking a capacity for intellectual growth and a capacity for a necessary power of detachment which does not obliterate the individuality of the particular mind, he must inevitably write a very uneven poetry and traffic in very miscellaneous ideas. The empathetic power that moves him to blend with the sparrow pecking gravel cannot finally sustain an *Endymion* or *Hyperion*.

His greatest triumphs, such as the odes, result from a return to the self after a brief flight as the chameleon winged by that deceiving elf, the imagination. He wished to be the Saint Francis of Assisi as poet, obliterating the self through a generous embrace of the particular Other. But the significant, the moving parts of Keats, do not result in things entered upon in themselves, the inscapes of nature.

They are rather a dramatization of the very attempt of a personality to enter upon things. There is a distinction to be made here between the inscapes of Keats and Hopkins; the latter is sustained by a metaphysics which Keats came late to lament not having. A distinction as well from that most captivating of all chameleon poets, Shakespeare. For the Shakespearean virtue which so attracted Keats is indeed a magic power, but one for entering into all states and conditions of *man*. Shakespeare's is an ability to become Iago or Imogen, but Keats's is captivated by "things"—by multiplicity itself. His imagination is indiscriminate of its objects, though his is not a willfully perverse election of multiplicity over unity or simplicity. In consequence Keats's achievement as poet must finally rest upon his person, which reflects his generous love of the world and its things, though his reach forever fails to match the capacity of his desire.

It seems, finally, that Keats is devoted to separateness at the expense of order and wholeness, a perverse side to his Platonic idealism not always given its destructive due in our reading of him. He may speak of the "innumerable compositions and decompositions which take place between the intellect and its thousand materials before it arrives at that trembling delicate and snail-horn perception of Beauty." And we may see evidence of that operation in changes in the text—"sheltered fold" giving way to "wooly fold," and old Angela's "tottering along," giving way to "shuffling along." But those thousand materials somehow seldom come to be one thing. They don't become a texture of any *essential* depth. We are, for instance, left with a cold pastoral quality to *Hyperion* which does not sufficiently warm either the intellectual or the sensual dimensions of our mind with a fullness or wholeness.

One has only to read his letters to see how often the word *thing* appears when he is concerned with his imaginative acts, and how indiscriminate its use. Particularly does it seem so in the light of Coleridge's and Wordsworth's concern over the question of the *life* of things, the mode of an object's existence in the mind of its Creator. And we recall in contrast Eliot's similar concern for the Word within the word. We have already noticed that to Keats the "poetical Character . . . is every thing." The poet himself, as distinguished from things in nature, including woman, is "the most unpoetical of any thing in existence." As poet then, Keats is somewhat like Eliot's floating Tiresias, but a Tiresias often freed from puzzlement by wonder, freed from thought by sensation. "I have never yet been able to perceive how any thing can be known for truth by consecutive reasoning—yet it must be," meaning surely: and yet we are burdened in some inexplicable way by the temptation to rational perceptions. "However it may be," he concludes, "O for a Life of Sensation rather than of Thought!" For, when "thoughts of self come on, how crude and sore / The journey homeward to habitual self."

Keats's zest for life, obscured from us somewhat by our recollections of him as dying consumptive poet, led him as directly to the Elizabethans as Eliot's concern for order, perspective, and continuity was later to lead him there. His interest in Spenser (which he shares with Wordsworth and Eliot), his overwhelming love of Shakespeare, is attested by verse and letter. But again, it is the particular or incidental influence we notice, not finally a largeness or enlargement of his comprehension of the world such as sustains allegory in Spenser or that God's plenty of mankind in Shakespeare. Where Spenser commands large metaphors of idea, Keats struggles with figures abstracted from myth to guide him toward idea. In *Endymion* and *Hyperion* Keats finds no adequate Virgil, and his Beatrice proves treacherous. Shakespeare has that inexplicable power to be many things and many people *at once;* Keats must repeatedly adapt himself to the particular thing or person. He tends, consequently, to be episodic and not dramatic. We finally have Keats at his best as sparrow and not as sparrowness. He is impressive (to quote Douglas Bush) for a "local beauty and power of word, line, image, and rhythm."

The voices in Keats, then, are finally one voice, whose characteristic distinction is the presence of a tension between the desire to know and the fear of knowing. Whatever stasis is momently achieved has a residue of melancholy about it, a melancholy out of his failure to "burst our mortal bars," as he thought the poet capable of doing. Another source of that melancholy is his fear of an inherent insufficiency in his power to burst those bonds. Joy's grape is a dream to the fine palate of sensations, not a recollection nor vision strongly believed. Even his love of Fanny Brawne failed of consummation less because of ill health and the dark future attendant upon it than because of his fear of consummation as the death of wonder, that eternal fountain of poetic feeling to Keats; even his opposition to thought in favor of sensation suggests a suspicion in Keats of an insufficiency which he speaks of again and again in his letters.

A more certain evidence of his fear of self-inadequacy as poet is his growing concern over the lack of metaphysical foundations, which with characteristic innocence he speaks of as if a piece of equipment acquired handily, a tool to poetry such as image or meter simply taken. He writes to Reynolds in April of 1818 that he is about to learn Greek and perhaps Italian, "and in other ways prepare myself to ask Hazlitt in about a years time the best metaphysical road I can take—for although I take poetry to be Chief, there is something else wanting to one who passes his life among Books and thoughts on Books—." Metaphysics, like Eliot's early discovery of myth, seems a convenient path, an instrument for measuring the country of books or poems. To Wordsworth or Eliot or Milton or Shakespeare such a use of metaphysics is incidental, however particular ones of them may have failed to come finally to a satisfying metaphysical position. One has only to contrast the depth of Wordsworth's concern with the question of whether the imagination half creates as it half perceives. The same question as Keats approaches it (separate from the momentary elevation of verses of which the major odes are example) has to do with creating poems, never a sufficient end to Wordsworth. And as for that natural world in which Wordsworth perceives some interfusing spirit, Keats is rather given to interfusing his own spirit through that faculty he calls negative capability. His implicit metaphysical approach to the world, though not his mode, is very like Wallace Stevens's. For Stevens's is absolutist: the imagination is omnipotent, and it is omnipotently declared the creator of a supreme world of imagination, which uses the empty world of nature. That is, the natural world is separate from its perception and there is no sustaining spirit in it. The difference is that Stevens seizes a metaphysics implicit in Keats but to which Keats cannot give himself because he does not believe strongly enough in the power of his own mind. He can never quite bring himself to declare *non serviam* with Joyce's Stephen, though he can declare the poet capable of creations greater than "our Creator himself made."

A metaphysical position, whether Eliot's or Wallace Stevens's—two which are diometrically opposed—requires a fundamental commitment which makes vision and thought tenable. One can then sustain with some authority both order and form, either "Notes toward a Supreme Fiction" or the *Four Quartets,* out of such commitment. We notice that it is Wordsworth's and Coleridge's attempts at a metaphysical structuring of life that prompts Keats's reaction to them. In that passage of his letter to his brothers in which he defines negative capability, he specifically sets Coleridge apart from it: "Coleridge, for instance, would let go by a fine isolated verisimilitude caught from the Penetralium of mystery from being incapable of remaining Content with half knowledge . . . with a great poet the sense of Beauty overcomes every other consideration, or rather obliterates all consideration." For Coleridge's distinction between the primary and secondary imaginations is an attempt to tie mind to the transcendent, to find a way of rescuing the poet as creator from the arrogance of Stephen Dedalus' indifferent creator or Wallace Stevens's Emperor of Ice-Cream. Coleridge may be contented only by moving to the innermost sanctuary of the Penetralium.

We may, at this point, recall once more Eliot's early

"Tradition and the Individual Talent," which attacks Wordsworth, and particularly recall his statement that he, Eliot, struggles to attack a metaphysical concept of the essential unity of the soul. That essay is in many ways reminiscent of Keats in those years when he sought to escape personality in his poetry. But Dante and Lancelot Andrews were to prove more influential on Eliot than Keats's theologian friend Benjamin Bailey, who tried to persuade Keats into the influence of Dante's metaphysical system. The consequence is that Eliot revises his judgment of Wordsworth to an almost shocking degree. He elevates Wordsworth over Coleridge (1933) as critic, for "it was Wordsworth who knew better what he was about: his critical insight, in this one *Preface* and the *Supplement,* is enough to give him the highest place."

One must always be careful in determining the nature of and degree of those influences on Keats exercised by Shakespeare or Dante or Milton or Wordsworth. These are the figures looming most largely in his background. But Keats, unlike each of these in their several ways, could win through to no still point nor spots of time. Neither could he reach that stasis of mind which Joyce provides biography to in *A Portrait of the Artist as a Young Man,* a stasis which Stephen posits after his Keatsian development beyond negative capability. Stephen reaches a point where the poet confidently assumes a position as creator of things greater than "our Creator . . . himself made." The position is one reasonably invulnerable, if not convincing, since it is removed from and indifferent to the world, even the one the poet creates while trimming inexplicable nails.

Eliot, in his essay on "Shelley and Keats," expresses no reservations in his praise of Keats. That he felt an affinity is evident. It is an interesting coincidence that Eliot, at a point in his career parallel to Keats's development, undergoes a crisis similar in its external particulars of situation and even of place. Keats, having finished his medical apprenticeship, writes that he is "not over capable in my upper Stories" and so "set off pell mell for Margate." There, seeing the ocean, a gull in the wind, sails at sea, and disappointed that in these images and through them he is not somehow consumed by Apollo, he considers darkly his future as poet. "I see that nothing but continued uphill Journeying." The "labyrinthian path to eminence in Art" seems impossible of passage. As Keats ponders the calling to art, which must lead him into strange deserts, as opposed to the more open profession of medicine in London, he is attempting *Endymion*. At a parallel point in his life, Eliot has finished his dissertation on "Knowledge and Experience" and is torn between his London banker's job and his own calling as poet. But that calling turns out to be larger than to poetry in Eliot's case, leading to a spiritual crisis. Not "over capable in his upper Stories," Eliot too goes to Margate sands, before going on to Switzerland. Each poet wrestles with the problems faced by the poet in the modern city's complex society; their separate retreat has radically separate outcome. It is at this point in Keats's life that Benjamin Bailey urges him to turn to Dante, Bailey realizing the depths of the crisis Keats faced as Pound did not Eliot's. Pound of course attempted a subscription among friends and patrons to get Eliot out of the bank, a generous but not perceptive view of Eliot's dilemma. A more telling reading of Eliot's condition is that recorded by Conrad Aiken, who recalls Eliot with his copy of Dante always in hand unable to write his own poetry, tormented by the prospect of his continued uphill journeying. With Aiken as mediator, the American analyst Homer Lane sent Eliot word (Aiken tells us) that he was balked by the fear of "putting anything down that is short of perfection. He thinks he is God." Aiken attributes Eliot's subsequent outburst of poetry, from which "Gerontion" and *The Waste Land* result, to the shock of this message.

One wonders whether Keats might not have been shocked by a similar bold frankness from Bailey, a man too kind perhaps for Keats's own good. Keats does read Dante, in large part because the Cary translation is in three small, convenient volumes. The nature of the reception each affords

259

that greatest poet of the egotistical sublime is decisive upon subsequent journeys of the two pilgrims from London. For it is Dante who leads Eliot through his wasteland. From Margate sands where he can connect nothing with nothing, there is a sharp uphill turn into the arid desert and toward the possibility of fire and water. Thence on toward the *Four Quartets*. Keats's indebtedness to Dante, on the other hand, is measured in small things. The debt, in fact, is far more to Cary's English details than to the *Divine Comedy*. He reports to George and Georgiana Keats that "the reading of Dante is well worth the while" required to learn Italian, but the main point is to prepare himself to ask Hazlitt next year for a convenient metaphysics. He is most impressed by canto 5 of *The Inferno*, the prospect of Hell in the second circle where the incontinent lovers are punished. And in a dream he delights in the condition of Paolo and Francesca. "The dream was one of the most delightful enjoyments I ever had in my life—I floated about the whirling atmosphere."

We are not in Dante's poem to any depth here. We are rather closer to that state of languor to which the "Ode on Indolence" owes its existence, with its own floating figures. Still, in those months of languor preceding the composition of the great odes, Keats reflects that because poetry involves bad as well as good energies "it is not so fine a thing as Philosophy—For the same reason an eagle is not so fine a thing as a truth." The disinterestedness of negative capability is undergoing a qualification. Keats is being pressed to acknowledge that commonplace of ethical necessity with which Donne begins a facetious poem: "Good we must love, and hate ill." The languor of this period in Keats's life speaks of the frustration to the poet out of a compulsion to know, and having given oneself to knowledge, to judge. That is, a compulsion to give of oneself, under the weight of responsibility for judgment, in a movement of the self larger than negative capability encompasses. We might note that Keats's judgments of the social world about him lack the weight the odes carry, that he is not incisive. His feeling of responsibility for the social world is far removed from Wordsworth's. That the political position he speaks is superficial needs only his statement to an intimate that he is thinking about supporting himself by journalism and will write "on the liberal side of the question." To have to tell one's friends what side of the question one will publicly defend says a great deal about the intensity of one's convictions and the depths of one's understanding of his place in the world of men.

Keats measures himself at this point, more judiciously than our sympathies for him allow us to acknowledge as just; "I am three and twenty with little knowledge and middling intellect. It is true that in the height of enthusiasm I have been cheated into some fine passages." The height of enthusiasm, a way of expressing that escape of self-awareness, that personality; an enthusiasm otherwise described as "negative capability." It is his gift, but one which allows no profound entry into the riddle of the "burden of the Mystery" of existence. For as he says in the dark *Fall of Hyperion,* negative capability is the particular power of the dreamer, not of the true poet. Moneta, memory, rebukes Keats's pilgrim as severely as Beatrice does Dante at the gates of Purgatory summit. For Keats there is no crossing over:

> The poet and the dreamer are distinct,
> Diverse, sheer opposite, antipodes.
> The one pours out a balm upon the world,
> The other vexes it.

And again she says, with a bitterness from which Keats's personality is not entirely absent: "Only the dreamer venoms all his days, / Bearing more woe than all his sins deserve." Here is a suspicion in the poet that negative capability may not entirely hide an element of the egotistical, even if it is not the egotistical sublime. It is an egotism which rejects or refuses a consummation, a peace which passes understanding, a quiet rest at a pole quite opposite indolence.

After the great odes there is one ode yet, a harvest home as it were. And after that Keats writes nothing of significance. His "Ode to Autumn" is the one poem which we may describe as out of that classical mind Keats speaks of to his brother George, in which, the passions being controlled, a calm elevation is possible above the terror of nature's or the mind's corruptions. April has been for Keats the cruelest month up to this point: clouds hide the green hills in April shroud; the fruits of autumn have not been the source of those heights of enthusiasm in his characteristic poetry, but rather April's budding rose. Joyce's Stephen on the threshold of vision, seeing the girl standing in the water like a heron, moves on from there. But this is the same moment which Keats, until the "Ode to Autumn," would suspend, though he cannot do so beyond the momentary enthusiasm. In this autumnal reconciliation with his limitations, Keats can say that the stubble fields are warm, "better than the chilly green of spring," as he says in a September letter to Reynolds. We have come, in this last moment, to an acceptance of what the sunset in "The Eve of St. Agnes" spoke of: that "chilly sunset faintly told / Of unmatured green vallies cold."

Here is a final reflection by Keats in the fall of 1819, not long before the end:

> Some think I have lost that poetic ardour and fire 't is said I once had—the fact is perhaps I have; but instead of that I hope I shall substitute a more thoughtful and quiet power. I am more frequently, now, contented to read and think—but now & then, haunted with ambitious thoughts. Quieter in my pulse, improved in my digestion; exerting myself against vexing speculations—scarcely content to write the best verses for the fever they leave behind. I want to compose without this fever. I hope I one day shall.

The "Ode to Autumn," is a result of the new quietude, which is rather clearly not the same as that state of indolence he wrote brother George about much earlier, the one following the cricket match and the black eye. That state he described as a "state of effeminacy" which "I must call . . . Laziness." There is, nevertheless, in this closing autumn still a turning into the self. The harvested fields are not to Keats what the yew trees were to Wordsworth, allowing an opening outward from the self. He is rather still like Stephen Dedalus in the last pages of Joyce's *Portrait*. Indeed he writes in the letter quoted above, "You would scarcely imagine I could live alone so comfortably 'Kepen in solitarinesse.' " It is not exactly the same state as Stephen's. This self-exile which Keats finds restful is not that of Joyce's young poet who, about to leave for the continent, writes self-assuredly to himself in a journal. There is rather in Keats the feeling of an ending, in the current letters and in "Ode to Autumn," as in the letters and actions following. One might ascribe it to the disease he suffered, and if one is a Thomas Mann make a convincing fictional case for it as in *The Magic Mountain*. But Keats fails to transcend the burden of process in nature and also that elementary faculty in the art of poetry, negative capability. Eliot, revisiting the terrors of April with its sweet showers, comes to an agreement with personality, with his own particularity, which eases the problem of the relation of private emotion to art; the necessity of a persona for formal control dissolves after *The Waste Land*.

There was to be no breakthrough for Keats into that great poetry he longed to write, a poetry with depths and heights such as those known to Shakespeare. But it was not because he died young. It seems impossible that he could ever have sustained "a few fine Plays." Nor does there seem possible to him that accommodation of the self to nature and history which moves an Eliot toward the *Four Quartets* or Wordsworth into that ruined cathedral, *The Excursion*. He could, with Eliot, still recognize the bad influence upon English poetry occasioned by *Paradise Lost,* coming also to a kinder evaluation of Milton. He writes, again not long before his death, "The Paradise lost though so fine in itself is a corruption of our Language—it should be kept as it is unique—a curiosity. A beautiful and grand Curiosity. . . .

263

A northern dialect accommodating itself to greek and latin inversions and intonations." But it is still the surface of Milton's attempt that he treads upon. The limit of Keats's powers are in his best poems, three or four odes, "The Eve of St. Agnes," "La Belle Dame Sans Merci," and in fragments of the more ambitious attempts. In the latter, as Douglas Bush says, his "negative capability or empathy...for the most part works best on inanimate objects or scenes." It leads to his highest accomplishments in short bursts of enthusiasm in which he almost forgets the dangers to the poet of the consummation of desire and is in his own words "cheated into some fine passages."

If one has no power beyond the power of empathy, he can be little more, finally, than a spiritual parasite upon this world. To simulate some other is to dissimulate oneself. It is finally to pervert that second and great commandment which is pertinent to poets since they are men, that commandment whose prerequisite to effective community with the world and to an essential unity of soul is a proper love of oneself, the opposite of Prufrock's self-love. Such is the high pursuit in Dante, in Chaucer, Shakespeare, Wordsworth, in Eliot. That pursuit failing, the terrors of a return to one's soul self brings one shockingly to the question of personality, however valiantly he has tried to escape it. To a concern with personality as it applies more largely than to the execution of a poem. For the capacity "of being in uncertainties, Mysteries, doubts" is not tolerated for long by that "irritable reaching after fact & reason." One is not satisfied by a fall into the languor of melancholy, that pale shadow of a high spiritual estate proclaimed in Eliot's still point, in Wordsworth's spots of time, in Dante's blinding moment in the presence of the multifoliate rose and the pure light shed upon it. Its opposite is in that moving despair in *Hyperion*. When "thoughts of self come on, how crude and sore / The journey homeward to habitual self."

Wordsworth, Eliot, and the General Mess of the Imprecision of Feeling

Michael Polanyi, *The Tacit Dimension*

> The most striking feature of our existence is our sentience. The laws of physics and chemistry include no conception of sentience, and any system wholly determined by these laws must be insentient.

Eliot, "East Coker"

> And so each venture
> Is a new beginning, a raid on the inarticulate
> With shabby equipment always deteriorating
> In the general mess of imprecision of feeling,
> Undisciplined squads of emotion.

In his "Tradition and the Individual Talent," Eliot does not name William Wordsworth directly as an antagonist, as if by that omission he might remove the personal from his critical attack upon the hoary Romantic establishment. But his argument is pointedly counter to Wordsworth's own attack upon the establishment of his day, made in the famous prefaces to *Lyrical Ballads.* He quotes Wordsworth's "emotion recollected in tranquility" and examines the phrase, thus underlining Wordsworth as his prinicpal adversary and the prefaces as the particular evidence for his case against the romantics. Given our fifty-year perspective upon Eliot's first major engagement with established tradition, we may see him in a position paradoxically parallel to Wordsworth's at the time of *Lyrical Ballads.* Eliot's direct point of attack, in both the poems of *Prufrock and Other Observations* and this essay, is upon the relation of "emotion" to personal experience, the effect of the personal upon the poet's art. It is as if he is making certain that Coleridge's sharp examination of Wordsworth's poetics be remembered with less critical tranquility than the intervening years had afforded. At the same time, he is rescuing Dr. Johnson, whom he sees in 1917 as his eighteenth-century counterpart, from Wordsworth's severe strictures. But if Coleridge, in the *Biographia Literaria,* did not correct Wordsworth's arguments for all time, Eliot's further critical corrections have not themselves proved decisive, as passages of Yvor Winters's *In Defense of Reason* and Karl Shapiro's *In Defense of Ignorance* indicate. What is overlooked by counter-criticisms of Eliot in general is that Eliot has affinities with Wordsworth, affinities which he himself came to recognize as he moved on from that early attack upon Wordsworth which as sequel became established as the new critical position on romanticism. Ironically, as we have seen, Eliot moves closer and closer to the Wordsworth of the early prefaces.

In the 1802 "Appendix" to *Lyrical Ballads,* Wordsworth argues insistently that the decay of "poetic diction" is the result of a deliberate distortion by false poets. False poets are those who desire the reputation of poet (the sin Shapiro accuses Eliot of), and to satisfy that desire they remove poetry from "real life" by mechanical manipulation of poetry's devices. Dr. Johnson is particularly to be chided since he failed to relate the sense of the poem to its technique. Thus he was, as critic, in no position to rebuke false poets. For the false poets disregard "the real events" which excite the true poet and set about manipulating the emotions by "a mechanical adoption of ... figures of speech ... applied ... to feelings and thoughts with which they had no natural connection whatever." As Eliot would have it, Wordsworth is arguing for the presence of the "personality" of the poet in the poem. And against "personality" as the essence of the poet's nature, Eliot poses the poet as "a more finely perfected medium in which special, or even varied, feelings are at liberty to enter into a new combination." But Wordsworth, too, argues for the new poet as "medium"; he is attacking rather passionately what Eliot is to tag as the "dissociation of sensibilities," while at the same time attempting to solve the technical problem Eliot considers solved by objective correlatives. Eliot says, "Impressions and experiences which are important in the poetry may play quite a negligible part in the man, the personality," but he is closer than he seems aware to Wordsworth's insistence that in a poem the situation derives whatever importance it has from the emotions and not from the situation itself. For it is the particulars of a situation that define personality. Eliot, in his statement, is preparing to introduce the term *feelings* to replace Wordsworth's *emotions,* feeling being a characteristic of the poet's mind as distinguished from the ordinary mind. Wordsworth's emotions have an anchor in common life, in a real situation whose magnitude he denies as relevant to the force of the poem that is the recollection. Eliot dissociates the poet's impressions and experiences as of little importance to the poetry except as they are manipulated by the poet's feelings. In other words, Eliot wants to cut the poem loose from emotion and situation as either term may be anchored in what Wordsworth calls "real life."

In the light of his subsequent development, Eliot's argument is of interest not so much because of its insistence upon the poet's "impersonality," but because it carefully avoids confronting any question of transcendent validity in those impressions and experiences that are the material the poet uses. For instance, he is being extremely careful to guard against couching his arguments in a way that may be taken to involve myth's relation to religion. His essay centers on the psychology of the poet's mind, upon the poetic process whereby a poem comes to be. It is as if Eliot is consciously avoiding the trap of that commitment which he would later record in *Little Gidding,* a poem carrying a precise statement of Eliot's later poetics. *Little Gidding* would require of the man, who is also the poet, a submission possible through that "condition of complete simplicity" which costs one "not less than everything," a condition Wordsworth was in pursuit of in his phrase "wise passiveness." The poet may then know that

> Every phrase
> And sentence that is right (where every word is at home
> Taking its place to support the others,
> The word neither diffident nor ostentatious
> An easy commerce of the old and new,
> The common word exact without vulgarity,
> The formal word precise but not pedantic,
> The complete consort dancing together)
> Every phrase and every sentence is an end and a beginning,
> Every poem an epitaph.

Wordsworth sought early the "common word exact without vulgarity" and in his odes and in "Tintern Abbey," the "formal word precise but not pedantic."

One of the costs of such surrender as Wordsworth made early to poetry is scorn from the enlightened intelligentsia. In Wordsworth's case it is a scorn summarized in Pound's "old shepe Wordsworth." And the early Eliot was perhaps afraid of appearing "at times almost the fool." *Emotion* is a word dangerous to use in certain intellectual circles if one has a care not to be scoffed at. But though Eliot is surely in some degree sensitive to the dangers of emotional response which makes one vulnerable (and he is closer to Prufrock in his early years than we generally allow), he is even more concerned with the threat of subjectivism to poetry. That is a principal reason he is intent on the distinction between emotion and feeling. Eliot seems to mean by emotion the literal response of a man to Wordsworth's "real life." That is, though emotion in a particular poem may have a direct relation to the experience of a particular man, the man is not necessarily the poet, nor is the particular experience necessarily common to poet and audience. The particular emotion, conjured out of impressions and experiences, is the material of the art, but it is quite subordinate to the concern for form in the poem. Or rather, the proper or effective access to emotion lies in the indirection of form. Put another way: emotion, as a concern in the poetic process, is a remote effect whose agent is feeling. The personality, the literal emotion aroused in poet or reader, are aspects of history; it is through the impersonality of feeling that the poet recognizes and controls the likely or possible. In other words, Eliot is making a distinction appropriate to a poetry which is short of being drama, a distinction analogous to that made by Aristotle in separating poetry from history. He enlarged that concern subsequently in those essays concerned with the objective correlative and the variety of voices in poetry. One sees a corollary to his distinction between emotion and feeling in his interest in *The Golden Bough, From Ritual to Romance,* and *Archetypal Patterns in Poetry,* an interest in the symbolic as concrete figurings of feeling. It is not so much, in his early interest, that the feelings suggest the universal or transcendent—the concern focused in the *Four Quartets*—but a concern that the personal not confuse the poet's control of his material. (There is also something of the Stephen Dedalus about the early Eliot, each so intent upon form's relation to feeling.) The *actual* or historically personal, insofar as it attaches to the poet's experience, is dangerous to poetry since it is contaminated by the specifically private aspects of the

269

actual. A refinement is necessary, whereby the mind of the poet collects and prepares objects, actions, events, situations which may be disposed in a pattern of words in such a way as to allow, ultimately, a proper historical response in the reader; that is, to allow an emotional response to actually occur as the poem is experienced. In other words, feeling is an impersonal aspect of the poet's mind transferred impersonally through words in such a way as to arouse personal emotion in the reader so as to make experience complete in him. Unless the poet dissociate his own emotion, the transferal is impure. Given Eliot's point in history, the actual seemed inevitably private and hence subjective because of the fragmented world. It was the old dilemma of the Wordsworthian romantic as Eliot saw it. Feeling, as opposed to emotion, is by its nature a quality "inhering for the writer in particular words or phrases or images," and so presumably inhering for the reader as well.

Thus Eliot felt it necessary to separate feeling and make it pristine. But emotion is not denied; it is reduced to a subordinate but not unimportant concern. When he then turns to consider the poetic process, it is to inorganic chemistry that he turns for analogy, as if once more countering not only Wordsworth, but his apologist Coleridge as well. We recall that Wordsworth, in "Tintern Abbey," is intensely concerned with the mind's abstracting from experience for future use. He too reflects upon "feelings," in a context implying feeling as an afterglow of an emotional involvement with the actual to be rekindled by recollection. The mind to Wordsworth is a "mansion for all lovely forms, . . . a dwelling-place / For all sweet sounds and harmonies" to be summoned by memory at future moments of intellectual or emotional despair. But Wordsworth's concern is not so much with the poet's mind as distinct from other men's. Eliot to the contrary asserts that "The poet's mind is . . . a receptacle for seizing and storing up numberless feelings, phrases, images, which remain there until all the particles which can unite to form a new compound are present together."

The poet's progress "is a continual self-sacrifice, a continual extinction of personality.... It is in this depersonalization that art may be said to approach science." The creative process is analogous to that action which results when "a bit of finely filiated platinum is introduced into a chamber containing oxygen and sulphur dioxide." The medium thus distinguished is quite unaffected by the emotions attendant upon its writing a poem. Eliot's depersonalizing the medium, the poet's mind, requires a neuter pronoun. Keats, who like Eliot had difficulty coming to terms with Wordsworth, describes the poetic mind in terms very close to those of Eliot. Writing to his friend Bailey (November 1817), he too attempts to define the difference between the poet and other men: "Men of Genius are great as certain ethereal Chemicals operating in the Mass of neutral intellect—[but] they have not any individuality, any determined Character." He almost says with Eliot that they "have no personality to express." Wordsworth, to the contrary, would have the poet's mind differ from the ordinary mind—"the Mass of neutral intellect" of Keats's formula—in that it "has a disposition to be affected more than other men by absent things as if they were present; an ability of conjuring up in himself passions" which then, because his mind is not a catalyst unaffected by the process as in Eliot's view, must be controlled in a state of tranquility. Unless tranquility attend the composition of the poem, the imagination gives way to fancy. For excess of emotion makes a disproportion between the emotion and that which calls the emotion forth; the composing mind could not select and order, discover the proper objective correlatives necessary to the poem. There is a disparity at this point between Wordsworth's conception of the poet's mind and Eliot's, for to Eliot the mind of the mature poet differs from the mind of other poets or other men "by being a more finely perfected medium in which special, or very varied, feelings are at liberty to enter into new combinations."

To put the disparity between the arguments in perspective, we might say that the poet in Wordsworth's view stands in relation to other men as the economist to the business-man in real life. But such an analogy brings the poet closer to real life than Eliot is prepared to do. He rather prefers to examine the creative process of the poet's mind in terms of an analogy to a purer science than economics. "The mind of the poet," he says, "is the shred of platinum" in the process of poetry. "It may partly or exclusively operate upon the experience of the man himself; but, the more perfect the artist, the more completely separate in him will be the man who suffers and the mind which creates; the more per-fectly will the mind digest and transmute the passions which are its materials."

Eliot's chemical analogy has about it a subtle wit, when we recall Wordsworth's prophecy that the poet would and must ally himself with science, following into the "remotest discoveries of the Chemist, the Botanist, or Mineralogist." But wit can be self-deceiving. Biology creeps into Eliot's argument, bringing with it all the complications of digestion and transmutation involved. Nevertheless, if one takes the making of a poem as analogous to the making of sulphurous acid, and the poet's relation to the process as that of a catalyst, a very neat separation occurs whereby one can analyze the poet's mind without infringing upon the poem. It is precisely this procedure that Eliot uses in this essay, his "Preface" to the *Prufrock* volume carefully detached from that volume. His is a procedure now become a funda-mentalist dogma of one segment of our criticism which would require the poet to speak of his own work through the indirection of careful analysis of the work of other poets. It is an approach which finds scant tolerance in a Karl Shapiro, who remarks that F. O. Matthiessen, as the "most intensely political mind among the English professors of his day [the 1930s], and a leftist ... *chose to cut himself off from the politics of Eliot's poetry and criticism to talk about 'forms'* " (Shapiro's italics). One quite agrees with Shapiro in this Wordsworthian position that Matthiessen accepts "a false dualism ... between art and social action." But it is a question whether it was "a split that Eliot had invented for himself." Intellectual disinterestedness such as Eliot is attempting does not assure infallibility, any more than a commitment to the emotions at the expense of intellect means inevitable revelation.

Eliot's attack is upon the active commitment of the poet to those causes of the poem, social or other, which may be separated from the creative process itself. One properly identifies the poet's feelings, not his involvement, through his techniques. Thus Poe's essay on composition gains a new level of authority, dealing as it does with the role of the feelings (adhering in the qualities of words, phrases, images divorced of a particular situation). "For," says Eliot, "it is not the 'greatness,' the intensity, of the emotions, the components, but the intensity of the artistic process, so to speak, under which the fusion takes place, that counts." Our praise of the poet must lie in his process, in his language as wit. Here Eliot's argument approaches Stephen Dedalus' practice, his "green roses" and "day of dapple sea-blown clouds." The great poet by Eliot's argument is very like the false poet by Wordsworth's: that poet who makes, as Wordsworth says, a "mechanical adopting of [words or phrases or images] to feelings and thoughts with which they had no natural connection whatever." Eliot, leading up to a specific divorcing of his position from Wordsworth's, says near the end of his essay:

> The business of the poet is . . . to express feelings which are not in actual emotions at all. And emotions which he has never experienced will serve his turn as well as those familiar to him. Consequently, we must believe that "emotion recollected in tranquility" is an inexact formula. For it is neither emotion, nor recollection, nor without distortion of meaning, tranquility.

So Wordsworth is openly introduced into "Tradition and the Individual Talent" as Eliot's antagonist. But we must look back to Wordsworth's "Preface" once more to see whether Eliot has read him accurately. There the poet is described as "pleased with his own passions and voli-

273

tions . . . *habitually impelled to create them where he does not find them*" (my italics). That is not only part of his nature, but part of his training toward those rare moments when he finds passion and volition of firmer origin than the conjurings of fancy. For the poet does have "an ability of conjuring up in himself passions, which are indeed far from being the same as those produced by real events, yet . . . do more resemble the passions produced by real events than anything which . . . other men are accustomed to feel themselves." There is necessary a control of such conjuring which prevents emotion in the poet himself from completely dominating the form: the poet's skill of language which he has acquired "from practice." Wordsworth is clearly aware of the necessity of what Eliot calls feelings as a control of the poet's literal involvement with the real world. Later, Eliot makes a great issue of the importance to the poet of his practicing his art even when that practice produces only second-rate work. He is justifying Pound's lesser work as having a claim upon our attention (in his introduction of Pound's *Selected Poems*). It is, he argues, preparation toward the poet's rising to those occasions when he accomplishes the peak of his powers, rare moments in the career of any poet. By 1928, then, Eliot's argument is another form of Wordsworth's statement on the importance of continual practice, through which (Wordsworth says in the "Preface") the poet acquires a "greater readiness and power in expressing what he thinks and feels, and especially those thoughts and feelings which, by his own choice, or from the structure of his own mind, arise in him without immediate external excitement." Wordsworth too, we see, requires of the poet the capacity of disengagement, in which capacity he can provide the materials of art—emotional response to possible human engagements with life—through which his practiced art shapes a poem which is an expression (as Aristotle says) of "what is possible according to probability or necessity." Eliot says, in his essay on Pound, that "the business of the poet is to be more conscious of his own language than other men, to be more sensitive to the feeling, more aware of the history of language and of every word he uses than other men." He requires as most necessary a familiarity with languages other than that native to the poet, which once more reminds us of Wordsworth's training in school, plus his stay in France, the avowed intent of which was to gain a thorough familiarity with French. (His familiarity with classical writers, particularly the Roman, is a further parallel to Eliot's own training.)

What now requires attention is the nature of "emotion recollected in tranquility" as it is attacked as an "inexact formula" by Eliot. Wordsworth's formula differs from Eliot's argument only in this respect: that Wordsworth holds as necessary a commitment of the man who is the poet to the emotion the poem embodies. He has objected to a language "insensibly produced, differing from the real language of men in *any situation*." The emphasis is Wordsworth's, and the phrase calls our attention to Aristotle's *Poetics* which is not far from Wordsworth's mind. For neither Wordsworth nor Aristotle would deny that "day of dapple sea-blown clouds" or "But somewhere there must be a place of green roses" is real language. We see it is real language because Joyce has allowed those words to a character already established in our confidence so that we can imagine Stephen saying precisely—and inevitably—these very words, given the circumstances. They are, indeed, a species of Stephen's recollection in some degree of tranquility, though not memory elevated as it is in section 3 of *Little Gidding*.

> This is the use of memory:
> For liberation—not less of love but expanding
> Of love beyond desire, and so liberation
> From the future as well as the past.

Memory is not an expansion in Stephen, as of gold to airy thinness beat, but a contraction upon the self. So too of Eliot in his "Tradition and the Individual Talent." His essay would deny the relevance of love which twenty years later he insists upon in the *Four Quartets*.

Wordsworth's phrase "recollected in tranquility" surely concerns itself with the creative process, with a revisiting of emotion in which the mind's control prevents the emotions from dominating. His, like Eliot's, is an argument for imagination's use of memory toward a liberation from the future no less than from the past. The phrase is an argument based on that demonstration of the process exhibited by "Tintern Abbey." "Recollection in tranquility" is Wordsworth's formula for the necessary control of the poem by the poet's mind. Early in his career, Eliot would have it that "the more perfect the artist, the more completely separate in him . . . the man who suffers and the mind which creates." The end of the process is a perfection of wit in the poet, expressed by an object called the poem, but the objects to which that poem relates become rather hazy in Eliot's argument: the artist is a man and a mind: his feelings are another name for what Wordsworth calls his peculiar powers of language. To Eliot, his significance as man is quite beside the point. To Wordsworth, on the other hand, poetry is emotion comprehended in the act of composition, and Wordsworth's emphasis is upon the accommodation of the particular man who is the poet to whatever of real life initiates his emotion and involves him in the act of composition. Poetry is to Wordsworth in his "Preface," if not always in his practice, the act through which one arrives at the starting place and sees it for the first time. If we recall the argument from earlier essays concerning Dante's and Wordsworth's struggles to become poets transcending and so ordering personal experience, we may conclude that though Wordsworth is not finally so successful as Dante he is much closer to Dante in the "Preface" than is Eliot in "Tradition and the Individual Talent."

We spoke earlier of Wordsworth's concern for language "really spoken by men" and of his concern for "real life" and its relation to poetry. Wordsworth does not mean by his phrase language transcribed from the literal speech of particular men. Already in those "earlier poets" he speaks of we have the poet conceived of as capable of refined utterance. His language was that which "the Poet himself had uttered when he had been affected by the events he described, or which he had heard uttered by those around him." It was a heightened utterance, whose intensity was caused by the events described. Meter, says Wordsworth, is an addition to "the genuine language of Poetry," and he warns that the addition of meter already begins to separate the speech of poetry from common life. It is, indeed, meter which is "the great temptation to all the corruption" of poetic diction. This last warning of Wordsworth's needs emphasis since its germ is the meat of Eliot's first essay on Milton, whose failure Eliot states to be the "hypertrophy of the auditory imagination" in Milton. And we should remember Wordsworth as a precursor to that more determined and specific assault upon iambic pentameter meter by Eliot and Pound.

But Wordsworth's criticism cuts in several directions. Those false poets who have come between the true poet and his reader, says Wordsworth,

> became proud of modes of expression which they themselves had invented, and which were uttered only by themselves. In process of time meter became a symbol of promise of this unusual language [in consequence of which] the taste of men became gradually perverted, this language was received as a natural language, and at length, by the influence of books upon men, did to a certain degree really become so.

Thus the rise of false diction which became more corrupt, "thrusting out of sight the plain humanities of nature by a motley masquerade of tricks, quaintnesses, hieroglyphics, and enigmas." The passage might be an argument directed against "The Love Song of J. Alfred Prufrock" by an unsympathetic reader such as Karl Shapiro, and it does aim itself at Eliot's favorites among the English poets, the metaphysicals. It is an attack upon the new personal heresy emanating from Eliot: the conception of the poet as a unique creature whose virtues reside in his feelings, rather than his emotions, in which consequently the virtues of poetry

277

reside. Wordsworth calls it false diction because it is language deliberately divorced from "the plain humanities of nature" by its emphasis on a "motley masquerade of tricks, quaintnesses, hieroglyphics, and enigmas."

Coleridge particularly praises Wordsworth's "Appendix" to the 1802 "Preface" for his insistence upon the value of "the *dramatic* propriety of those figures and metaphors in the original poets, which, stripped of their justifying reasons, and converted into mere artifices of connection or ornament, constitute the characteristic falsity in the poetic style of moderns" (*Biographia Literaria,* 2). He sees that Wordsworth's concern for the particular image or metaphor is that such figures be anchored in a reality stronger than the mere drapings of fancy which end in poetic sentimentality. Wordsworth wants his images to be those really seen—a concern for historical experience such as Hemingway's fiction turns so largely upon—so that they will be discovered a part of the reader's experience or potential experience as separate from the verses. The commonplace is consequently preferable to the exotic, as well as to the commonplace inflated to the exotic. Such an attention to image or metaphor allows for a control of the emotions in poetry and theoretically forms ground on which to arouse similar emotions in the reader. Thus it is that somewhat later than the "Appendix" Wordsworth writes a contemporary, R. P. Gilles, criticizing his poetry partly for its "turning so much upon internal feelings," but mainly because those feelings are "of a peculiar kind, without a sufficiency of incident or imagery to substantiate them." One is very close in this statement to Eliot's definition of the objective correlative, to a "set of objects, a situation, a chain of events which shall be the formula of that *particular* emotion." The details differ, but only because Eliot is speaking primarily of the drama, while Wordsworth speaks of verses on the page.

Wordsworth, after long reflection on the problem, sees the image as a medium through which one captures characteristics, not the accidental or spectacular detail which is transient and most limited by subjectivity. "In every scene [by which he means panorama in the natural world, as an example of the point] many of the more brilliant details are but accidental. A true eye for Nature does not note them, or at least does not dwell on them." These are Wordsworth's remarks to Aubrey de Vere, late in life, as he reflects upon his place in English poetry. Dryden had failed, in Wordsworth's view of him, because he had not fixed a true eye on nature, seeing neither the accidental nor the essential. Among his own contemporaries, many fixed eyes on nature only to exploit its brilliant but transient aspect which was not suitable to poetic images beyond a limited reflection of "feelings of a peculiar kind." Pound, we may note, is substantially in agreement with Wordsworth in Wordsworth's evaluation of Dryden. And Wordsworth has anticipated as well Pound's criticism of the imagists in the objection to the details of nature stripped of their justifying reasons and converted, in consequence, to artifices. Pound, more stringent in his expectations of language than Wordsworth, does not abandon image but rather attempts its rescue from the distortions of metaphor.

Wordsworth does not deny that the poetry of "brilliant detail" gives pleasure to a reader. But, as he says, in that passage Coleridge singles out for praise, the primary reason it does so is "its influence in impressing a notion of the peculiarity and exaltation of the Poet's character, and in flattering the Reader's self-love by bringing him nearer to a sympathy with that character." The result, however far from really bringing the reader to know poetry's relationship to "the plain humanities of nature" which he shares with the poet, actually sets him further from poetry, since it gives him a false impression of both poetry and the poet. False diction's effect "is accomplished by unsettling ordinary habits of thinking, and thus assisting the Reader to approach to that perturbed and dizzy state of mind in which if he does not find himself, he imagines that he is *balked* of a peculiar enjoyment which poetry can and ought to bestow." For the true poet's habits of thinking as compared to the "ordinary habits of thinking" involve a difference of degree. The false poet tries to lead the reader to suppose the poet's thinking different in kind.

Wordsworth's argument is for the poet as medium no less than Eliot's, though a medium (mediator) of the "plain humanities of nature." And there is more solid substance to his position than Eliot accorded him in his early attack. One has only to reflect upon the difficulty of facing students reared on Poe's music (which produces a perturbed and dizzy state of mind altogether delightful) and Edgar Guest's philosophy. The argument Wordsworth advances is as applicable to a Guest on the one hand, or the abuses of advertising jingles, as to the most experimental anarchist. Perhaps Eliot was more sensitive to the validity of Wordsworth's charges than we suppose. Certainly he was rightly concerned for the dangers of uncollected emotions, the threat of sentimentality which has been the abiding fear of most of the great names of modern letters from James through Conrad to Joyce, Pound, Eliot, and Hemingway. Eliot's intense concern for the dangers of the emotion brought him to those close concerns with technique. It involves him in new meters, which would not necessarily have offended Wordsworth. For Wordsworth's argument as we have seen is essentially that there has come about a dissociation of sensibilities in English poetry. Indeed Wordsworth points to that dissociation in the eighteenth century, as Eliot does. He cites, in the "Appendix," two passages from the King James translation of the Old Testament, and measures them against two renderings in verse, one by Prior and the other by Samuel Johnson. The gist of his argument is the one Pound made to Harriet Monroe a hundred years later, that poetry must be at least as good as prose. Though we cannot know how Wordsworth would have reacted to a "Love Song of J. Alfred Prufrock," we do know that he was dissatisfied with Shelley and Keats in a way he was not with Browning, the immediate antecedent of Eliot and Pound. Certainly if we may believe him committed to his arguments of the relation of science and poetry which he advances in his "Preface," and if we may suppose him cognizant of the new arguments concerning the nature of the mind made from William James through Jung, we must conclude that he would welcome "Prufrock" as an instance of how poetry ("the breath and finer spirit of all knowledge" and "the impassioned expression which is in the countenance of all Science") accompanies science as handmaid. For he insists upon the poet's obligation to be ready, when the scientist has created revolutions "in our condition, and in the impressions which we habitually receive," to follow the man of science and be at his side "carrying sensation into the midst of the objects of science itself."

When Eliot concludes his essay with the insistence that "sincere emotion" is suspect in poetry and that "*significant* emotion" is the true measure of the superior poetry (significant emotion being "emotion which has its life in the poem and not in the history of the poet") he has succeeded in disregarding Wordsworth's basic insistence that significant emotion has its reference not in the unique experience of the poet (in which instance Wordsworth himself would consider it private and unacceptable) but in the general experience of mankind. Wordsworth is not so easy a target as Eliot's essay takes him to be. Still, it is not finally Wordsworth who is the fundamental protagonist of Eliot's essay on the individual talent. The most profound presence in Eliot's essay is that Fury which he names as the "metaphysical theory of the substantial unity of the soul" which he is "struggling to attack." He will come, as we know, to a poetry which is technically (that is, in its feelings) very impersonal but essentially (that is, in regard to its emotions) a very personal poetry indeed. In the later poetry the masks made by the "feelings" are abandoned. Prufrock and Tiresias are abandoned in that ultimate surrender "costing not less than everything." A change in Eliot's thinking moved him away from Coleridge's insistence that the question of "*legitimate* poetry" has a concern only for the relevance of parts to whole and for meter to this relationship. Eventually his position holds "Every poem an epitaph" of the dead self because, through an expansion of love, which is the natural action of that surrender, the self is constantly enlarged. *Being* is a continuous enlargement which is of the first importance, and the *words* of a being are secondary. Words are man's way to arrive after the journey of exploration at the place "where we started / And know the place for the first time."

Eliot's later discarding of the principal literary arguments I have selected from his "Tradition and the Individual Talent" may be found in a variety of places besides his poetry itself. The process is underway very obviously in *For Lancelot Andrewes*. It is in the introduction to Pound's *Selected Poems;* it is in "From Poe to Valéry." It is in that essay of the fifties, "The Frontiers of Criticism," when he says one *Road to Xanadu* and one *Waste Land* are quite enough. Not long before his death he objected to Valéry's poetry, in an introduction to a collection of Valéry's prose, on grounds which in the early twenties he would have defended it upon. For Valéry's concern with "feelings," even as Poe's, leads to a poetry which is arrested in its development because it has so little significance beyond "feelings." It is a poetry which is of American origins, as Eliot has pointed to in relation to Poe's influence: the literature of permanent adolescence. In his "Essay upon Epitaphs," Wordsworth addressed himself to that conception of poetry Poe later chose to argue in "The Philosophy of Composition." But Poe specialized Wordsworth's arguments, making Abstracted Epitaph, inhabited by the poet's feeling, the only province of poetry. In doing so Poe disconnected not only death from significant life, but poetry from mankind. The poetry which results from this position, as Eliot said of Valéry's, has an insufficient relation to "life." Wordsworth's earlier phrase is "real life," whose significant capacity is "the plain humanities of nature." The Wordsworth of the prefaces and the Eliot of the late essays and the *Quartets* are struggling to say essentially the same thing.

Emotion Recollected in Tranquility
WORDSWORTH'S LEGACY TO ELIOT, JOYCE,
HEMINGWAY

Wordsworth, *The Prelude*

>   The array
> Of outward circumstance and visible form
> Is to the pleasure of the human mind
> What passion makes it.

Karl Shapiro, *The Bourgeois Poet*

> The world is my dream, says the wise child, ever so wise
> not stepping on lines. I am the world, says the wise-eyed
> child. I made you, mother. I made you, sky.

In respect to his turning attention toward a new hero to replace lost heroes, Wordworth anticipates much of our fiction, though the change in the nature of the hero is one coming to fiction relatively late, after the death of Wordsworth at mid-century. The final impetus is given by new scientific and philosophical ideas and by a skillful development of techniques, but the aesthetic theory is already stated by Wordsworth by 1800. The progress in fiction moves from our having a character in a situation (place and circumstances), as in Hardy's *Jude the Obscure,* a late holdout against the new mode, to our having the situation of place and circumstance a part of character. We move from an author's looking at the world of his fiction and at the character who inhabits the world to the author's looking at the world through the eyes of the character without the awkward intrusion. It is the difference between Hardy's "It seemed to Jude that..." and Joyce's "When you wet the bed, first it is warm then it is cold." However, it is not a shift merely to technique in point of view, though it is that also, but a shift toward making the subjective and private sufficient to fiction; the revelation of psychological and emotional states replaces action, which otherwise demands ends beyond simply adjustment to or failure to adjust to the world and, as fiction develops in this line, it tends to become short. The story blooms, and the short novel, and even when the novel is long in words, its tendency is toward concentration in time and limitation of character, "development sideways," as Frank O'Connor says. Not the sweep of a lifetime as in Hardy's *Jude,* but the day in Joyce's *Ulysses.*

In short, the revolution in fiction has been in the direction of the lyric as defended by Wordsworth, who proposes that "it is not the action or situation which gives importance to the emotion, but the emotion which gives importance to the action and situation." The fiction writer has moved toward submerging himself into a character, toward expressing the character's world with the character's emotions. He selects aspects of knowledge in terms of the character he allows himself to become and makes a world as seen by that character. Imagery, symbolism, juxtaposition of scenes in the manner of the two terms of a metaphor become more important to the architecture of fiction than does plot or any generally accepted set of values against which to measure action. Given the absence of large intellectual and religious structures with which an author can identify himself—myth and accepted social order—it is no doubt inevitable that the tendency is for fiction to move toward becoming autobiographical in content, lyrical in mode. The necessary approach under the circumstances implies for fiction as for lyric poetry a serious concern for states of mind as the central drama; it considers questions of the mechanics of emotion in the mind in a manner more limited than Aristotle's concern in examining the nature of catharsis, which is finally a religious concern as much as aesthetic. But in spite of the elaborate modern myth supplied by Freud and welcomed by the fiction writer since it allows seemingly final answers to a character's definition—an ultimate authority held in common with the reader—it is an uncertain task to create a character separate from the author's own self when the primary burden of the fiction becomes authoritative psychological definition. The fiction's persona, once identified against ethical and moral structures in a theater of action, moves out of the theater into the test tube. The most reliable referent of such tests lies in the tester's experience of himself; the immediate technical problem is to project the analysis without the stain of personal subjectivity, the autobiographical tinge that has so concerned critic and writer in this most autobiographical century of our literature.

That Wordsworth is aware of the technical, as well as the philosophical and "scientific," problems of making the individual mind's mechanics accessible to the reader appears not only in the "Preface," to which I shall presently once more return, but in such practice as "Strange Fits of Passion Have I Known," an experiment in the mind's workings which considers the effect of the moon's setting on the observer's emotions. His investigations go wider and are more effective as he analyzes the influences on his "subconscious"

285

in greater poems like "Tintern Abbey." In those poems the source of emotional effect is pursued outside the mind. Lacking a Freud to supply theory for his intimations, he turns to Plato and such reconciliations of sensibility as appear in the "Intimations Ode."

From Wordsworth, through such fictions of character as represented in Browning's "Porphyria's Lover," "Soliloquy of the Spanish Cloister," and "The Bishop Orders His Tomb at Saint Praxed's Church," we come on great modern fiction in Wordsworth's mode: Lawrence, Joyce, Hemingway. The effect on the mind of absent things as though present, says Wordsworth, leads to the poem. Or, we might add, to the epiphany in fiction, which is fiction's high lyric moment—the moment of a character's self-awareness or the reader's awareness of a character's obliviousness. Stephen Dedalus' concern for swallows over his head in *A Portrait of the Artist as a Young Man;* Paul's recognition of the whole sweep of life in the changing colors of the sunset in *Sons and Lovers;* Jake Barnes's concern for the way it really was in Paris or at Pamplona in *The Sun Also Rises.* These are the moments the fiction writer must enter into to make them effective, and it requires the kind of talent Wordsworth ascribes to the poet, the ability to respond to "absent things as though present." In fiction, Joyce steps into Dedalus and sees the effect of fictionally present things upon the emotional state. So do Lawrence and Hemingway. But the significant relationship is that each of the fiction writer's characters is an art image of himself, and the act of putting the character's emotion in us is the act of recollecting, with artistic tranquility, personal emotions from old experiences. When we read "Tintern Abbey," we see the same process at work, with the exception that Wordsworth is himself dramatically present—looking at two earlier versions of William Wordsworth. As we read Wordsworth's poem this way, we see a relationship of the poet—a character in his poem—to a Stephen Dedalus standing at a desk, seeing the word *foetus* carved there, from which experiences are summoned absent things which are beheld by him as though present. Or consider Stephen, confronted by Herron and Herron's insistent word *confess:* again, absent things as though present—the summoning of old experiences with a kind of tranquility which puzzles Stephen. Why, he wonders, isn't he angry at Herron now as earlier? The answer would seem to be that he has become enough of a poet to control experience of emotions and maintain a tranquility of deportment in the process of recollection that prevents Stephen, the artist, from excessive emotionalism at the present moment of memory. Such control is prerequisite, in Wordsworth's theory, to good artistry, to prevent the emotional excess that the innocent romantic is susceptible to. Stephen's is a portrait of the romantic poet as defined by Wordsworth, just as Joyce is himself such a romantic poet, albeit more sophisticated and worldly than Wordsworth. Wordsworth is present in "Tintern Abbey"; Joyce less apparently so in the episode here cited. Still we remember that the fence is identified in Dublin upon which Stephen's Herron thrust Joyce himself.

Fiction then—one stream of it—has moved closer to the lyric. The novel has moved more toward becoming autobiography using lyric's techniques, while at the same time, because of the development of technical skills, it seems less autobiographical. The modern counterparts of Wordsworth's *Prelude* and *Excursion* are Joyce's *Portrait of the Artist as a Young Man* and *Ulysses.* The city replaces the country; aloneness increases as society condenses and individuals coagulate. And critically, it becomes less satisfactory to separate fiction from lyric poetry in our concern with the two, both in their manner and content. If Hemingway's several artistic disguises of himself are somewhat less obvious than Wordsworth's, they are more obvious than Eliot's. Eliot says, in *The Three Voices of Poetry:* "The poet, speaking as Browning does, in his own voice, cannot bring a character to life: he can only mimic a character otherwise known to us. And does not the point of mimicry lie in the recognition of the person mimicked, and in the incompleteness of the illusion?" Just so. That is part of our fascination with Joyce's *Portrait,*

Stephen giving us an incomplete illusion of Joyce the Romantic, or with Hemingway's *Sun Also Rises*, Jake Barnes giving us an incomplete illusion of Hemingway as a case of "arrested development." That is also part of the fascination in Prufrock, who mimics Eliot far more than the Bishop of St. Praxed's mimics Browning in that poem so like Eliot's in its devices. For circumstantial proof, consider Pound's saying of Eliot, in regard to their service to modern letters, that it was Pound's job to throw a brick through the front window while Eliot slipped around back and got the "swag." The cutting edge to Pound's words lies not so much in his associating the slang *swag* with Eliot, who has become the proper Englishman, but with Eliot as Prufrock. Eliot, as compared to Pound, played it safe—at least on the surface level. Hemingway, less generous than Pound, who understood both approaches to the Establishment necessary, ridicules Eliot in *A Moveable Feast*. In recalling Pound's attempt to raise funds for Eliot, to get him out of the bank in London, he says: "I mixed things up a little by always refering to Eliot as Major Eliot pretending to confuse him with Major Douglas an economist about whose ideas Ezra was very enthusiastic." But putting aside Hemingway's schoolboy attitude toward both Pound and Eliot in this and following sentences of his account, Eliot's kinship to Prufrock still haunts one. Consider the comedy attendant upon Eliot's being given a ten-gallon hat on his visit to Texas several years ago. The effect would have been quite different had the visitor been such an Englishman as Winston Churchill.

A further point concerning Eliot's kinship to Wordsworth: consider along with Wordsworth's problem of representing his country peasants, Eliot's presentation of his Sweeneys. "He can only mimic a character otherwise known to us" with his Sweeneys, in comparison to which Prufrock comes dramatically alive. The voice there is more convincing of the character, as is the voice of the *Quartets,* though the *Quartets* is in a different scale. Eliot's range of human sympathies is as limited as is Wordsworth's, though he buttresses that limitation with resources of wit and irony denied Wordsworth. (Another differentia that allies them, and they with Milton, is an absence of humor in each. Milton and Eliot do possess wit to a degree denied Wordsworth.) Wordsworth says in his "Preface" that he sets out to use the language really used by men. But he doesn't mean here quite what one thinks him to mean at first sight, not even what he thought himself to mean in an earlier part of the "Preface" when he considers going to the simple folk for his language. At this particular point in his essay, Wordsworth is aware (as is Eliot in his concern for the three voices of poetry) of the differences between the poet speaking in his own voice, the poet speaking through an adopted mask (as Eliot says Browning does), and the character speaking in his own right, at which point one enters upon drama. Wordsworth says: "Few persons of good sense... would not allow that the dramatic parts of composition are defective in proportion as they deviate from the real language of nature, and are colored by a diction of the poet's own, either peculiar to him as an individual poet or belonging simply to poets in general." It isn't merely the problem of the dramatic voice necessary to a Shakespeare's or a Hemingway's dialogue which concerns Wordsworth here, but further the problem which exists in lyric, narrative, or dramatic literature—the problem of finding in language Eliot's objective correlative, "the only way of expressing emotion in the form of art... a set of objects, a situation, a chain of events which shall be the formula of that *particular* emotion, such that when the external facts, which must terminate in sensory experience, are given, the emotion is immediately evoked." Thus, again, Eliot's definition. It is an experiment in pursuit of the objective correlative that lies behind such a poem as "The Solitary Reaper," as it does Eliot's "Love Song of J. Alfred Prufrock." It is impossible for both Wordsworth and Prufrock to say just what they mean, though Prufrock comes closer with his *teacups* and *dooryards* and *coffee spoons* than Wordsworth with his "melancholy strain" and "single in the field."

In the particular passage of the "Preface" just quoted, Wordsworth is concerned with the problem of speaking in his own person. He says also: "The poet is chiefly distinguished from other men by a greater promptness to think and feel without immediate external excitement, and a greater power in expressing such thoughts and feelings as are produced in him in that manner." Nevertheless, these passions, thoughts, feelings are "the general passions and thoughts and feelings of men," being connected with "our moral sentiment and animal sensations." The poet must "express himself as other men express themselves." Wordsworth has moved away from his earlier talk about the "language really spoken by men" and begins now to talk about that imagery and diction which the poet must choose "to connect the passion," that is, the emotion, so that it is accessible to the reader. He is close to talking as Archibald MacLeish does in his famous essay-poem on the objective correlative, "Ars Poetica," about the necessity of a poem's "being" and not "meaning." Through this passage Wordsworth laments the poetic diction that is decayed from misuse by poor poets, the images that have become clichés. He is concerned, not with dialect as a source of poetic language, but with the possibility of setting down, as MacLeish says the poem must, "For love / The leaning grasses and two lights above the sea." He seeks the means of arousing the emotion through images in such poems as "She Dwelt among the Untrodden Ways," naming an almost neglected country maiden as "A violet by a mossy stone / Half-hidden from the eye!" Wordsworth is concerned in such lines, surely, with the possibility of giving, in MacLeish's words, "For all the history of grief / An empty doorway and a maple leaf." That he can be magnificently successful in the attempt is shown by such a poem as "A Slumber Did My Spirit Seal," with its subtle play on the word *thing* as applied to the living person first, and then implied in the association of the same person dead with "rocks and stones and trees," the effect being to take us to the heart of the speaker's grief, as we are not so moved by "Elegiac Stanzas."

Perhaps Wordsworth is so seldom mentioned in investigations of the origins of the modern developments in our literature because he seems far simpler than in fact he is. His theory about the language really spoken by men as appropriate to literature, if taken superficially, as it is and has been, leads only to journalism and to Eddie Guest or his successor, Rod McKuen. Good followers, though, know how to build on foundations. In new country, one builds whatever log cabin he can against the elements and the natives, and the sons that follow make windows of glass, put in puncheon floors, eventually perhaps even install air conditioning. Perhaps in this new house of art there are possible fluorescent lights such as those almost perfected by Joyce in his stream of consciousness, or Eliot's magic lantern that casts the inner Prufrock in patterns on old walls. So Wordsworth prepares the way for these improving sons, and for a Hemingway, about whose work, however, hovers the same naiveness, the same uneasiness of the stranger in a world he never made, that one finds in Wordsworth following *Lyrical Ballads.* Literary kinship must be remembered and examined toward understanding one's capacity for his inheritance so that violence may not be done to the worthy, so that new houses rest on "good" foundations, to borrow a favorite Hemingway word. That has been the burden of Pound's and Eliot's teaching, different though they may be as to the foundations they recommend, the one more concerned with the stones of Venice, the other with an Eternal City. How one may reduce his possibilities by not seeking his forebears seems borne out by such a rebel as Hemingway. It takes courage to accept and try to understand the given, as Lucifer failed to appreciate and—on a diminished scale—as Hemingway failed to comprehend. The passage from *A Moveable Feast* concerning "Major" Eliot and Pound's "Bel Esprit" makes my point. It is an absence of this more difficult courage in Hemingway that makes him so intent upon the courage of a moment's bravery of body. In spite of all the attention given to the effect of immediacy in his fiction and other prose—the moment of commitment to battle or love—Hemingway's is the reflective mode of one man's quest rather than the dramatic mode of everyman's. Personal emotion recollected in tranquility. But it is philosophical reflection without philosophy. It is escape literature. To illustrate, let us consider Hemingway's version of "Tintern Abbey."

He writes, in *A Moveable Feast,* of sitting in a Paris Cafe in the twenties writing "about up in Michigan." "[In] the story the boys were drinking and this made me thirsty and I ordered a rum St. James." The boys indeed. Hemingway, in the midst of what one presumes to be a personal recollection of the actual event of the story's composition, pretends the absence from it of autobiography, except as an immediate effect of negative capability. This is in itself no terrible indictment, but it is an indication of Hemingway's fear of really coming to grips with the moment itself, as his heroes sometimes do. This is not really the way it is. A Wordsworth would have written, "In the story I was remembering the time I was drinking up in Michigan and it made me thirsty again." It is Hemingway's pretense at honesty here (as in his account in the same book of his relationship to the Fitzgeralds and of the failure of his first marriage) that is to be questioned. He shies away from being open with us as Wordsworth is, not asking "whither is fled the visionary gleam," but pointing our attention to others' failures, or in this passage concerning the cafe episode, to a girl who comes in the cafe, he getting all excited about her. This particular passage, through his finishing the episode, is dramatically parallel to "Tintern Abbey," except that Wordsworth is less frightened by the past, and consequently less intimidated by the future. There is less of the frenzy of the moment in Wordsworth—less excited concern for catching it the "way it really was" and more concern for understanding why it was the way it was. In his writing, when the moment of *why* threatens, Hemingway quickly brings in either a woman or a bull. Thus he fakes a stoic pose. It would appear that he is finally frightened by tranquility when it attempts to accompany his recollections, for with tranquility comes the why which sends one deeper into the past and into the self than Hemingway is willing to go.

A Moveable Feast as a whole might, as I have suggested, be taken as Hemingway's "Tintern Abbey." But the epigraph which gives the book its title indicates in miniature the difference between what I call Wordsworth's honest openness and Hemingway's self-delusion. "If you are lucky enough to live in Paris as a young man then wherever you go for the rest of your life it stays with you, for Paris is a moveable feast." Here is insistence on lifetime innocence, one moment unchanged, to which one might compare the passage in Aldous Huxley's devastating portrait of the disengaged critic Mr. Mercaptan in *Antic Hay:* "Satan, it is said, carries hell in his heart ... wherever he [Mercaptan] was, it was Paris. 'Dreams in nineteen twenty-two ...' he shrugged his shoulders." Wordsworth, on the other hand, takes the present moment, a revisiting which Hemingway shies from, as one in which "there is life and blood / For future years" no less than were the earlier moments. On revisiting the Wye, Wordsworth recognizes and accepts himself as changed "after many wanderings, many years of absence." But the present moment is more dear than before. Hemingway's great fear, finally, is always of the present moment, in the instance of his *Feast,* the moment in the 1950s when recollecting Paris some thirty years earlier. That is why it is a fortress from distress to seize on a moment of morning glory—Paris in the twenties—and try to give it "the way it was." Present tense is absent from Hemingway, which is a major difference between Hemingway as romantic poet and Wordsworth. Or for that matter John Keats, who though he looked upon the morning rose to glut his sorrow was aware that he was doing so.

Concerning the echoes of Wordsworth in Hemingway, consider one final instance from his last book. In *A Move-*

able Feast Hemingway gives an account of a visit with Gertrude Stein, during which she singled out his story "Up in Michigan" as one she didn't like.

> "It's good," she said. "That's not the question at all. But it is *inaccrochable*. That means it is like a picture that a painter paints and then he cannot hang it when he has a show and nobody will buy it because they cannot hang it either."
>
> "But what if it is not dirty, but it is only that you are trying to use words that people would actually use? That are the only words that can make the story come true and that you must use them? You have to use them."

There lies the old problem, but presented with an innocence that well might argue Hemingway of a lost generation. Recollected forty years after the event (and who can say how much of *A Moveable Feast* is history and how much fiction), it still rings in the old man's voice with innocence. The old man is far less removed from that young Hemingway arguing with Miss Stein than Wordsworth from his youth on revisiting (in Wordsworth's late twenties) the banks of the Wye. Dante, "Major" Eliot in his essay on Dante, Wordsworth in his "Preface," Chaucer in his "Prologue" make sounder arguments on the same point, but they are arguments that involve giving up youthful innocence as tranquilizer, the private moment glorified as immortal. Hemingway says he learned from Pound, who also is descended from Wordsworth as well as from Browning, and he would have profited by looking into his antecedents more thoroughly, rather than—like Chaucer's Monk in whom there are several likenesses to Hemingway—letting old things pass.

A writer is not absolutely free to choose his literary parents, as Wordsworth discovered in imitating *Othello* in *The Borderers,* nor of ignoring them, as William Carlos Williams and Hemingway in their separate ways wanted to do. The peculiar qualifications of a writer's mind and talent prohibit it. A Hemingway is of Wordsworth's tribe, a Faulkner of Chaucer's and Shakespeare's willy-nilly.

He must at least show a proper regard for those he is descended from. He fails to do so at his own peril. Certainly the literary stream that flows through Joyce, Eliot, Pound, and Hemingway flows in part through and from Wordsworth. There is an indebtedness that has been largely overlooked, partly because Wordsworth is so embarrassing in his failures. We mustn't of course ignore the shortcomings of our literary fathers. We have to live with the awkward shuffling of aged parents as eventually with our own—with false teeth, even wooden legs. But if Wordsworth's poetics and practice sometimes go on wooden leg, he has helped show a way, and even with false teeth muddling the words, he has told us something of the country we inhabit and of a possible house we may find ourselves in. Whether it is your or my proper house or not, it is someone's. And as James might remind us, the city of art has room for many different houses, particularly houses with many different windows.

Bibliography

Eliot, *The Use of Poetry and the Use of Criticism*

I . . . affirm all human affairs are involved with each other, that consequently all history involves abstraction, and that in attempting to win a full understanding of the poetry of a period you are led to the consideration of subjects which at first sight appear to have little bearing upon poetry. These subjects have accordingly a good deal to do with the criticism of poetry.

Intellectual ecology is more important in a scholar or critic—and more difficult to characterize—than we generally acknowledge. For that reason, among others, I have chosen to be somewhat unorthodox in this bibliography so that through it a reader may better know how to take me. Even bibliographies are subject to the personal heresy. I am fundamentally indebted to the labors of such scholars as de Selincourt, Darbishire, Coburn, Rollins, Garrod—to their labors which have made available to us the poems and letters and notebooks of the principals of these essays. I am deeply greatful. But I have chosen also to make an acknowledgment of a more general but equally important indebtedness as well, incurred in my attempt to win a full understanding of poetry. In addition to the primary sources, and those secondary sources I have drawn upon for points of departure, I have included examples of those more remote works which have pushed and led me on this venture, works not always evident in the text itself though very much a part of the climate of my thought. I hope thereby to suggest how wide a range of material I consider helpful, necessary to, and inevitably a part of one's consideration of the problems of literary criticism.

Abrams, M. H. *The Mirror and the Lamp: Romantic Theory and the Critical Tradition.* New York: Oxford University Press, 1953.

Ardrey, Robert. *African Genesis: A Personal Investigation into the Animal Origins and Nature of Man.* New York: Dell, 1961.

———. *The Territorial Imperative: A Personal Inquiry into the Animal Origins of Property and Nations.* New York: Dell, 1966.

Auden, W. H. *The Dyer's Hand and Other Essays.* New York: Random House, 1968.

Augustine, Saint. *The City of God.* Translated by the Reverend Marcus Dods. *A Selected Library of the Nicene and Post-Nicene Fathers,* vol. 2. Edited by Philip Shaff. Grand Rapids, Mich.: William B. Eerdmans, 1956.

———. *The Confessions.* Translated and edited by John K. Ryan. New York: Image, 1960.

Barnary, Mary. *The Mythmakers.* Athens, Ohio: Ohio University Press, 1966.

Barth, J. Robert, S. J. *Coleridge and Christian Doctrine.* Cambridge, Mass.: Harvard University Press, 1969.

Bate, Walter Jackson. *John Keats.* Cambridge, Mass.: Harvard University Press, 1963.

Bowra, C. M. *Primitive Song.* New York: Mentor, 1962.

Brett, R. L. *Fancy and Imagination.* London: Methuen, 1969.

Bullet, Gerald, ed. *Silver Poets of the Sixteenth Century.* London: J. M. Dent and Sons, 1947.

Bury, J. B. *The Idea of Progress: An Inquiry into Its Growth and Origin.* New York: Macmillan, 1932.

Bush, Douglas. *John Keats.* London: Weidenfeld and Nicolson, 1966.

Butcher, S. H. *Aristotle's Theory of Poetry and Fine Art.* 4th ed. London: Macmillan, 1907.

Butler, Don Cuthbert. *Western Mysticism: The Teaching of Augustine, Gregory and Barnard on Contemplation and the Contemplative Life.* New York: Harper Torchbook, 1966.

Coleridge, Samuel Taylor. *Collected Letters of Samuel Taylor Coleridge.* Edited by Earl Leslie Griggs. 4 vols. Oxford: Oxford University Press, 1956.

———. *The Letters of Samuel Taylor Coleridge.* Edited by Ernest Hartley Coleridge. 2 vols. London: Heinemann, 1895.

———. *The Literary Remains of Samuel Taylor Coleridge.* Edited by Henry Nelson Coleridge. 4 vols. New York: AMS, 1967.

———. *The Notebooks of Samuel Taylor Coleridge.* Edited by Kathleen Coburn. New York: Pantheon, 1957.

———. *Samuel Taylor Coleridge: Biographia Literaria, Edited with His Aesthetical Essays.* Edited by John Shawcross. 2 vols. London: Oxford University Press, 1965.

Collingwood, R. G. *The Idea of History.* New York: Oxford University Press, 1956.

———. *The Principles of Art.* New York: Oxford University Press, 1958.

Davidson, Donald. *The Attack on Leviathan: Regionalism and Nationalism in the United States.* Chapel Hill, N.C.: University of North Carolina Press, 1938.

Durrant, Geoffrey. *William Wordsworth.* London: Cambridge University Press, 1969.

Eliot, T. S. *Collected Poems, 1909–1962.* New York: Harcourt, Brace & World, 1963.

———. *Knowledge and Experience in the Philosophy of F. H. Bradley.* New York: Farrar, Straus, 1964.

———. *Selected Essays.* New York: Harcourt, Brace & World, 1960.

———. *The Use of Poetry and the Use of Criticism: Studies in the Relation of Criticism to Poetry in England.* London: Faber and Faber, 1933.

———, ed. *Literary Essays of Ezra Pound.* New York: New Directions, 1954.

Farnham, Willard. *The Medieval Heritage of Elizabethan Tragedy.* Oxford: Basil Blackwell, 1963.

Fredrickson, George M. *The Inner Civil War: Northern Intellectuals and the Crisis of the Union.* New York: Harper & Row, 1965.

Gilson, Etienne. *Forms and Substances in the Arts.* Translated by Salvator Attanasis. New York: Charles Scribner's Sons, 1966.

Heffernan, James A. W. *Wordsworth's Theory of Poetry: The Transforming Imagination.* Ithaca, N.Y.: Cornell University Press, 1969.

Heller, Erich. *The Artist's Journey into the Interior and Other Essays.* New York: Vintage, 1968.

Hesse, Mary B. *Models and Analogies in Science.* Notre Dame, Ind.: University of Notre Dame Press, 1966.

Joyce, James. *The Critical Writings of James Joyce.* Edited by Ellsworth Mason and Richard Ellmann. New York: Viking, 1959.

———. *Letters of James Joyce.* Edited by Stuart Gilbert. New York: Viking, 1957.

Keats, John. *The Letters of John Keats.* Edited by H. E. Rollins. 2 vols. Cambridge, Mass.: Harvard University Press, 1958.

————. *The Poetical Works of John Keats.* Edited by H. W. Garrod. London: Oxford University Press, 1956.

Knowles, David. *The Nature of Mysticism.* New York: Hawthorne, 1966.

Kuhn, Thomas S. *The Structure of Scientific Revolutions.* 2d ed. *International Encyclopedia of Unified Science,* vol. 2. Chicago: University of Chicago Press, 1970.

Lacy, Norman. *Wordsworth's View of Nature and Its Ethical Consequences.* Hamden, Conn.: Archon, 1965.

Langbaum, Robert. *The Poetry of Experience: The Dramatic Monologue in Modern Literary Tradition.* New York: W. W. Norton, 1957.

Lapp, Ralph E. *The New Priesthood: The Scientific Elite and the Uses of Power.* New York: Harper & Row, 1965.

Lewis, C. S. *The Problem of Pain.* New York: Macmillan, 1962.

Litz, A. Walton, *The Art of James Joyce: Method of Design in "Ulysses" and "Finnegans Wake."* New York: Oxford University Press, 1964.

Maritain, Jacques. *The Peasant of the Garonne.* Translated by Michael Cuddihy and Elizabeth Hughes. New York: Holt, Rinehart & Winston, 1968.

May, Rollo, et al. *Existence: A New Direction in Psychiatry and Psychology.* New York: Basic, 1958.

Montgomery, Marion. *Ezra Pound: A Critical Essay.* Grand Rapids, Mich.: William B. Eerdmans, 1970.

————. "Richard Weaver against the Establishment." *Georgia Review* 23 (1969): 433–59.

————. *T. S. Eliot: An Essay on the American Magus.* Athens, Ga.: University of Georgia Press, 1969.

Muecke, D. C. *Irony.* London: Methuen, 1970.

O'Connor, Flannery. *Mystery and Manners.* New York: Farrar, Straus & Giroux, 1970.

Ortega y Gasset, José. *Meditations on Quixote.* Translated by Evelyn Rugg and Diego Marín. New York: W. W. Norton, 1961.

Polanyi, Michael. *The Study of Man.* Chicago: University of Chicago Press, 1959.

————. *The Tacit Dimension.* New York: Doubleday, 1967.

Pound, Ezra. *A B C of Reading.* New York: New Directions, 1960.

———. *The Cantos.* New York: New Directions, 1970.

———. *Guide to Kulchur.* New York: New Directions, n.d.

———. *The Letters of Ezra Pound.* Edited by D. D. Paige. London: Faber and Faber, 1951.

———. *Personae: Collected Shorter Poems.* New York: New Directions, n.d.

———. *The Spirit of Romance.* New York: New Directions, n.d.

Ricoeur, Paul. *The Symbolism of Evil.* Translated by Emerson Buchanan. New York: Harper & Row, 1967.

Singh, Jagjit. *Great Ideas and Theories of Modern Cosmology.* New York: Dover, 1961.

Singleton, Charles S. *An Essay on "The Vita Nuova."* Cambridge, Mass.: Harvard University Press, 1958.

Sinnott, Edmund W. *The Biology of the Spirit.* New York: Viking, 1955.

———. *Matter, Mind and Man: The Biology of Human Nature.* New York: Atheneum, 1962.

Stewart, Randall. *American Literature and Christian Doctrine.* Baton Rouge, La.: Louisiana State University Press, 1958.

Stone, Lawrence. *The Crisis of the Aristocracy, 1558–1641.* London: Oxford University Press, 1965.

Strauss, Leo. *Natural Right and History.* Chicago: University of Chicago Press, 1953.

Teilhard de Chardin. *The Phenomenon of Man.* Translated by Bernard Wall. New York: Harper & Bros., 1959.

Telford, Kenneth A. *Aristotle's Poetics: Translation and Analysis.* Chicago: Henry Regnery, 1961.

Tillyard, E. M. W., and Lewis, C. S. *The Personal Heresy: A Controversy.* London: Oxford University Press, 1939.

Twelve Southerners. *I'll Take My Stand.* New York: Harper & Bros., 1930.

Vossler, Karl. *Mediaeval Culture: An Introduction to Dante and His Times.* Translated by William C. Lawton. 2 vols. New York: Frederick Ungar, 1929.

Walters, Clifton, trans. *The Cloud of Unknowing.* Baltimore: Penguin, 1961.

Watson, George. *The Study of Literature.* New York: Charles Scribner's Sons, 1969.

Weaver, Richard M. *Ideas Have Consequences.* Chicago: University of Chicago Press, 1948.

————. *The Southern Tradition at Bay: A History of Postbellum Thought.* Edited by George Core and M. E. Bradford. New Rochelle, N.Y.: Arlington, 1968.

Werblowsky, R. J. Z. *Lucifer and Prometheus: A Study of Milton's Satan.* London: Routledge and Kegan Paul, 1952.

Wordsworth, John. *The Letters of John Wordsworth.* Edited by Carl H. Ketcham. Ithaca, N.Y.: Cornell University Press, 1969.

Wordsworth, William. *The Literary Criticism of William Wordsworth.* Edited by Paul M. Zall. Lincoln, Neb.: University of Nebraska Press, 1966.

————. *Lyrical Ballads.* Edited by R. L. Brett and A. R. Jones. London: Methuen, 1965.

————. *Wordsworth: Poetical Works.* Edited by Thomas Hutchinson and Ernest de Selincourt. London: Oxford University Press, 1966.

————, and Wordsworth, Dorothy, *The Letters of William and Dorothy Wordsworth: The Middle Years, 1806–1820.* Edited by Ernest de Selincourt. 2 vols. Oxford: Oxford University Press, 1937.

Zinsser, Hans. *Rats, Lice and History.* Boston: Little, Brown, 1935.

Index

Adams, John, 96
Aeschylus, 43, 51, 54–55, 73, 77–78, 232; *Agamemnon*, 54, 70, 73, 76; *Oresteia* trilogy, 23
Aiken, Conrad, 22, 259
Andrews, Lancelot, 258
Aquinas, Thomas, 63, 110, 156, 188
Archetypal Patterns in Poetry (Maud Bodkin), 269
Aristotle, 54, 64–65, 67, 70, 72, 156, 164, 175, 183, 188, 269, 274, 285; *Ethics*, 76; *Poetics*, 71, 90
Arnold, Matthew, 53, 185; "Dover Beach," 30, 45
Atlantic Monthly, 94
Auden, W. H., 131; *The Dyer's Hand*, 131
Augustine, Saint, 26, 96, 110, 154–155, 188; *The City of God*, xiii

Bacon, Sir Francis, 11, 29, 90, 165–168, 178
Bailey, Benjamin, 250, 253, 258–259, 271
Barth, J. Robert, 190; *Coleridge and Christian Doctrine*, 190
Baudelaire, Charles, 8, 20, 177, 200
Beaumont and Fletcher, 116; *The Maid's Tragedy*, 116
Beaupuis, Michael, 225
Beckett, Samuel, 43; *Endgame*, 61; *Molloy*, 109; *Waiting for Godot*, 60
Bible, The (King James version), 280
Blake, William, 21
Boccaccio, 12
Boyer, James, 185
Bradley, F. H., 244
Brawne, Fanny, 248, 250
Brown, Calvin, 56
Browning, Robert, 5, 93, 109, 177, 221, 280, 287–289; "The Bishop Orders His Tomb at Saint Praxed's Church," 286; "Porphyria's Lover," 286; "Soliloquy of the Spanish Cloister," 286
Burke, Edmund, 96, 219; *Reflections upon the French Revolution*, 219–220
Bush, Douglas, 255, 264
Butcher, S. H., 72–73
Byron, George Gordon, Lord, 2, 5, 121

304

Fredrickson, George M., 94; *The Inner Civil War: Northern Intellectuals and the Crisis of the Union,* 94
Freud, Sigmund, 22, 121, 239, 285–286
From Ritual to Romance (Jessie L. Weston), 269
Frost, Robert, 43; "The Gift Outright," 43

Gilles, R P., 278
Gilpin, Thomas, 101; *Tour of the Wye,* 101
Gilson, Etienne, 52; *Forms and Substances in the Arts,* 52
Ginsberg, Allen, 39
Goethe, Johann Wolfgang von, 177
Golden Bough (Sir James Frazer), 269
Grant, U. S., 94
Guest, Edgar, 280, 291

Hardy, Thomas, 12, 45, 57; *Jude the Obscure,* 284
Hartley, David, 185, 203
Hawthorne, Nathaniel, 41–42, 44–45, 93–94, 96, 242; "Young Goodman Brown," 96
Hayne, Paul Hamilton, 44
Hazlitt, William, 260
Heffernan, James A. W., 9, 158, 215; *Wordsworth's Theory of Poetry: The Transforming Imagination,* 9, 214
Hemingway, Ernest, xiv, 4, 31, 39, 43, 48, 58, 119, 123, 184, 278, 280, 286–288, 291, 294; *A Moveable Feast,* 31, 123, 288, 291–294; *The Sun Also Rises,* 123, 286, 288; "Up in Michigan," 294
Henry III, 218
Henry V, 91
Herrick, Robert, 63; "The Argument of His Book," 33
Herzog (Saul Bellow), 109
Hobbes, Thomas, 12, 187–188
Holinshed, 228
Homer, 9, 22, 37, 55, 78, 132–133, 214, 232; *The Iliad,* 23, 51; *The Odyssey,* 133
Hopkins, Gerard Manley, 29, 31, 48, 55–56, 163, 165, 200, 254
Howard, Henry, Earl of Surrey, 44
Hunt, Leigh, 2, 92–93, 253
Hutchinson, Mary, 83, 215–216, 223
Huxley, Aldous, 27, 43; *Antic Hay,* 98, 293; *Point Counter Point,* 109

James I, 93
James, Henry, 36, 44–45, 58, 95–96, 109, 121–123, 184, 242, 250, 280, 295; *The American,* 34
James, William, 29, 281

MacLeish, Archibald, 290; "Ars Poetica," 290
McLuhan, Marshall, xiii
Madame Bovary (Gustave Flaubert), 95
Madge, Charles, 8
Mallarmé, Stéphane, 52
Mann, Thomas, 263
Matthiesscn, F. O., 272
May, Rollo, 162
Milton, John, xi, 2, 5–7, 9, 18, 29, 31, 37, 55–57, 64, 66, 68–69,
    75, 86, 90–91, 98, 102–104, 106, 108, 110, 112, 114, 118–119,
    121, 123, 151–153, 172–173, 175–177, 182, 209, 211, 225–230,
    232, 240, 256, 258, 277, 289; *Il Penseroso*, 103, 105–106, 118;
    L'Allegro, 102–106, 118; "Lycidas," 106, 110–111, 125, 159; "Of
    That Sort of Dramatic Poem Which Is Called Tragedy," 65;
    Paradise Lost, 7, 30, 55, 74, 105, 108, 111–112, 151–152, 159,
    173–174, 227, 263; *Paradise Regained*, 98; *Reason of Church
    Government*, 111, 227; *Samson Agonistes*, 64–65, 112
Monet, Claude, 8
Monroe, Harriet, 280
Montgomery, Marion, 244; *T. S. Eliot: An Essay on the American
    Magus*, 244
Moore, Marianne, 25
Moore, Thomas, 2
Moses, Grandma, 31

New English Dictionary, 68
Newton, Sir Isaac, xiv, 12, 165, 169, 184, 187–188
Nietzsche, Friedrich Wilhelm, 22

O'Connor, Flannery, 45–46, 170
O'Connor, Frank, 284
Origen, 26, 29

Paine, Thomas, 227
Petrarch, 12; *De Remediis Ultriusque Fortunae*, 113
Pinter, Harold, 170
Plato, xiv, 44, 155, 164, 169, 183, 188, 200, 286; *Phaedo*, 193;
    The Republic, 182
Plutarch, 228
Poe, Edgar Allan, 237, 242, 273, 280, 282; "The Philosophy of
    Composition," 282
Polanyi, Michael, 40; *The Study of Man*, 162; *The Tacit Dimension*,
    40, 265
Pope, Alexander, 57, 165, 209; *Essay on Man*, 187

Index